# HISTORY OF RACISM

## FIRST EDITION

**Edited by Lezlee Hinesmon-Matthews**
*California State University, Fullerton*

cognella™
San Diego, CA

First published in the United States of America in 2010 by Cognella, a division of University Readers, Inc.

Trademark Notice: Product or corporate names may be trademarks or registered trademarks, and are used only for identification and explanation without intent to infringe.

14 13 12 11 10          1 2 3 4 5

Printed in the United States of America

ISBN: 978-1-935551-72-0

www.cognella.com  800.200.3908

# CONTENTS

# PART 2
# SPECIFIC WAYS THAT RACISM BECOMES MANIFEST

# PART 3
# STRATEGIES OF ADDRESSING RACISM

# Preface

## Lezlee Hinesmon-Matthews

THIS ANTHOLOGY ABOUT the history of racism in America centers on a provocative subject that requires readers to closely examine a troubling chapter in the book of America's past. Whether racism exists today in the same manner as it did historically is an open question. For this collection, the main question is whether racism directed towards African Americans, and other marginalized racial groups, can be understood through individual, cultural, and institutional dimensions. The text is laid out along these lines with the belief that such a framework is useful and valid.

This is in contrast to the argument that telling the history of racism must focus solely on a historical peek at key episodes or organizations. That is, let the work be a who's who of notable or infamous people, groups, and activities. Such a collection would highlight the nefarious actions of the slave captors who brought Africans to these shores during the Middle Passage. It would recount the worst attributes of plantation overseers who made life nearly unbearable for those of skin with a darker hue. The terrorizing reign of the Ku Klux Klan would loom large in stories about black life in post-slavery America. The belittling effect of second-class status in the Jim Crow South would figure prominently in this story as well. The centerpiece of this saga would be the church's role in the civil rights movement, protest marches, boycotts, and Black Panther-led efforts to resist structural racism. Anti- and pro-affirmative action policy debates, mandatory bussing skirmishes, reaction to Hurricane Katrina's devastation, and the racism-tainted rhetoric during the campaign to elect America's first African American president would round out the organizational structure of such a text. However, I argue that this retelling of the history of racism leaves readers lacking much in the way of understanding the individual, social, and structural mechanisms that perpetuate racism in American history.

Although this book points out notable eras in America's historic struggle with questions of racial prejudice, discrimination, and bigotry, it is nonetheless primarily organized to present the history of racism as a series of events that are at once unique to their times and yet share common features with episodes that occur at different times. My position is that attitudes, behaviors, and social structures can best be understood when the history of racism is examined on individual, cultural, and institutional levels. The advantage of this approach for teaching is that it provides students with an un-paralleled exploration of the ideological premises and historical events associated with racism.

## ORGANIZATION

The reader is organized in three parts: (1) key terms and concepts, (2) ways racism becomes manifest, and (3) strategies to address racism. The first part gives foundational knowledge, part two provides concrete historical examples, and part three elucidates solutions. The end of each reading includes several probing questions designed to prompt students to recall salient points and reflect upon their meaning. Following the last section is an appendix of film and web resources so that readers may learn more about the topic through multimedia formats and obtain information for further research.

# Acknowledgments

THE WORK WAS made possible by the supportive team at *University Readers*. The team's patience, professionalism, and advice helped crystallize my ideas on the subject of the history of racism. Their creativity, from book cover design to layout, led me to envision myriad possibilities to extend the anthology's audience. Special thanks to Tracey Barraza for responding with such enthusiasm to my initial inquiry; to Marissa Waggoner for selling the possibility of partnering with *University Readers* in such an enticing way; and to Jessica Knott for editing the project, guiding me through the production process, and responding to my queries with thoroughness and tact.

I would also like to thank the faculty, staff, and administrators at California State University, Fullerton for encouraging my scholarly interests, as well as for talking and listening to me while I developed my ideas about this book and related anti-racism curriculum. Thanks also to the women of color support groups at Cal State Fullerton and San Diego State University for support and encouragement. Special thanks to Armone, for believing in me and debating with me the relative merits of teaching racism from this perspective. And to Adrian for his special place in my heart.

—*LEZLEE HINESMON-MATTHEWS*

# Introduction

## Lezlee Hinesmon-Matthews

THIS INTRODUCTION EXPLAINS the three parts comprising this work. Part One deals with key terms and concepts; Part Two relates to the ways in which racism is manifest; and Part Three discusses strategies to address racism. The reader's interests may guide emphasis on any section or all of them. The purpose of Part One is to help the reader understand the common language used to discuss issues of racism. The terms may be unfamiliar to the new reader. The concepts may be used differently in other areas of study. In this way, the reader is sure to have a solid foundation on which to uncover this remarkable history, in both its shame and triumph.

In Reading 1, the preeminent sociologist and scholar W. E. B. Du Bois investigates the meaning of race and its implications for African Americans in "The Conservation of Races." Du Bois's analysis presents racial categories and national origins historically associated with them. Beyond a strict interpretation of racial categories as skin deep, Du Bois reveals the close association people began to make between concrete notions of skin color and hair texture, to more abstract ideals of nationality, spirituality, and philosophy. Du Bois then lays out his plan for addressing the pressing social conditions of African Americans in his day, largely based on establishing institutions governed and led by them. Reading 2, Joe R. Feagin's "Racist America: Racist Ideology as a Social Force," concerns itself with the concept of racist ideology and its reproduction across generations in broader American society. This ideology is maintained, Feagin argues, through deeply embedded practices in society's institutions, including government, education, and employment. Feagin then supports his thesis of the permeation of racist ideology in American institutions by giving examples from a broad sweep of American history, dating from the country's founding in the 1600s to the present. In contrast to Du Bois's remedy for racism through establishing Black institutions, Feagin's prescription is for Americans (and other Western societies) to admit and address inequalities within the social institutions that are a legacy of racist ideology. Feagin's work is also more in line with a conflict perspective that links the consequences of racism to the oppression of Blacks at the hands of White colonizers and imperialists. Du Bois, on the other hand, appears willing to engage White society on its own terms through African American institutions.

One element of Feagin's work is the connection it draws between antiblack ideology, scientific racism in the 1700s, and social Darwinism in the 19th and 20th centuries. In Reading 3, Sven Lindqvist's "The Skull Measurer's Mistake" succinctly argues against these types of scientific claims by pointing out shortcomings of the biological approach to understanding race. Specifically, Lindqvist reveals the overreliance on flawed data to explain racial differences, most notably data produced about skull measurements from people all over the world. In the process, he debunks scientific claims of racial hierarchies. Lindqvist's analysis is significant because it counters scientific theories based on these research projects and is used to justify the discriminatory treatment of Blacks.

Reading 4 examines Steve Garner's work, "Whiteness as Contingent Hierarchies: Who Counts as White and Why." It is fascinating because it reveals the distinctions the dominant society makes even between those who on the outside appear to fit into the racial group known as "White." This reading is included because it gives specific examples of ethnic groups who were treated with the same low social status associated with those with darker skin color, or non-Whites. Garner uses international and American examples of this differential treatment. The importance of these choices lies in the fact that those at the top of such hierarchies—Anglo-Saxons—were thought to possess superior intellect and abilities. The text reveals how those on top of the racial hierarchy treated those at the bottom (usually immigrants) and strategies that newcomers used for fitting in. Garner also uses his work to introduce the commingling of these ideas with the American eugenics discourse.

Elements of this subject can be found in Reading 5, Neil Foley's "Becoming Hispanic: Mexican Americans and Whiteness." Here Foley examines the process by which Mexicans fought for recognition as "White" and against association with "Mexican" (rather than reflecting nationality, historically this has meant a racially inferior category). A part of this dynamic played out not only in the decennial census, but also in court cases. Foley explains how the census category changed over time for Mexican Americans. Foley's work exposes an internal struggle within the Mexican American community. It is one based on their desire for equal treatment with Whites, but at times comes at the cost of separating themselves from other racially marginalized groups. Like the Whites who distinguished themselves from immigrants in Garner's reading about differences between White ethnic groups, Foley's work is a case study in how Mexican Americans have struggled to overcome racism and gain the privileges of White skin color.

Reading 6 continues a theme raised by Feagin about inequality in American social institutions. In "Housing and Education: The Inextricable Link," Deborah L. McKoy and Jeffrey M. Vincent explore the history of racism in two institutions that impact many lives. The reading contrasts little known and famous legal cases waged by plaintiffs to fight school segregation in secondary and higher education. The basis for their analysis was the trend toward racially segregated communities that, in turn, resulted in racially segregated schools. Evidence suggests that since the 1980s, poor Black and Latino students and their families have become trapped in communities with inferior schools because they cannot afford to move out. Institutional racism is implicit in the school and housing nexus because of discriminatory real estate industry practices.

## PART TWO: SPECIFIC WAYS IN WHICH RACISM BECOMES MANIFEST

The readings in Part Two deal with the various ways in which racism becomes manifest in daily life. Although the previous section included examples of how racism occurs, the purpose was to give more breadth and depth to key terms and concepts. That information provides a foundational knowledge upon which to build our analysis of the individual, cultural, and institutional examples of racism throughout American history. This part begins with individual and cultural racism.

Nell Irvin Painter also explores the insidious use of stereotypes in Reading 7, "Hill, Thomas, and the Use of Racial Stereotype." Painter vividly reveals historic stereotypes embedded in media and public discourse during the hearings to confirm U.S. Supreme Court Justice Clarence Thomas. The stereotypes relate to Thomas and Anita Hill, an attorney and former employee under Thomas. Hill testified about being sexually harassed by Thomas when they worked together. Painter is mainly concerned about stereotypes that are demeaning to women, but she also discusses some that cast aspersions on African American men. The stereotypes present in testimony and media coverage during the hearing evoked for Painter historical themes about African American deficiencies on the bases of race and gender.

Also in this section is work by Joseph Barndt in Reading 8. His "Individual Racism" reveals four elements of his theory of conditioning and race socialization. He primarily argues that racism is perpetuated through individual attitudes and behaviors. This reading is different from others in this collection because of its limited use of examples from history. Instead, the author relies on a largely social-psychological approach to interpret racism by individuals. Similar in the way Painter's reading raises traditional stereotypes to explain a dimension of cultural racism, Barndt reveals how attitudes can lead people to behave in racist ways. Barndt and Painter also share their emphasis on the divisive nature of racism on Black and White relations.

In "Are Jews White? Or, the History of the Nose Job" in Reading 9, Sander Gilman deviates from this pattern and contrasts the experiences of Whites to Jews, a historically marginalized White ethnic group. Gilman discusses changes in the physical appearance of Jews over time and the stigma associated with their features, which to some appeared more phenotypically Black than White. Gilman reports that some Jews changed their physical features by having children with non-Jews or, more recently, by undergoing plastic surgery. These behaviors promote understanding about the pressure that groups with non-White features may feel to adopt mainstream beauty standards.

Aside from individual and cultural manifestations, racism has historically also existed in American social institutions. These institutional contexts include housing, education, employment, and criminal justice. The first two readings, one by Raymond A. Mohl and the other by Feagin, explore racism in housing. In Reading 10, Mohl discusses the history of public and private sector policies, which resulted in racially segregated communities. The FHA and private sector realtors established underwriting criteria to protect homeowner investments, but contributed to racially discriminatory practices such as redlining. Feagin in Reading 11, "A House Is Not a Home: White Racism and U.S. Housing Practices," includes firsthand accounts of African Americans about the meaning of home. The analysis is a suitable counterpart to the Mohl reading because it reveals the consequences of the discriminatory policies for African Americans. Beyond this, Feagin's work details how homes are havens from racial discrimination.

Another institution is education. In Reading 12, "Asian Americans and the Shifting Politics of Race," Rowena Robles deals with a policy issue—affirmative action—at the forefront of cultural wars in this country. The reading is noteworthy for its commentary about the institution of education and American culture. That is, the culture in our communities that acknowledges racially segregated schools, but allows them to continue because of the assertion that White students, and their Asian American counterparts, are naturally smarter and therefore more deserving of placement in the best schools. This idea that one racial or ethnic group is inherently superior to another persists in American culture. Robles reveals the complex argument waged by Chinese American students who reject affirmative action on the grounds that it will unfairly increase African American representation, but who feel victimized by policies denying them admission to elite public schools when they qualify in high numbers. The article further gives insight into the cultural wars waged on the grounds of neoconservative politics, notions of a color-blind society, and the "model minority" myth. Robles raises questions about the instrumental use of stereotypes to portray one racial minority as deserving and the other as undeserving.

A third institutional context for racism is employment. Reading 13 has William Rhoden exploring the world of highly paid professional athletes in "The $40 Million

Slave: The Dilemma of Wealth Without Control." He raises interesting parallels between employment conditions for professional athletes and the enslaved. Rhoden draws provocative conclusions about workers' rights in freedom and in bondage. The consistent thread, he argues, is the impact of racism and discrimination on working conditions and on relations between labor and management.

The final readings in this section are devoted to the institution of criminal justice. Reading 14, Renford Reese's "The Race Card," analyzes data on American incarceration rates by race. His analysis is contextualized by a review of the history of the uneasy relationship between race and criminal justice in America. This analysis of racial disparities in incarceration is supported by a table that depicts rates of incarceration for Whites, Blacks, and Hispanics, as well as ratios for each group. His concern is the apparent inequality evident in the system, with very high rates of incarceration for African American males nationwide. The dilemma discussed is whether actual crime or an unjust system is at the heart of these incarceration levels. The implications such levels have for the ultimate penalty—the death penalty—is at the heart of Reading 15, "Capital Punishment as Legal Lynching?" by Timothy Kaufman-Osborn. He analyzes the circumstances surrounding spectacle lynching at the turn of the 20th century. He draws parallels between the outlawed practice, one characterized by mob violence, and state-sanctioned killing under capital punishment law. The link to the study of racism is apparent in the inequalities of how capital punishment is decided for African American offenders, especially those accused of harming Whites.

## PART THREE: STRATEGIES OF ADDRESSING RACISM

The purpose of the readings in Part Three is to lead readers to a place of reconciliation. That is, one may be inclined to feel hopeless about the prospects for racial reconciliation and justice after examining ways that racism has manifested itself in American ideas and actions. However, there *is* hope, and this section provides a path to achieving racial equity in individual, cultural, and institutional spheres.

The work devoted to addressing racism on a group level is in Reading 16, bell hooks's "Racism and Feminism." hooks (lower case preferred by author) discusses Black and White women and their challenges with respect to feminism. She compares and contrasts Black women's experiences in women's clubs, the suffrage movement, the women's rights movement, and the feminist movement. hooks is highly critical of White women's exclusion of Blacks in their social movements and related leadership positions, but she is also mindful of trends toward excluding Black women's concerns within feminist writing and activity. A remedy to this exclusion, hooks argues, is for White women to address both the gender and race concerns of African American women.

Kenneth Andrews' "The Mississippi Civil Rights Movement and Its Legacy" in Reading 17 seeks to reveal how the civil rights movement transformed social institutions and relations between individuals in a locale that was infamous for its vehement racial animosity. The work is interesting for critically analyzing the strategies used not only by national organizers, but by everyday people on local levels to effect societal change.

In Reading 18, Cornel West's "Beyond Affirmative Action: Equality and Identity" is particularly relevant to the topic of arenas for individual and group strategies because it discusses a major public policy—affirmative action—in the context of highlighting its strengths and weaknesses. This is a call for African Americans and Whites to join forces to bring about broad societal change. West is hopeful that Americans can achieve this objective, but he is vigilant about the need to bring an end to notions of White supremacy. Melvin Oliver and Thomas Shapiro continue West's optimistic tone in Reading 19, "Getting Along: Renewing America's Commitment to Racial Justice." The authors embrace the idea that forums to decrease racism exist on individual and institutional levels. Their concern is that wealth is passed along, but the negative status that is associated with even the most successful African Americans hinders this group's chances of personal fulfillment and the likelihood of passing wealth along across generations. Group and institutional mechanisms are offered to reduce this race-based inequality.

# PART 1

---

## KEY TERMS

# CHAPTER 1

## Understanding and Conceptualizing Racism

# The Conservation of Races

## W. E. B. DuBois

THE AMERICAN NEGRO has always felt an intense personal interest in discussions as to the origins and destinies of races: primarily because back of most discussion of race with which he is familiar, have lurked certain assumptions as to his natural abilities, as to his political, intellectual and moral status, which he felt were wrong. He has, consequently, been led to deprecate and minimize race distinctions, to believe intensely that out of one blood God created all nations, and to speak of human brotherhood as though it were the possibility of an already dawning to-morrow.

Nevertheless, in our calmer moments we must acknowledge that human beings are divided into races; that in this country the two most extreme types of the world's races have met, and the resulting problem as to the future relations of these types is not only of intense and living interest to us, but forms an epoch in the history of mankind.

It is necessary, therefore, in planning our movements, in guiding our future development, that at times we rise above the pressing, but smaller questions of separate schools and cars, wage discrimination and lynch law, to survey the whole question of race in human philosophy and to lay, on a basis of broad knowledge and careful insight, those large lines of policy and higher ideals which may form our guiding lines and boundaries in the practical difficulties of every day. For it is certain that all human striving must recognize the hard limits of natural law, and that any striving, no matter how intense and earnest, which is against the constitution of the world, is vain. The question, then, which we must seriously consider is this: What is the real meaning of Race; what has, in the past, been the law of race development, and what lessons has the past history of race development to teach the rising Negro people?

When we thus come to inquire into the essential difference of races we find it hard to come at once to any definite conclusion. Many criteria of race differences have in the past been proposed, as color, hair, cranial measurements and language. And manifestly, in each of these respects, human beings differ widely. They vary in color, for instance, from the marble-like pallor of the Scandinavian to the rich, dark brown of the Zulu, passing by the creamy Slav, the yellow Chinese, the light brown Sicilian and the brown Egyptian. Men vary, too, in the texture of hair from the obstinately straight hair of the Chinese to the obstinately tufted and frizzled hair of the Bushman. In measurement of heads, again, men vary; from the broad-headed Tartar to the medium-headed European and the narrow-headed Hottentot; or, again in language, from the highly-inflected roman tongue to the monosyllabic Chinese. All these physical characteristics are patent enough, and if they agreed with each other it would be very easy to classify mankind. Unfortunately for scientists, however, these criteria of race are most exasperatingly intermingled. Color does not agree with texture of hair, for many of the dark races have straight hair; nor does color agree with the breadth of the head, for the yellow Tartar has a broader head than the German; nor, again, has the science of language as yet succeeded in clearing up the relative authority of these various and contradictory criteria. The final word of science, so far, is that we have at least two, perhaps three, great families of human beings—the whites and Negroes, possibly the yellow race. That other races have arisen from the intermingling of the blood of these two. This broad division of the world's races which men like Huxley and Raetzel have introduced as more nearly true than the old five-race scheme of Blumenbach, is nothing more than an acknowledgement that, so far as purely physical characteristics are concerned, the differences between men do not explain all the differences of their history. It declares, as Darwin himself said, that great as is the physical unlikeness of the various races of men their likenesses are greater, and upon this rests the whole scientific doctrine of Human Brotherhood.

Although the wonderful developments of human history teach that the grosser physical differences of color, hair and bone go but a short way toward explaining the different roles which groups of men have played in Human Progress, yet there are differences—subtle, delicate and elusive, though they may be—which have silently but definitely separated men into groups. While these subtle forces have generally followed the natural cleavage of common blood, descent and physical peculiarities, they have at other times swept across and ignored these. At all times, however, they have divided human beings into races, which, while they perhaps transcend scientific definition, nevertheless, are clearly defined to the eye of the Historian and Sociologist.

If this be true, then the history of the world is the history, not of individuals, but of groups, not of nations, but of races, and he who ignores or seeks to override the race idea in human history ignores and overrides the central thought of all history. What, then, is a race? It is a vast family of human beings, generally of common blood and language, always of common history, traditions and impulses, who are both voluntarily and involuntarily striving together for the accomplishment of certain more or less vividly conceived ideals of life.

Turning to real history, there can be no doubt, first, as to the widespread, nay, universal, prevalence of the race idea, the race spirit, the race ideal, and as to its efficiency as the vastest and most ingenious invention for human progress. We, who have been reared and trained under the individualistic philosophy of the Declaration of Independence and the laisser-faire [sic] philosophy of Adam Smith, are loath to see and loath to acknowledge this patent fact of human history. We see the Pharaohs, Caesars, Toussaints and Napoleons of history and forget the vast races of which they were but epitomized expressions. We are apt to think in our American impatience, that while it may have been true in the past that closed race groups made history, that here in conglomerate America *nous avons changer tout cela*—we have changed all that, and have no need of this ancient instrument of progress. This assumption of which the Negro people are especially fond, cannot be established by a careful consideration of history.

We find upon the world's stage today eight distinctly differentiated races, in the sense in which History tells us the word must be used. They are, the Slavs of eastern Europe, the Teutons of middle Europe, the English of Great Britain and America, the Romance nations of Southern and Western Europe, the Negroes of Africa and America, the Semitic people of Western Asia and Northern Africa, the Hindoos of Central Asia and the Mongolians of Eastern Asia. There are, of course, other minor race groups, as the American Indians, the Esquimaux and the South Sea Islanders; these larger races, too, are far from homogeneous; the Slav includes the Czech, the Magyar, the Pole and the Russian; the Teuton includes the German, the Scandinavian and the Dutch; the English include the Scotch, the Irish and the conglomerate American. Under Romance nations the widely-differing Frenchman, Italian, Sicilian and Spaniard are comprehended. The term Negro is, perhaps, the most indefinite of all, combining the Mulattoes and Zamboes of America and the Egyptians, Bantus and Bushmen of Africa. Among the Hindoos are traces of widely differing nations, while the great Chinese, Tartar, Corean and Japanese families fall under the one designation—Mongolian.

The question now is: What is the real distinction between these nations? Is it the physical differences of blood, color and cranial measurements? Certainly we must all acknowledge that physical differences play a great part, and that, with wide exceptions and qualifications, these eight great races of today follow the cleavage of physical race distinctions; the English and Teuton represent the white variety of mankind; the Mongolian, the yellow; the Negroes, the black. Between these are many crosses and mixtures, where Mongolian and Teuton have blended into the Slav, and other mixtures have produced the Romance nations and the Semites. But while race differences have followed mainly physical race lines, yet no mere physical distinctions would really define or explain the deeper differences—the cohesiveness and continuity of these groups. The deeper differences are spiritual, psychical, differences—undoubtedly based on the physical, but infinitely transcending them. The forces that bind together the Teuton nations are, then, first, their race identity and common blood; secondly, and more important, a common history, common laws and religion, similar habits of thought and a conscious striving together for certain ideals of life. The whole process which has brought about these race differentiations has been a growth, and the great characteristic of this growth has been the differentiation of spiritual and mental differences between great races of mankind and the integration of physical differences.

The age of nomadic tribes of closely related individuals represents the maximum of physical differences. They were practically vast families, and there were as many groups as families. As the families came together to form cities the physical differences lessened, purity of blood was replaced by the requirement of comicile, and all who lived within the city bound became gradually to be regarded as members of the group; i.e., there was a slight and slow breaking down of physical barriers. This, however, was accompanied by an increase of the spiritual and social differences between cities. This city became husbandmen, this, merchant, another warriors, and so on. The ideals of life for which the different cities struggled were different. When at last cities began to coalesce into nations there was another breaking down of barriers which separated groups of men. The larger and broader differences of color, hair and physical proportions were not by any means ignored, but myriads of minor differences disappeared, and the sociological and historical races of men began to approximate the present division of races as indicated by physical researches. At the same time the spiritual and physical differences of race groups which constituted the nations became deep and decisive. The English nation stood for constitutional liberty and commercial freedom; the German nation for science and philosophy; the Romance nations stood for literature and art, and the other race groups are striving, each in its own way, to develop for civilization its particular message, its particular ideal, which shall help to guide the world nearer and nearer that perfection of human life for which we all long, that

"one far off Divine event."

This has been the function of race differences up to the present time. What shall be its function in the future? Manifestly some of the great races of today—particularly the Negro race—have not as yet given to civilization the full spiritual message which they are capable of giving. I will not say that the Negro race has yet given no message to the world, for it is still a mooted question among scientists as to just how far Egyptian civilization was Negro in its origin; if it was not wholly Negro, it was certainly very closely allied. Be that as it may, however, the fact still remains that the full, complete Negro message of the whole Negro race has not as yet been given to the world: that the messages and ideal of the yellow race have not been completed, and that the striving of the mighty Slavs has but begun. The question is, then: How shall this message be delivered; how shall these various ideals be realized? The answer is plain: By the development of these race groups, not as individuals, but as races. For the development of Japanese genius, Japanese literature and art, Japanese spirit, only Japanese, bound and welded together, Japanese inspired by one vast ideal, can work out in its fullness the wonderful message which Japan has for the nations of the earth. For the development of Negro genius, of Negro literature and art, of Negro spirit, only Negroes bound and welded together, Negroes inspired by one vast ideal, can work out in its fullness the great message we have for humanity. We cannot reverse history; we are subject to the same natural laws as other races and if the Negro is ever to be a factor in the world's history—if among the gaily-colored banners that deck the broad ramparts of civilization is to hang one uncompromising black, then it must be placed there by black hands, fashioned by black heads and hallowed by the travail of 200,000,000 black hearts beating in one glad song of jubilee.

For this reason, the advance guard of the Negro people—the 8,000,000 people of Negro blood in the United States of America—must soon come to realize that if they are to take their just place in the van of Pan-Negroism, then their destiny is not absorption by the white Americans. That if in America it is to be proven for the first time in the modern world that not only Negroes are capable of evolving individual men like Toussaint, the Saviour, but are a nation stored with wonderful possibilities of culture, then their destiny is not a servile imitation of Anglo-Saxon culture, but a stalwart originality which shall unswervingly follow Negro ideals.

It may, however, be objected here that the situation of our race in America renders this attitude impossible; that our sole hope of salvation lies in our being able to lose our race identity in the commingled blood of the nation; and that any other course would merely increase the friction of races which we call race prejudice, and against which we have so long and so earnestly fought.

Here, then, is the dilemma, and it is puzzling one, I admit. No Negro who has given earnest thought to the situation of his people in America has failed, at some time in life, to find himself at these cross-roads; has failed to ask himself at some time: What, after all, am I? Am I an American or am I a Negro? Can I be both? Or is it my duty to cease to be a Negro as soon as possible and be an American? If I strive as a Negro, am I not perpetuating the very cleft that threatens and separates Black and White America? Is not my only possible practical aim the subduction of all that is Negro in me to the American? Does my black blood place upon me any more obligation to assert my nationality than German, or Irish or Italian blood would?

It is such incessant self-questioning and the hesitation that arises from it, that is making the present period a time of vacillation and contradiction for the American Negro; combined race action is stifled, race responsibility is shirked, race enterprises languish, and the best blood, the best talent, the best energy of the Negro people cannot be marshalled to do the bidding of the race. They stand back to make room for every rascal and demagogue who chooses to cloak his selfish deviltry under the veil of race pride.

Is this right? Is it rational? Is it good policy? Have we in America a distinct mission as a race—a distinct sphere of action and an opportunity for race development, or is self-obliteration the highest end to which Negro blood dare aspire?

If we carefully consider what race prejudice really is, we find it, historically, to be nothing but the friction between different groups of people; it is the difference in aim, in feeling, in ideals of two different races; if, now, this difference exists touching territory, laws, language, or even religion, it is manifest that these people cannot live in the same territory without fatal collision; but if, on the other hand, there is substantial agreement in laws, language and religion; if there is a satisfactory adjustment of economic life, then there is no reason why, in the same country and on the same street, two or three great national ideals might not thrive and develop, that men of different races might not strive together for their race ideals as well, perhaps even better, than in isolation. Here, it seems to me, is the reading of the riddle that puzzles so many of us. We are Americans, not only by birth and by citizenship, but by our political ideals, our language, our religion. Farther than that, our Americanism does not go. At that point, we are Negroes, members of a vast historic race that from the very dawn of creation has slept, but half awakening in the dark forests of its African fatherland. We are the first fruits of this new nation, the harbinger of that black to-morrow which is yet destined to soften the whiteness of the Teutonic to-day. We are that people whose subtle sense of song has given America its only American music, its only American fairy tales, its only touch of pathos and humor amid its mad money-getting plutocracy. As such, it is our duty to conserve our physical powers, our intellectual endowments, our spiritual ideals; as a race we must strive by race organization, by race solidarity, by race unity to the realization of that broader humanity which freely recognizes differences in men, but sternly deprecates inequality in their opportunities of development.

For the accomplishment of these ends we need race organizations: Negro colleges, Negro newspapers, Negro business organizations, a Negro school of literature and art, and an intellectual clearing house, for all these products of the Negro mind, which we may call a Negro Academy. Not only is all this necessary for positive advance, it is absolutely imperative for negative defense. Let us not deceive ourselves at our situation in this country. Weighted with a heritage of moral iniquity from our past history, hard pressed in the economic world by foreign immigrants and native prejudice, hated here, despised there and pitied everywhere; our one haven of refuge is ourselves, and but one means of advance, our own belief in our great destiny, our own implicit trust in our ability and worth. There is no power under God's high heaven that can stop the advance of eight thousand thousand honest, earnest, inspired and united people. But—and here is the rub—they must be honest, fearlessly criticizing their own faults, zealously correcting them; they must be earnest. No people that laughs at itself, and ridicules itself, and washes to God it was anything but itself ever wrote its name in history; it must be inspired with the Divine faith of our black mothers, that out of the blood and dust of battle will march a victorious host, a mighty nation, a peculiar people, to speak to the nations of earth a Divine truth that shall make them free. And such a people must be united; not merely united for the organized theft of political spoils, not united to disgrace religion with whoremongers and wardheelers; not united merely to protest and pass resolutions, but united to stop the ravages of consumption among the Negro people, united to keep black boys from loafing, gambling and crime; united to guard the purity of black women and to reduce that vast army of black prostitutes that is today marching to hell; and united in serious organizations, to determine by careful conference and thoughtful interchange of opinion the broad lines of policy and action for the American Negro. This, is the reason for being which the American Negro Academy has. It aims at once to be the epitome and expression of the intellect of the black-blooded people of America, the exponent of the race ideals of one of the world's great races. As such, the Academy must, if successful, be

    (a) Representative in character.
    (b) Impartial in conduct.
    (c) Firm in leadership.

It must be representative in character; not in that it represents all interests or all factions, but in that it seeks to comprise something of the best thought, the most unselfish striving and the highest ideals. There are scattered in forgotten nooks and corners throughout the land, Negroes of some considerable training, of high minds, and high motives, who are unknown to their fellows, who exert far too little influence. These the Negro Academy should strive to bring into touch with each other and to give them a common mouthpiece.

The Academy should be impartial in conduct; while it aims to exalt the people it should aim to do so by truth—not by lies, by honesty—not by flattery. It should continually impress the fact upon the Negro people that they must not expect to have things done for them—they MUST DO FOR THEMSELVES; that they have on their hands a vast work of self-reformation to do, and that a little less complaint and whining, and a little more dogged work and manly striving would do us more credit and benefit than a thousand Force or Civil Rights bills.

Finally, the American Negro Academy must point out a practical path of advance to the Negro people; there lie before every Negro today hundreds of questions of policy and right which must be settled and which each one settles now, not in accordance with any rule, but by impulse or individual preference; for instance: What should be the attitude of Negroes toward the educational qualification for voters? What should be our attitude toward separate schools? How should we meet discriminations on railways and in hotels? Such questions need not so much specific answers for each part as a general expression of policy, and nobody should be better fitted to announce such a policy than a representative honest Negro Academy.

All this, however, must come in time after careful organization and long conference. The immediate work before us should be practical and have direct bearing upon the situation of the Negro. The historical work of collecting the laws of the United States and of the various States of the Union with regard to the Negro is a work of such magnitude and importance that no body but one like this could think of undertaking it. If we could accomplish that one task we would justify our existence.

In the field of Sociology an appalling work lies before us. First, we must unflinchingly and bravely face the truth, not with apologies, but with solemn earnestness. The Negro Academy ought to sound a note of warning that would echo in every black cabin in the land: Unless we conquer our present vices they will conquer us; we are diseased, we are developing criminal tendencies, and an alarmingly large percentage of our men and women are sexually impure. The Negro Academy should stand and proclaim this over the housetops, crying with Garrison: I will not equivocate, I will not retreat a single inch, and I will be heard. The Academy should seek to gather about it the talented, unselfish men, the pure and noble-minded women, to fight an army of devils that disgraces our manhood and our womanhood. There does not stand today upon God's earth a race more capable in muscle, in intellect, in morals, than the American Negro, if he will bend his energies in the right direction; if he will

> Burst his birth's invidious bar
> And grasp the skirts of happy chance,
> And breast the blows of circumstance,

And grapple with his evil star.

In science and morals, I have indicated two fields of work for the Academy. Finally, in practical policy, I wish to suggest the following Academy Creed:

1.  We believe that the Negro people, as a race, have a contribution to make to civilization and humanity, which no other race can make.
2.  We believe it the duty of the Americans of Negro descent, as a body, to maintain their race identity until this mission of the Negro people is accomplished and the ideal of human brotherhood has become a practical possibility.
3.  We believe that, unless modern civilization is a failure, it is entirely feasible and practicable for two races in such essential political, economic and religious harmony as the white and colored people of America, to develop side by side in peace and mutual happiness, the peculiar contribution which each has to make to the culture of their common country.
4.  As a means to this end we advocate, not such social equality between these races as would disregard human likes and dislikes, but such a social equilibrium as would, throughout all the complicated relations of life, give due and just consideration to culture, ability, and moral worth whether they be found under white or black skins
5.  We believe that the first and greatest step toward the settlement of the present friction between the races—commonly called the Negro problem—lies in the correction of the immorality, crime and laziness among the Negroes themselves, which still remains as a heritage from slavery. We believe that only earnest and long continued efforts on our own part can cure these social ills.
6.  We believe that the second great step toward a better adjustment of the relations between the races, should be a more impartial selection of ability in the economic and intellectual world, and a greater respect for personal liberty and worth, regardless of race. We believe that only earnest efforts on the part of the white people of this country will bring much needed reform in these matters.
7.  On the basis of the foregoing declaration, and firmly believing in our high destiny, we, as American Negroes, are resolved to strive in every honorable way for the realization of the best and highest aims, for the development of strong manhood and pure womanhood, and for the rearing of a race ideal in America and Africa, to the glory of God and the uplifting of the Negro people.

## DISCUSSION QUESTIONS

1. How does Du Bois characterize African Americans' response to the question of race in his day? And what response does he advocate in its place? Why?
2. How does the author define race, and how does this differ from commonplace or even not-so-commonplace definitions of race today?
3. What is the rationale for the American Negro Academy, and how does that rationale and the American Negro Academy's mission mesh with recent arguments for and against affirmative action policies?

# Racist America
## *Racist Ideology as a Social Force*

Joe R. Feagin

## CREATING A RACIST IDEOLOGY

THE DRAMATIC EXPANSION of Europe from the 1400s to the early 1900s eventually brought colonial exploitation to more than 80 percent of the globe. The resulting savagery, exploitation, and resource inequalities were global, and they stemmed, as W. E. B. Du Bois has noted, from letting a "single tradition of culture suddenly have thrust into its hands the power to bleed the world of its brawn and wealth, and the willingness to do this."[1] However, for the colonizing Europeans it was not enough to bleed the world of its labor and resources. The colonizers were not content to exploit indigenous peoples and view that exploitation simply as "might makes right." Instead, they vigorously justified what they had done for themselves and their descendants. Gradually, a broad racist ideology rationalized the oppression and thereby reduced its apparent moral cost for Europeans.

An ideology is a set of principles and views that embodies the basic interests of a particular social group. Typically, a broad ideology encompasses expressed attitudes and is constantly reflected in the talk and actions of everyday life. One need not know or accept the entire ideology for it to have an impact on thought or action. Thus, each person may participate only in certain fragments of an ideology. Ideologies are usually created by oppressors to cover what they do, and counterideologies are often developed by the oppressed in their struggle against domination. Here we examine a critical aspect of the social reproduction of systemic racism from one generation to the next. The per-

Selected for The Social Issues Collection™ by Pawan Dhingra. Excerpted and adapted by Joe R. Feagin from Feagin, *Racist America: Roots, Current Realities, and Future Reparations*, 69–104 (Routledge, 2007).

petuation of systemic racism requires an intertemporal reproducing not only of racist institutions and structures but also of the ideological apparatus that buttresses them.

The early exploitative relationships that whites developed in regard to African Americans and Native Americans were quickly rationalized, and they became enduring racist relations. From the beginning, racial oppression has been webbed into most arenas of American life, including places of work and residence, and activities as diverse as eating, procreating, and child rearing. Racist practices in these life worlds create, and are in turn shaped by, basic racist categories in the language and minds of Americans, especially white Americans. A racist ideology has overarching principles and beliefs that provide an umbrella for more specific racist attitudes, prejudices, and stereotypes.

Major ideological frameworks, including racist frameworks, are typically created, codified, and maintained by those at the top of a society, although this construction takes place in ongoing interaction with the views and practices of ordinary citizens. Those with the greater power have the greater ability to impose their own ideas on others. As Karl Marx and Friedrich Engels long ago pointed out, "the ideas of the ruling class are in every epoch the ruling ideas: i.e. the class, which is the ruling material force of society, is at the same time its ruling intellectual force."[2] Elites have dominated the creation, discussion, and dissemination of system-rationalizing ideas in business, the media, politics, education, churches, and government. While there is indeed much popularly generated racist imagery and discourse, even this is usually codified and embellished by the elites. As with most important ideas, if the elites had been opposed to the development of the racist ideology, they would have actively combated it, and it would likely have declined in importance. Thus, in his detailed analysis of the racist ideas and actions of presidents from George Washington to Bill Clinton, Kenneth O'Reilly has shown that conventional wisdom about presidents following a racist populace is wrongheaded. The historical evidence shows that most of the men who control U.S. political institutions have worked hard "to nurture and support the nation's racism."[3] Racist thought did not come accidentally to the United States. It was, and still is, actively developed and propagated.

## THE EMERGING ANTIBLACK IDEOLOGY: EARLY VIEWS

For several centuries white ministers, business people, political leaders, academics, scientists, and media executives have developed and disseminated to all Americans a complex and variegated racist ideology that defends the theft of land and labor from Americans of color. The antiblack version of this ideology is the most developed; it has included a variety of religious, scientific, and psychosexual rationalizations for oppression. Although the ideology has been elaborated and changed somewhat over time, in all its variations it has operated to rationalize white power and privilege.

From the 1600s to the 1800s English and other European Protestants dominated the religious scene on the Atlantic coast of North America, and their religious views incorporated notions of European superiority and non-European inferiority. The early English Protestants regarded themselves as Christian and civilized, but those they conquered as unchristian and savage. Religious and cultural imperialism accompanied economic imperialism.

Most of the new colonists from Europe saw themselves as Christian people of virtue and civilization. From the first century of American colonization these Europeans frequently portrayed themselves as "virtuous republicans." They did not, or should not, have the instinctual qualities of the "creatures of darkness," the black and red Calibans they saw in their stereotyped images. Europeans were rational, ascetic, self-governing, and sexually controlled, while the African and Native American others were irrational, uncivilized, instinctual, and uncontrolled.[4] The first non-Europeans with whom many European colonists came into contact were Native Americans. Rationalizing the often brutal destruction of Native American societies, European colonists developed early on some negative images of Native Americans. Native Americans were "uncivilized savages" to be killed off or pushed beyond the boundaries of European American society. Moreover, much white thinking about indigenous peoples in the first centuries alternated between great hostility, such as can be seen in the Declaration of Independence's complaint about "merciless Indian savages," and the paternalism seen in the image of a "noble savage" who was independent of the vices of Europeans. Novelists such as James Fenimore Cooper heralded what they saw as the diversity in character of the "native warrior of North America. In war, he is daring, boastful, cunning, ruthless … in peace, just, generous, hospitable, revengeful, superstitious, modest, and commonly chaste."[5]

## EARLY COLOR CODING: THE LINK TO SLAVERY

In the first century of North American slavery the antiblack ideology was becoming ever more developed and comprehensive. The emerging ideology increasingly focused not only on the blackness of the others but also on the whiteness of Europeans. Africans and African Americans were viewed as physically, aesthetically, morally, and mentally inferior to whites—differences that were regarded as more or less permanent. "Whiteness" was created in opposition to "blackness," in comparison to which it was not only different but quite superior. Indeed, from the seventeenth century forward black women, men, and children were "constructed as lazy, ignorant, lascivious, and criminal; Whites as industrious, knowledgeable, virtuous, and law-abiding."[6]

Significantly, the antiblack image was not "out there," but rather in the white mind and emotions. In their thinking and imaging, some whites went so far as to view the dark skin of Africans as a "natural infection" or as "pollution." A leading medical educator of the late 1700s, Dr. Benjamin Rush, thought the dark skin color of African Americans resulted from a type of leprosy that could be cured with medical treatment.[7]

The U.S. Constitution recognized the slave economy and implicitly incorporated an ideology of white supremacy in such provisions as the one that counted an African American as only "three-fifths" of a person. After the new nation was created, the unifying of growing numbers of immigrants from various European countries was done in part through the legal and political doctrines buttressing white privilege and superiority. In the first naturalization law in 1790, the new U.S. Congress made the earliest political statement on citizenship. Naturalization was restricted to "white persons." Whiteness thereby became an official government category; only European immigrants could qualify to become citizens of the new United States. The legal doctrines established by Congress and the courts helped to shape and unify the white consciousness, including that of the nation's leadership.[8]

## EMOTIONAL UNDERPINNINGS

From the seventeenth century to the present the ideology justifying antiblack oppression, while overtly cognitive and legally enshrined, has had a strong emotional base. Antiblack attitudes and actions among whites have long been linked to or supported by such emotions as hate, fear, guilt, and repulsion. W. E. B. Du Bois suggested that color barriers are created not only out of overt maliciousness but also by "unconscious acts and irrational reactions unpierced by reason."[9]

For instance, many whites have been emotionally obsessed with what they term "racial mixing." Strong and irrational emotions are evident in the taboos and laws against interracial sex and marriage, which have long been considered to be extremely "unnatural" and "abominable" by many whites. In 1662 the colony of Virginia established the first law against interracial sex, and in 1691 a law against interracial marriage was enforced by banishment. White Virginians, scholars have noted, were very "disturbed by the racial intermingling, especially white-Negro mixtures, and introduced laws to prevent what they saw as the 'abominable mixture and spurious issue' by penalizing whites who engaged in interracial sex."[10] Mixed-ancestry Americans were viewed not only as inferior but also as degrading what Benjamin Franklin called a "lovely" whiteness. As Franklin argued, white "amalgamation with the other color produces a degradation to which no lover of his country, no lover of excellence in the human character can innocently consent."[11] Like most whites of the eighteenth century, Franklin seems to have developed a deep fear of black Americans. A slaveholder for several decades, then a leading abolitionist later in life, Franklin openly opposed slavery not because of its inhumanity but because of its negative impact on the whiteness of the American population. Ironically and significantly, for most of American history it was white men who were the most likely to cross the color line and force sex on black women.

Strong emotions are evident in the white violence that has long targeted black Americans. While most of the bloodthirsty lynchings of black Americans took place after the Civil War, they were preceded before that war by barbaric beatings, rape, torture, and mutilation of Africans and African Americans on slave ships, farms, and plantations. The early white notion that African Americans were "dangerous savages" and "degenerate beasts" played a role in rationalizing this violence. To deserve such treatment "the black man presumably had to be as vicious as the racists claimed; otherwise many whites would have had to accept an intolerable burden of guilt for perpetrating or tolerating the most horrendous cruelties and injustices."[12] After slavery, the racist ideology legitimated lynchings, whose sadistic character suggests deep and shared white emotions of guilt, hatred, and fear.

Fear is central to the ideology and attitudes woven through the system of antiblack oppression. Significantly, of the three large-scale systems of social oppression—racism, sexism, and classism—only racism involves the dominant group having a deep and often obsessively emotional fear of the subordinate group. This is not generally true for men, who dominate women in the system of sexism, nor is it true for the capitalists who exploit workers in the class-stratified capitalist system.

## DEVELOPING AN EXPLICIT IDEOLOGY OF "RACE"

The ideology rationalizing exploitation did not develop all at once, but was elaborated as colonialism expanded around the globe. First, as we saw above, the "others" were viewed as religiously and culturally inferior. This brought an early accent on a hierarchy of inferior and superior groups. Later on, those oppressed were seen as distinctive "races" that were inferior in physical, biological, and intellectual terms to Europeans. A clearly delineated concept of "race" as a distinctive pseudobiological category was developed by northern Europeans and European Americans about the time of the American Revolution.

By the late 1700s these hierarchical relations were increasingly explained in overtly bioracial terms. This biological determinism read existing European prejudices back into human biology; then it read that biology as rationalizing social hierarchy. Those at the bottom were less than human; they were alleged to have smaller, and thus inferior, brains. Reflecting on European imperialism in the late nineteenth and early twentieth centuries, Frantz Fanon stressed the point that this colonialism was about much more than labor or resource exploitation, for it involved broad social domination constructed in racist terms. European colonialism created the modern idea of "race" across the globe. "In the colonies the economic substructure is also a superstructure. The cause is the consequence; you are rich because you are white, you are white because you are rich."[13] This new racist ideology had three important elements: (1) an accent on physically and biologically distinctive categories called "races"; (2) an emphasis on "race" as the primary determinant of a group's essential personality and cultural traits; and (3) a hierarchy of superior and inferior racial groups.

America's prominent theorist of liberty, Thomas Jefferson, contended that black Americans were an inferior "race." In *Notes on the State of Virginia*, written in the late eighteenth century, Jefferson articulated what were the first developed arguments by an American intellectual for black inferiority. Blacks are said to be inferior to whites in reasoning, imagination, and beauty. Blacks are alleged to favor white beauty "as uniformly as is the preference of the Oranootan [Orangutan] for the black women over those of his own species." Blacks are alleged to be more adventuresome than whites because they have a "want of forethought," to be unreflective, and—perhaps most amazing—to feel life's pain less than whites. Blacks are alleged to have produced no important thinkers, poets, musicians, or intellectuals. Improvement in black minds comes only when there is a "mixture with whites," which Jefferson argues "proves that their inferiority is not the effect merely of their condition of life."[14]

## SCIENTIFIC RACISM

As early as the 1730s the Swedish botanist and taxonomist, Carolus Linneaus, distinguished four categories of human beings—black, white, red, and yellow. Though he did not explicitly use the idea of "race," he associated skin color with cultural traits—with whites being superior and blacks inferior. Between the 1770s and the 1790s the prominent German anatomist and anthropologist, Johann Blumenbach, worked out a racial classification that became influential. At the top of his list of "races" were what Blumenbach called the "Caucasians" (Europeans), a term he coined because in his judgment the people of the Caucasus were the most beautiful of the European peoples. Lower on the list were the Mongolians (Asians), the Ethiopians (Africans), the Americans (Native Americans), and the Malays (Polynesians). "White" was viewed as the oldest color of mankind, and white had degenerated into the darker skin colors.[15]

The new scientific racism firmly encompassed the notion of a specific number of races with different physical characteristics, a belief that these characteristics were hereditary, and the notion of a natural hierarchy of inferior and superior races. In their broad sweep these racist ideas were not supported by careful scientific observations of all human societies but rather were buttressed with slanted reports gleaned by

European missionaries, travelers, and sea captains from their experiences with selected non-European societies. Most scientists of the late eighteenth and early nineteenth centuries, while presenting themselves as objective observers, tried to marshal evidence for human differences that the white imperialists' perspective had already decided were important to highlight.[16]

## CELEBRATING AND EXPANDING THE RACIST IDEOLOGY

In the United States distinguished lawyers, judges, and political leaders promoted scientific racism and its white-supremacist assumptions. In the first half of the nineteenth century whites with an interest in slavery dominated the political and legal system. This influence was conspicuous in the infamous *Dred Scott v. John F. A. Sandford* (1857) decision. Replying to the petition of an enslaved black American, a substantial majority of the U.S. Supreme Court ruled that Scott was not a citizen under the Constitution and had no rights. Chief Justice Roger Taney, a slaveholder, argued that African Americans "had for more than a century before [the U.S. Constitution] been regarded as beings of an inferior order, and altogether unfit to associate with the white race, either in social or political relations; and so far inferior, that they had no rights which the white man was bound to respect; and that the negro might justly and lawfully be reduced to slavery for his benefit. He was bought and sold, and treated as an ordinary article of merchandise and traffic, whenever a profit could be made by it. This opinion was at that time fixed and universal in the civilized portion of the white race."[17] The Dred Scott decision showed that the racist ideology was both elaborate and well established.

Senators and presidents played their role in articulating and spreading this ideology. President James Buchanan, a northerner, urged the nation to support the racist thinking of the *Dred Scott* decision. Moreover, several years before he became president, in his debate with Senator Stephen A. Douglas, Abraham Lincoln argued that the physical difference between the races was insuperable, saying, "I am not nor ever have been in favor of the social and political equality of the white and black races: that I am not nor ever have been in favor of making voters of the free negroes, or jurors, or qualifying them to hold office or having them to marry with white people. ... I as much as any other man am in favor of the superior position being assigned to the white man."[18] Lincoln, soon to be the "Great Emancipator," had made his white supremacist views clear, views later cited by southern officials in the 1960s struggle to protect legal segregation and still quoted by white supremacist groups today.

With the end of Reconstruction in 1877 came comprehensive and coercive racial segregation in the South. Distinguished judges, including those on the Supreme Court, played a key role in solidifying the extensive segregation of black Americans and in unifying white defenses of institutionalized racism. In *Plessy v. Ferguson* (1896) a nearly unanimous Supreme Court legitimated the fiction of "separate but equal" for black and white Americans in a case dealing with racially segregated railroad cars. This separate-but-equal fiction was legal for more than half a century, until the 1954 *Brown v. Board of Education of Topeka* decision and until broken down further by the civil rights laws of the 1960s. There was widespread agreement in the elites and in the general white population about the desirability of thorough and compulsory segregation for black men, women, and children.

## SOCIAL DARWINISM

In his influential writings Charles Darwin applied his evolutionary idea of natural selection not only to animal development but also to the development of human "races." He saw natural selection at work in the killing of the indigenous peoples of Australia by the British, wrote of blacks as a category between whites and gorillas, and spoke against social programs for the "weak" because they permitted the least desirable people to survive. The "civilized races" would eventually replace the "savage races throughout the world."[19]

During the late 1800s and early 1900s a perspective called "social Darwinism" developed the ideas of Darwin and argued aggressively that certain "inferior races" were less evolved, less human, and more apelike than the "superior races." Prominent social scientists like Herbert Spencer and William Graham Sumner argued that social life was a life-and-death struggle in which the best individuals would win out over inferior individuals. Sumner argued that wealthy Americans, who were almost entirely white at the time, were products of natural selection and essential to the advance of civilization. Black Americans were seen by many of these openly racist analysts as a "degenerate race" whose alleged "immorality" was a racial trait.[20]

By the late 1800s a eugenics movement was spreading among scientists and other intellectuals in Europe and the United States. Eugenicists accented the importance of breeding the "right" types of human groups. Britain's Sir Francis Galton argued for improving the superior race by human intervention. Like Galton, U.S. eugenicists opposed "racial mixing" (or "miscegenation") because it destroyed racial purity. Allowing "unfit races" to survive would destroy the "superior race" of northern Europeans. Those from the lesser races, it was decided, should be sterilized or excluded from the nation. Such views were not on the fringe, but had the weight of established scientists, leading politicians, and major business leaders. Thus, in 1893 Nathaniel S. Shaler, a prominent scientist and dean at Harvard University, argued that black Americans were inferior, uncivilized, and an "alien folk" with no place in the body politic. In social Darwinist fashion, he spoke of their eventual extinction under the processes of natural law.[21]

Scientific racism was used by white members of Congress to support passage of discriminatory congressional legislation, including the openly racist 1924 immigration law excluding most immigrants other than northern Europeans. In this period overtly racist ideas were advocated by all U.S. presidents. Former president Theodore Roosevelt openly favored scientific racism.[22] President Woodrow Wilson was well-known as an advocate of the superiority of European civilization over all others, including those of Africa. As president, Wilson increased the racial segregation of the federal government. Significantly, no less a racist leader than Adolf Hitler would later report having been influenced by Wilson's writings. (In its contemporary sense, the term *racism* first appeared in a 1933 German book by Magnus Hirschfeld, who sought to counter the Nazi and other European racists' notion of a biologically determined hierarchy of races.)[23]

In 1921 President Warren G. Harding, who had once been linked to the Ku Klux Klan, said he rejected any "suggestion of social equality" between blacks and whites, citing a popular racist book as evidence the "race problem" was a global problem. Not long before he became president, Calvin Coolidge wrote in *Good Housekeeping* magazine, "Biological laws tell us that certain divergent people will not mix or blend. The Nordics propagate themselves successfully. With other races, the outcome shows deterioration on both sides."[24] Ideas of white supremacy and rigid segregation were openly advocated by top political leaders.

## PERPETUATING THE RACIST IDEOLOGY: CONTEMPORARY AMERICA

Periodically, the racist ideology framed in the first two centuries of American development has shifted somewhat in its framing or emphases. Those in charge have dressed it up differently for changing social circumstances, though the underlying framework has remained much the same. Some new ideas have been added to deal with pressures for change from those oppressed, particularly ideas about government policy. After World War II, aspects of the dominant racist ideology were altered somewhat to fit the new circumstances of the 1950s and 1960s, during which black Americans increasingly challenged patterns of compulsory racial segregation.

In recent decades white elites have continued to dominate the transmission of new or refurbished ideas and images designed to buttress the system of racial inequality, and they have used ever more powerful means to accomplish their ends. The mass media now include not only the radio, movies, and print media used in the past, but television, music videos, satellite transmissions, and the Internet.

Today, for the most part, the mass media are still controlled by whites. Just under 90 percent of the news reporters, supervisors, and editors at newspapers and magazines across the United States are white. On television whites are overrepresented in managerial jobs, and as on-air reporters; they are greatly overrepresented as "experts" in the mass media. Americans of color have only a token presence in the choice and shaping of news reports and media entertainment. The concentration of media control in a few corporations has increased dramatically in recent decades. In the early twenty-first century, fewer than two dozen corporations control much of the mass media, and that number is likely to decrease further. In addition, the mass media, especially television, are substantially supported by corporate advertisers, and advertisers have significant command over programming. Thus, information about racial matters is usually filtered and whitewashed through a variety of elite-controlled organizations. This filtering is not a coordinated conspiracy, but reflects the choices of many powerful whites socialized to the dominant framing in regard to racial issues.[25]

Looking for data and stories, reporters and journalists typically seek out established government, business, academic, and think-tank reports and experts. The right wing of the U.S. ruling class, a large segment, has historically been the most committed to the racist ideology and has pressed for repression of protests against oppression. The liberal wing of the white elite is much smaller and often more attuned to popular movements; it has been willing to liberalize the society to some degree and to make some concessions to protesters for the sake of preserving the society. (The center of the elite has waffled between the two poles.) In the late 1960s and 1970s many experts consulted by top executives in government and the mass media came from think tanks usually espousing the views of those in the center or on the left of the ruling elite. Becoming very concerned about this, wealthy conservatives began in the 1970s to lavishly fund right-wing think tanks and to press aggressively conservative views of U.S. society on universities, politicians, and media owners. In recent years the right-wing think tanks—including the American Enterprise Institute, the Manhattan Institute, and the Heritage Foundation—have been very successful in getting their experts into mainstream discussions and debates. Working alongside a large group of other conservative intellectuals, media experts, and activists, these right-wing think tanks continue to be successful in an indoctrination campaign aimed at shaping public views on racial and other social issues.[26]

Most Americans now get their news from commercial television and radio programs. The largest single source is local news programming.[27] Using these local and national media, the white elites have the capability to mobilize mass consensus on elite-generated ideas and views; this consensus often provides an illusion of democracy. These elites encourage collective ignorance by allowing little systematic information critical of the existing social and political system to be circulated through the media to the general population.

With the national racial order firmly in place, most white Americans, from childhood on, come to adopt the views, assumptions, and proclivities of previous generations and established white authorities. In this manner the system of racism is reproduced from one generation of whites to the next.

## INCREASED EQUALITY RHETORIC

From the 1960s onward the rhetoric of racial equality, or at least of an equality of opportunity, grew in volume among members of the white elite, including presidents and members of Congress. The black protests and rebellions of the 1950s and 1960s had an important effect in eradicating not only the system of the legal segregation but also most public defense of racial discrimination by the nation's white leadership. Since the late 1960s most leaders have proclaimed the rhetoric of racial and ethnic equality.

The structural dismantling of a large-scale system of compulsory segregation did require a new equality emphasis in the prevailing racial ideology. However, while the structural position of whites and blacks had changed somewhat, at least officially, most whites—in the elites and the general public—did not seem interested in giving up significant white power or privilege. Thus, the racist ideology was altered in some ways but continued to incorporate many of its old features, and it continued to rationalize white privilege—now under conditions of official desegregation. There had long been some fairness language in the prevailing ideology—for example, most whites thought blacks were treated fairly—but now notions of fairness and equality of opportunity were moved to the forefront. The acceptance by the white elite and public of the principles of equal opportunity and desegregation in regard to schools, jobs, and public accommodations did *not* mean that most whites desired for the federal government to implement large-scale integration of these institutions.

## A MORE CONSERVATIVE ORIENTATION: 1969 TO THE PRESENT

Beginning around 1969, with the arrival of Richard Nixon's presidential administration, the rhetoric of equality was increasingly accompanied by a federal government backing off from its modest commitment to desegregation and enforcement of the new civil rights laws. At the local level, there was increased police repression of aggressive dissent in the black community, such as the illegal attacks on Black Panthers and other militant black groups by local police and FBI agents. The old racist images of dangerous black men and black welfare mothers were dusted off and emphasized by prominent white leaders who often spouted the rhetoric of equality at the same time. Moreover, the liberal wing of the white elite, which had provided some funding for the civil rights movement and other social movements of the 1960s, significantly reduced its support for these movements.[28]

By the mid-1970s the right wing of the ruling elite was accelerating its attack on the liberal thinking associated with the new civil rights laws. Since the 1970s a growing number of conservative organizations have worked aggressively in pressing Congress, the federal courts, and the private sector to eviscerate or eliminate antidiscrimination programs such as affirmative action efforts, as well as an array of other government social programs. This signaled the increasing influence on national policy of a more conservative Republican Party that represented, almost exclusively, the interests of white Americans. Moreover, even at the top of the Democratic Party there was also some shift to the right, which could be seen in the relatively modest antidiscrimination policies of the Jimmy Carter and Bill Clinton administrations.

The shift away from government action to remedy discrimination was associated with a reinvigoration of notions about inferior black intelligence and culture. In the 1970s, and increasingly in the 1980s and 1990s, numerous white journalists, politicians, and academics were critical of what they saw as too-liberal views in regard to black Americans and remedies for discrimination and defended arguments about black intellectual or cultural inferiority. In public policy discussions, increasingly led by white conservatives, there was a renewed emphasis on the view that only the individual, not the group, is protected from discrimination under U.S. law.

The federal courts provide an important example of this conservative shift. In the decades since the 1970s these courts have often ruled that group-remedy programs against racial discrimination violate the U.S. Constitution, which they assert only recognizes the rights of individuals, not groups. For instance, in 1989 a conservative Supreme Court handed down a major decision, *City of Richmond, Virginia v. J. A. Croson Co.,* which knocked down a local program designed to remedy past discrimination against black and other minority businesses.[29] The high court ruled in favor of a white-run construction company, the plaintiff, which argued that the municipal government had unconstitutionally set aside business for minority companies. The court ruled that the city of Richmond had not made a compelling case for racial discrimination, even though the defendant's statistics showed that in a city whose population was one-half black, *less than 1 percent of the city government's business* went to black-owned firms.

## STILL ARGUING FOR BIOLOGICAL "RACES"

In recent years some social and behavioral scientists have joined with certain physical scientists to continue to press for the idea of biological races and to connect that idea to concerns over government social policies. Since the late 1960s several social scientists at leading universities, including Arthur Jensen and Richard Herrnstein, have continued to argue that racial-group differences in average scores on the so-called IQ tests reveal genetic differences in intelligence between black and white Americans. Their views have been influential, especially on white politicians and the white public. In 1969 the *Harvard Educational Review* lent its prestige to a long article by Jensen, a University of California professor. The arguments presented there and Jensen's later arguments in the next two decades have received much national attention, including major stories in *Time, Newsweek, U.S. News and World Report, Life,* and major newspapers. Jensen has argued that on the average blacks are born with less intelligence than whites, and that the "IQ" test data support this contention. In addition, he has suggested that high birth rates for black Americans could result in a lowering of the nation's overall intelligence level.[30]

Perhaps the most widely read example of biological determinism is a 1990s book, *The Bell Curve,* which sold more than a half million copies. Into the twenty-first century it is still being cited and read. Like Jensen, the authors of *The Bell Curve*—the late Harvard University professor Richard Herrnstein and prominent author Charles Murray—argue that IQ test data show that black (and Latino) Americans are inferior in intelligence to whites. Though the authors have no training in genetics, they suggest that this supposed inferiority in intelligence results substantially from genetic differences. Thus, biological differences account to a substantial degree for racial inequalities. The fact that the book has sold many copies and has been widely debated in the media—in spite of the overwhelming evidence against its arguments—strongly suggests that biologically oriented racist thinking is still espoused by a large number of white Americans, including those who are well-educated. Indeed, Herrnstein and Murray explicitly suggest that their views are *privately shared* by many well-educated whites, including those in the elite, who are unwilling to speak out publicly. This book was launched during a major press conference at the conservative American Enterprise Institute. This publicity insured that the book would get much national attention, while antiracist books have generally gotten far less media play.[31]

Racist arguments about contemporary intelligence levels are grounded in nearly four hundred years of viewing blacks as having an intelligence inferior to that of whites. Today, such views are much more than an academic matter. They have periodically been used by members of Congress and presidential advisors in the White House to argue against antidiscrimination and other government programs that benefit Americans of color. Given this elite activity, it is not surprising to find these views in the white public.

Another aspect of older racist views that can be found in new dress is the idea of what one might call "cultural racism"—the view that blacks have done less well than whites because of their allegedly deficient culture with its weak work ethic and family values. As early as the seventeenth century, black Americans were seen as inferior in civilization and morality to white colonists. These blaming-the-victim views have regularly been resuscitated among the white elites and passed along to ordinary Americans as a way of explaining the difficult socioeconomic conditions faced by black Americans.

Since the 1970s leading magazines have published articles accenting some version of this perspective on what came to be called the black "underclass"; the perspective accents the allegedly deficient morality and lifestyle of many black Americans. Prominent author Ken Auletta wrote an influential set of *New Yorker* articles, later expanded in his book *The Underclass*. He accented the black underclass and its supposed immorality, family disorganization, and substandard work ethic.[32] A later article in the *Chronicle of Higher Education* surveyed the growing research on the underclass, noting that "the lives of the ghetto poor are marked by a dense fabric of what experts call 'social pathologies'—teenage pregnancies, out-of-wedlock births, single-parent families, poor educational achievement, chronic unemployment, welfare dependency, drug abuse, and crime—that, taken separately or together, seem impervious to change."[33] To the present day, similar stories designed to explain black problems in cultural terms regularly appear in the local and national media across the nation.

## A WHITEWASHED WORLDVIEW

This antiblack ideology links in so many ways to so much of white thought and behavior that we might speak of it as a broad worldview. Seen comprehensively, all the mental images, prejudiced attitudes, stereotypes, fictions, racist explanations, and rationalizations that link to systemic racism make up a white racist worldview, one deeply imbedded in the dominant culture and institutions. The U.S. system of racism is not just something that affects black Americans and other Americans of color, for it is central to the lives of white Americans as well. It determines how whites think about themselves, about their ideals, and about their nation.

In the early 1900s European immigrants to the United States came to accept this worldview and its implicit assumption that being "American" means being white. This has not changed much in the intervening years. Today the term "American" still means "white"—at least for the majority of white Americans, and probably for most people across the globe. One can pick up most newspapers or news magazines and find "American" or "Americans" used in a way that clearly accents *white* Americans. Take this sentence from a news writer in a Florida newspaper: "The American Public isn't giving government or police officers the blind trust it once did."[34] Clearly, "American" here means "white American," for the majority of blacks have never blindly trusted the police.

One research analysis examined all the articles in sixty-five major English-language newspapers for a six-month period and estimated that there were thousands of references to "black Americans" or "African Americans" in the articles. However, in the same newspapers there were *only forty-six* mentions of "white Americans."[35] In almost every case these mentions by newspaper writers occurred in connection with "black Americans," "blacks," or "African Americans." (The exceptions were three cases in which "white Americans" was used in connection with "Native Americans" or "Korean Americans.") A similar pattern was found for major magazines. Not once was the term "white Americans" used alone in an article; if used, it was always used in relation to another racial category. The same study examined how congressional candidates were described in news articles in the two weeks prior to the November 1998 elections. In every case white congressional candidates were *not* described as "white," but black congressional candidates were always noted as being "black."[36] In the United States blackness is usually salient and noted, while whiteness generally goes unmentioned, except when reference is specifically made to white connections to other racial groups.

Being "American" still means, in the minds of many people, including editors and writers in the media, being white. This need not be a conscious process. For several centuries most whites have probably not seen the routines of their everyday lives as framed in white. "Race" is often not visible when one is at the top of the social hierarchy. Today, major social institutions, those originally created by whites centuries ago, are still dominated by whites. Yet from the white standpoint they are not white, just normal and customary. They are not seen for what they actually are—whitewashed institutions reflecting in many of their aspects the history, privileges, norms, values, and interests of white Americans. When whites live in these customary arrangements, they need not think in overtly racist terms. Nonetheless, when whites move into settings where they must confront people of color in the United States or elsewhere, they usually foreground their whiteness, whether consciously or unconsciously.

## FEAR OF A MULTIRACIAL, MULTICULTURAL FUTURE

Today, many white analysts still see Western civilization as under threat from groups that are not white or European. Racist thinking is more than rationalizing oppression, for it also represents a defensive response, a fear of losing power to Americans of color. In recent years many advocates of white superiority have directed their attacks at the values or cultures of new immigrants of color coming to the United States, as well as at black Americans. In one recent interview study elite numerous white men openly expressed some fear of the growth of Americans of color in the United States, seeing Western civilization as under threat.[37]

We observe examples of this fear among U.S. politicians and intellectuals. For example, in several speeches and articles Patrick Buchanan, media pundit and once a candidate for the Republican presidential nomination, has argued that "our Judeo-Christian values are going to be preserved and our Western heritage is going to be handed down to future generations and not dumped on some landfill called multiculturalism."[38] Once again, we see the linkage between religion and a strong sense of European supremacy. We also see a concern for the reproduction of the white-dominated system from current to future generations. In addition, Buchanan told one interviewer that "if we had to take a million immigrants in, say, Zulus next year or Englishmen, and put them in Virginia, what group would be easier to assimilate and would cause less problems for the people of Virginia? There is nothing wrong with us sitting down and arguing that issue that we are a European country, [an] English-speaking country."[39] The Zulus, who are Africans, seem to represent in his mind the specter of strange or savage hordes who would not assimilate well into the nation. Ironically, Africans have been in the nation longer than Buchanan's Irish ancestors, and Virginia has been home to African Americans for nearly four centuries.

## CONCLUSION

The systemic racism that is still part of the base of U.S. society is interwoven with a strong racist ideology that has been partially reframed at various points in U.S. history, but which has remained a well-institutionalized set of beliefs, attitudes, and concepts defending white-on-black oppression. Until the late 1940s commitment to a white supremacist view of the world was proud, openly held, and aggressive. Most whites in the United States and Europe, led by elites, took pride in forthrightly professing their racist perspectives on other peoples and their racist rationalizations for Western imperialistic adventures. Brutal discrimination and overt exploitation were routinely advocated. Indeed, white domination of the globe was "seen as proof of white racial superiority."[40]

Beginning in the late 1940s, however, the open expression of a white supremacist ideology was made more difficult by a growing American awareness of actions of the racist regime in Nazi Germany. In addition, by the 1950s and 1960s growing black civil rights protests against U.S. racism—with their counterideology of black liberation—and the U.S. struggle with the Soviet Union made the open expression of a white supremacist ideology less acceptable. The dominant racist ideology changed slowly to reflect these new conditions, with a new accent on equality of opportunity and some support for moderate programs to break down the nation's segregated institutions. Still, as we have seen, many aspects of the old racist ideology were dressed up in a new guise, and they persist, with some barnacle-like additions, to the present day. From the beginning, the age-old idea of the superiority of white (Western) culture and institutions has been the most basic idea in the dominant ideology rationalizing oppression.

For some time now, most whites have viewed the last few centuries of societal development in terms of a broad imagery equating "human progress" with Western civilization. We hear or see phrases like "Western civilization is an engine generating great progress for the world" or "Africans have only seen real advancement because of their contacts with Western civilization." Western imperialism's bringing of "civilization" or "democracy" to other peoples is made to appear as an engine of great progress, with mostly good results. However, this equating of "progress" with European civilization conceals the devastating consequences of imperialism and colonialism. The actual reality was—and often still is—brutal, bloody, oppressive, or genocidal in consequence for those colonized. When whites speak of Western civilization as equivalent to great human progress, they are talking about the creation of social systems that do not take into serious consideration the interests and views of the indigenous or enslaved peoples whose resources were ripped from them, whose societies were destroyed, and whose lives were cut short. Images of Western civilization, like the racist ideologies of which they are often part, are too often used to paper over the sordid realities of Western colonialism and imperialism.

## DISCUSSION QUESTIONS

1. What is a racist ideology, and when did it first develop in North America?
2. Are elites or the rank-and-file population most responsible for the growth and importance of the racist ideology?
3. Is the racist ideology still important today? How and where?
4. Have prominent presidents and scientists played any important role in the development of racist ideas and notions? If so, how and when?
5. What is social Darwinism, and is it still important in U.S. society today?

## NOTES

1. W. E. B. Du Bois, *Dusk of Dawn: An Essay Toward an Autobiography of a Race Concept* (New Brunswick, NJ: Transaction Books, 1984 [1940]), p. 144.
2. Karl Marx and Friederich Engels, *The German Ideology,* ed. R. Pascal (New York: International Publishers, 1947), p. 39.
3. Kenneth O'Reilly, *Nixon's Piano: Presidents and Racial Politics from Washington to Clinton* (New York: Free Press, 1995), p. 11.

4. Ronald T. Takaki, *Iron Cages: Race and Culture in 19th Century America* (Oxford: Oxford University Press, 1990), pp. 11–14.

5. James Fenimore Cooper, *The Last of the Mohicans* (1826), as quoted in Emily Morison Beck, ed., *John Bartlett's Familiar Quotations, 15th ed.* (Boston: Little Brown, 1980), p. 463.

6. Tomás Almaguer, *Racial Fault Lines* (Berkeley and Los Angeles: University of California Press, 1994), p. 28.

7. Takaki, *Iron Cages,* pp. 30–34.

8. See Frances Lee Ansley, "Stirring the Ashes: Race, Class and the Future of Civil Rights Scholarship," *Cornell Law Review* 74 (September, 1989): 993.

9. W. E. B. Du Bois, *Dusk of Dawn: An Essay Toward an Autobiography of a Race Concept* (New Brunswick, NJ: Transaction Books, 1984 [1940]), p. 6.

10. A. Leon Higginbotham, Jr., and Barbara K. Kopytoff, "Racial Purity and Interracial Sex in the Law of Colonial and Antebellum Virginia," *Georgetown Law Journal* 77 (August 1989): 1671.

11. Benjamin Franklin, quoted in Takaki, *Iron Cages,* p. 50; Claude-Anne Lopez and Eugenia W. Herbert, *The Private Franklin: The Man and His Family* (New York: Norton, 1975), pp. 194–95.

12. George Frederickson, *The Black Image in the White Mind* (Hanover, NH: Wesleyan University Press, 1971), p. 282.

13. Frantz Fanon, *The Wretched of the Earth* (New York: Grove Press, 1963), p. 32.

14. Thomas Jefferson, *Notes on the State of Virginia,* ed. Frank Shuffelton (New York: Penguin, 1999 [1785]), pp. 145, 147–48.

15. William H. Tucker, *The Science and Politics of Racial Research* (Urbana: University of Illinois Press, 1994), pp. 8–9; Ivan Hannaford, *Race: The History of an Idea in the West* (Baltimore: Johns Hopkins University Press, 1996), pp. 205–207.

16. Audrey Smedley, *Race in North America* (Boulder, CO: Westview Press, 1993), p. 26.

17. *Dred Scott v. John F. A. Sandford,* 60 U.S. 393, 407–408 (1857).

18. Abraham Lincoln, "The Sixth Joint Debate at Quincy, October 13, 1858," in *The Lincoln-Douglas Debates: The First Complete, Unexpurgated Text,* ed. Harold Holzer (New York: HarperCollins, 1993), p. 283.

19. Charles Darwin, quoted in Frederickson, *The Black Image in the White Mind,* p. 230.

20. See Joe R. Feagin, *Subordinating the Poor: Welfare and American Beliefs* (Englewood Cliffs, NJ: Prentice-Hall, 1975), pp. 35–36; and Frederick L. Hoffman,

"Vital Statistics of the Negro," *Arena* 5 (April 1892): 542, cited in Frederickson, *The Black Image in the White Mind,* pp. 250–51.

21. John Higham, *Strangers in the Land* (New York: Atheneum, 1963), pp. 96–152; Tucker, *The Science and Politics of Racial Research,* p. 35.

22. Tucker, *The Science and Politics of Racial Research,* p. 93.

23. See Theodore Cross, *Black Power Imperative: Racial Inequality and the Politics of Nonviolence* (New York: Faulkner, 1984), p. 157; Magnus Hirschfeld, *Racism,* trans. and ed. by Eden and Cedar Paul (London: V. Gollancz, 1938). The book was published in German in 1933.

24. Warren G. Harding and Calvin Coolidge, each quoted in Tucker, *The Science and Politics of Racial Research,* p. 93.

25. David K. Shipler, "Blacks in the Newsroom," *Columbia Journalism Review,* May/June 1998, pp. 81 26–29; Robert M. Entman et al., *Mass Media and Reconciliation: A Report to the Advisory Board and Staff, The President's Initiative on Race* (Washington, DC, 1998); Edward Herman, "The Propaganda Model Revisited," *Monthly Review* 48 (July 1996): 115.

26. Sidney Blumenthal, *The Rise of the Counter-Establishment* (New York: Times Books, 1986), pp. 4–11, 133–70; Peter Steinfels, *The Neoconservatives: The Men Who Are Changing America's Politics* (New York: Touchstone, 1979), pp. 214–77.

27. Franklin D. Gilliam Jr., and Shanto Iyengar, "Prime Suspects: the Effects of Local News on the Viewing Public," University of California at Los Angeles, unpublished paper, n. d.

28. Thomas Ferguson and Joel Rodgers, *Right Turn: The Decline of the Democrats and the Future of American Politics* (New York: Hill and Wang, 1986), pp. 65–66.

29. *City of Richmond, Virginia v. J.A.Croson Co.,* 488 U.S. 469 (1989).

30. Arthur R. Jensen, "How Much Can We Boost IQ and Scholastic Achievement?" *Harvard* 99 *Educational Review* 39 (1969): 1–123.

31. Jean Stefancic and Richard Delgado, *No Mercy: How Conservative Think Tanks and 100 Foundations Changed America's Social Agenda* (Philadelphia: Temple University Press, 1996), p. 34.

32. Ken Auletta, *The Underclass* (New York: Random House, 1982).

33. Ellen K. Coughlin, "Worsening Plight of the Underclass Catches Attention," *Chronicle of Higher Education,* March 1988, A5.

34. I draw here on Nick Mrozinske, "Derivational Thinking and Racism," unpublished research paper, University of Florida, fall, 1998.

35. The search algorithm did not allow searches for the word "whites" alone, because this picks up the surnames of individuals in the Lexis/Nexis database.

36. Mrozinske, "Derivational Thinking and Racism."

37.  Rhonda Levine, "The Souls of Elite White Men: White Racial Identity and the Logic of Thinking on Race," paper presented at annual meeting, Hawaiian Sociological Association, February 14, 1998.

38.  Patrick Buchanan, quoted in Clarence Page, "U.S. Media Should Stop Abetting Intolerance," *Toronto Star,* December 27, 1991, A27.

39.  Patrick Buchanan, quoted in John Dillin, "Immigration Joins List of '92 Issues," *Christian Science Monitor,* December 17, 1991, 6.

40.  Frank Furedi, *The Silent War: Imperialism and the Changing Perception of Race* (New Brunswick, NJ: Rutgers University Press, 1998), p. 1.

## SELECTED BIBLIOGRAPHY

Cross, Theodore. *Black Power Imperative: Racial Inequality and the Politics of Nonviolence* (New York: Faulkner, 1984).

Du Bois, W. E. B. *Dusk of Dawn: An Essay Toward an Autobiography of a Race Concept* (New Brunswick, NJ: Transaction Books, 1984 [1940]).

Furedi, Frank. *The Silent War: Imperialism and the Changing Perception of Race* (New Brunswick, NJ: Rutgers University Press, 1998).

O'Reilly, Kenneth. *Nixon's Piano: Presidents and Racial Politics from Washington to Clinton* (New York: Free Press, 1995).

Smedley, Audrey. *Race in North America* (Boulder, CO: Westview Press, 1993).

Takaki, Ronald T. *Iron Cages: Race and Culture in 19th Century America* (Oxford: Oxford University Press, 1990.

Tucker, William H. *The Science and Politics of Racial Research* (Urbana: University of Illinois Press, 1994).

# CHAPTER 2
## Theories of Racism

# The Skull Measurer's Mistake

## Sven Lindqvist

R ACIST IDEOLOGY BEGAN to appear in the early nineteenth century primarily as a defense of the trade in slaves and then of slavery itself.

The English Anti-Slavery Society was formed in 1823, and after a ten-year struggle, succeeded in having slavery banned in the British colonies. That same year, 1833, the American Anti-Slavery Society was formed to fight against slavery in the United States. The slave owners needed a scientific theory that would make slavery appear natural and justified.

During the 1830s, the last remains of the almost eradicated Native American population were moved from the eastern states of the United States to camps on the other side of the Mississippi. The forced resettlement was conducted in an outrageously cruel fashion, and mortality, particularly among children and old people, was terrifyingly high. A scientific theory was needed to explain why these measures were necessary.

At the time, the races were classified according to color. But skin color was hard to measure. Though inborn, it is clearly influenced by external circumstances—even the whitest skin darkens in the rays of the sun. And, most of all, the causal connection between skin color and slavery was not entirely self-evident.

During the search for permanent and measurable race differences, scholars increasingly changed to examining the skulls of dead people. The skull could be weighed and measured, and was more permanent in size and shape than other parts of the body, both in life and after death. In addition, it was intuitively easy to presume that a causal connection could be found between the capacious cranium and civilized behavior.

So skulls were collected and measured.

The largest collection in the world—six hundred human skulls—was in Philadelphia and belonged to the American Samuel Morton (1799–1851). He came from a Quaker family with an Irish background and had studied medicine in Edinburgh and Paris. He started collecting skulls when he was twenty, and in his forties published two monumental volumes of prints, of which *Crania Americana* (1839) is the best known.

Morton's conclusion from his measurements was unambiguous: white people's skulls were largest, which gave them "decided and unquestionable superiority over all the nations of the earth." That was why they had spread all over the world. "In Asia, in Africa, in America, in the torrid and the frigid zones, have not all the other races of men yielded and given place to this one … ?"

Yes, indeed. And Morton had the explanation: large skull.

One hundred and thirty years later, another scientist, Stephen Jay Gould, set about examining and checking Morton's figures. He found that Morton had made a number of faulty calculations, insignificant in themselves, but systematic in the sense that they all contributed to support Morton's conclusion.

Morton based his conclusions on averages for different races. But represented among his 144 Indian skulls were many different Indian peoples whose skulls were in themselves of very different sizes. If these groups are not weighed, the number of skulls from a certain group would quite randomly influence the final result. That randomness also contributed to supporting Morton's conclusion.

But the determining factor was something else: namely, that the size of the head is related to the size of the body to which it belongs. Men have on an average larger bodies than women. So, if white men's skulls are compared with those of black women, then you can be quite sure the result will be that whites have larger skulls than blacks.

On the other hand, if in Morton's collection men are compared with men, and women with women, it can be seen that black men have slightly larger skulls than white men, while black women have slightly smaller skulls than white women.

Morton did not bother to distinguish between the sexes. By comparing the female skulls of small Hottentots with male skulls of large Englishmen, he "proved" that black people were .stupid and inferior—which was what he wanted to prove.

Morton was not dishonest. He himself published all the raw data needed to establish which mistakes he made. But his scientific reputation was such that no one questioned his conclusion, discussed his methods, or even bothered to check the figures.

To Morton and his American contemporaries, the problem was not whether whites were or were not superior. Whites considered this as obvious as fresh butter is better than rancid. The problem was to measure this superiority. The point at issue was settled; what remained was to find a method to express that truth in figures.

They could not bring in body weight, for just as convincing as it seemed to maintain a connection between the skull and what is inside it, it would be just as ridiculous to maintain that intelligence was dependent on body weight. So no one paid any attention to the connection between the size of the body and that of the skull. No one, except Sven Lindqvist (1781–1861).

He came from Marburg in Germany. As a gynecological surgeon during the Napoleonic Wars, Tiedemann started studying the development of the skull of the fetus. In 1823, he became a professor in Heidelberg and continued his neurological studies, including some dolphins.

The study of dolphins taught Tiedemann that a small head can very well be combined with great intelligence. He also realized that an animal species that is "low" in the biological hierarchy can possess a far more complicated mental capacity than that of "higher" animal species.

In dolphins it was clear that the weight of brain varied with gender, body length, body weight, and acute body condition. The dolphins also taught Tiedemann not only to study averages in large groups, but also to take an interest in individuals and the variations between individuals as well as between groups and divisions of groups.

Tiedemann measured skulls by filling them with millet, then weighing the millet. The most capacious cranium in his collection—fifty-nine ounces—was from a Native American man. In second place came a white man with fifty-seven ounces. Third was an African, fourth a white, and fifth place was shared among three whites, a Mongol, and a Malay.

The most capacious female skull came from a Malay woman at forty-one ounces. A white and a Native American shared second place, and the third place was shared by one black and one white woman.

If, instead, the bottom placings are studied, fifteen percent of the Mongol skulls measured below the thirty-two-ounce level, together with thirteen percent of the Malayan and ten percent of the Native American. But only one single African and one single white measured below that level.

These results did not fit in with the current race hierarchy, in which whites were always to be at the top and blacks at the bottom. Tiedemann drew the conclusion that the anatomists and natural historians who ascribed to the African a smaller skull and smaller brain than the European and all other human races, were quite simply wrong.

As the human skulls were not accompanied by information on body length, body weight etc., then it was not clear what the figures really meant. Perhaps they entailed nothing more than that human beings of certain races are larger or better nourished than others, which does not necessarily influence intelligence.

And what quantity of brain matter was really necessary in order to be a human being? Was any more needed than we all had by nature? On the basis of his investigations, Tiedemann maintained that as far as the brain matter needed for mental faculties was concerned, nature had "equipped people of all the human races equally."

Tiedemann's researches had great influence in Europe and contributed to delaying the advance of racism.

Tiedemann had three sons who participated in the German revolution of 1848—one of them was executed by firing squad and the other two fled to America. There their father's research had not had the same impact as it had had in Europe. America believed Morton. His teachings on the inferiority of the colored races were scientifically inferior to Tiedemann's, but they filled a deeply felt need in white Americans.

The same year that Tiedemann died, 1861, Sanford B. Hunt summarized Morton's teaching as follows:

In history, we find that, so far as the welfare of nations is concerned, there is no such thing as equality; that the strong hand, guided by the intelligent brain, has ever conquered. So the small-brained South American Indians were driven out by the larger-brained North American Indians, who then in their turn were driven to their forest graves by Teutons with even larger brains. It was not conquest or subjugation, but annihilation.

In this race struggle, the "Indian" and the "Negro," according to Morton, were born losers. Nature had condemned them to be exterminated and enslaved. So racists, whatever violence they committed, were essentially innocent. Morton's teaching, as opposed to Tiedemann's, fulfilled the main task of a racist ideology: to justify violence against other races.

## DISCUSSION QUESTIONS

1. What was the skull measurer's mistake?
2. Why was measuring skulls a part of the scientific process?
3. How did society use scientific claims to explain racial differences in social outcomes, social class, or social status?

## BIBLIOGRAPHY

Friedrich Tiedemann, *Das Hirn des Negers mit dem des Europäers und Orang-outangs verglichen* (1837) (Marburg, 1984).

Samuel G. Morton, *Crania Americana, or Comparative View of the Skulls of Various Aboriginal Nations of North and South America, to which is Prefixed an Essay on the Varieties of the Human Species* (Philadelphia & London, 1839); An *Inquiry into the Distinctive Characteristics of the Aboriginal Race of America* (Philadelphia, 1844).

Stephen Jay Gould, *The Mismeasure of Man* (New York, 1981).

Robert E. Bieder, *Science Encounters the Indian 1820–1880* (Norman, 1986).

Sanford B. Hunt quoted after Bieder.

# CHAPTER 3
## Whiteness

# Whiteness as Contingent Hierarchies
## *Who Counts as White and Why*

Steve Garner

## WHAT IS THE POINT OF USING "WHITENESS" AS AN ANALYTICAL TOOL?

S o far we have observed that whiteness has been conceptualized in a number of complementary ways. In this chapter I will focus on the idea that in addition to a set of borders between people categorized as "white" and "non-white," there is another set of internal borders produced by racialization. In other words, there are socially observable degrees of whiteness between the groups that seem to be unproblematically white. Examples here include Southern, Central and Eastern European immigrant groups, Jews, Gypsy-Travellers/Roma, as well as the numerous and important divisions based on class, gender, sexuality, region, etc., identified in the literature on both America and Britain (Hartigan 2005, Nayak 2003, Daniels 1997). The reader may well be experiencing trepidation about the extent to which we are encroaching onto other areas of work. We already have concepts like "anti-semitism," "sexism" and "homophobia." Class divisions are already covered in other literatures. Considering that European migrants are white anyway, how is this to do with "race"? Isn't it ethnicity, another area abundantly, if not excessively, analyzed already? I do not want to be proscriptive. There are plenty of perspectives that can bring fruitful analyses to bear on these identities and social hierarchies, and using the whiteness problematic is one of them. However, I hope to convince you of its utility through the use of three of the broad areas of study dealt with in the literature: immigration into America in the nineteenth and early twentieth century (the "inbetween peoples" thesis); the "White

Australia" policy (1901–1972); and the related ideas of "white trash" in America, and the working class in the U.K.

Before we look at those case studies, I want to provide a brief outline of the history of "white" as a racial identity, in order to put them into perspective. We have to keep in mind that we are dealing with social interpretations of physical and cultural phenomena, and these interpretations can change over time and place, reflecting the political, economic and cultural distinctiveness of the context.

## WHERE DID WHITENESS COME FROM?

Primarily we have looked so far at the intersection of whiteness and its Others, those racialized identities created by white world's military, commercial and ideological domination of the globe since the sixteenth century. That is the story of how Europeans simultaneously created whiteness and otherness as collective identities. Although from the vantage point of the twenty-first century, the terms "white" and "black" seem to go without saying, these words have not always been used to identify human beings. Indeed use of the term "white" to describe people dates back only to the sixteenth century. At that time however it was one of a range of labels, and not the one most frequently used. Religion, nation, and social class were all deployed more than color. The literature on the period from 1500 to the end of the seventeenth century arrives at a rough consensus: the co-existence of religious labels of identity; "Christian" and "heathen" in the American colonies (Jordan 1968, Frederickson 1988) rendered color distinctions redundant until slaves began to convert to Christianity. Elsewhere in the New World, V.S. Naipaul (1969) notes that after the slave revolt in Berbice (then in Dutch Guiana, South America) in 1764, the dead were divided up in official reports neither as "black" and "white," nor even as "slave" and "free," but as "Christians" and "heathens."

Slavery is now irrevocably linked in popular understandings of history to the trans-atlantic slave trade and its institutions in the Americas, with Africans as its principal population. However, vital to the development of whiteness is the acknowledgement that in the Anglophone colonies, it was the end of the seventeenth century before the status of "free" and "unfree" labor corresponded perfectly to European and African workers respectively. This is because in the earlier days of colonization, white indentured laborers[1] were employed before, and then alongside Africans. When these indentured laborers became numerically inferior due to their access to landownership after indentureship, then the numbers of enslaved Africans started to rapidly over take them. So it was around the last decade of the seventeenth century that the only unfree laborers were Africans. There were free Blacks as well as free white laborers, and it is at this point that we see the emergence of colony-level legislation against voting rights for Blacks; "race" mixing; and the introduction of restrictions on property ownership for Black people. We can thus start the clock of "whiteness" as an explicit legitimized collective identity in North America and the Anglophone Caribbean from around that point. This was clearly not a historical coincidence. The sixteenth and seventeenth centuries was the period when Europeans were beginning to encounter people from Africa, the Americas and Asia on an ongoing basis, and notice the obvious if cosmetic physical differences between groups alongside the cultural ones.

In the period between then and the mid nineteenth century, the idea that some people's identities were "white" came to be attached to the new ways of understanding mankind that developed out of the Enlightenment (Eze 1997). These understandings were enshrined in elite scientific discourse as empirically provable racial differences explaining cultural, political and technological inequalities. While earlier eras had noted that physical appearance, climate and culture differed from place to place, there was no sustained intellectual effort to link these in a coherent philosophy of difference. This changed during the Enlightenment. Climate, it was argued, determined physical appearance, and in turn these determined the capacity of different people to evolve, that is, toward the goal of European norms. However, the mainstream discourse fixed the relationship of climate to civilizational capacity: only those living in temperate climates, that is, white Europeans, could properly attain the heights of civilization, and the others trailed behind. Versions of this logic appeared throughout the eighteenth and early nineteenth centuries. By the mid nineteenth century, this was no longer up for discussion, but was itself the basis for further discussion.

Indeed, as racial science and philosophy garnered credence, increasingly complex schemas were produced, in which there were subdivisions of whiteness. Notions of Anglo-Saxon supremacy (within the multi-layered "white race") began to gain intellectual support, bolstered by an amalgam of the press, a network of scientists engaged in somatic measurements (Horsman 1981) and internationally read work. Robert Knox and Joseph Arthur Comte de Gobineau developed the notion that within the white "race," Anglo-Saxons were particularly capable of civilization in comparison to Celts, Slavs and Latins[2]. This hierarchy within a hierarchy is the basis of the thesis developed by U.S. labor historians David Roediger and James Barrett, whose work we shall look at next.

## CASE STUDY 1: "INBETWEEN PEOPLE"?

In a set of influential publications (Roediger 1991, Barrett and Roediger 1997, 2004, 2005), Roediger and Barrett argue that in the period from the 1850s to the 1910s, incoming migrant Europeans were exposed to a situation where the American mainstream racialized values exerted forces that pushed Europeans to claim whiteness for themselves, in order to gain privileged access to resources, and psychological and social capital (Du Bois's "wages of whiteness")[3]. Barrett and Roediger (1997, 2004) maintain two principal and connected points. Firstly, "Whiteness" is to do with cultural and political power and, secondly, not all those who appear phenotypically white are incorporated equally into the dominant group.

Catholic and Jewish migrants from the various, Southern, Eastern and Central European countries, they argue, were not immediately accepted socially and culturally as white. Differential access to this resource was sought by successive waves of migrants learning the rules of the game, or "this racial thing," as one of Barrett and Roediger's respondents puts it (1997: 6). They label these groups of less dominant Europeans, who were temporarily disadvantaged in the U.S. context by class and culture, "inbetween people": not white, but not black either.

Scholarship in dialogue with the writers above has debated the extent to which various ethnic groups such as Jewish- (Brodkin 1994, 1998) and Italian-Americans (Guglielmo and Salerno 2003) can be considered "white." These arguments posit some parallels between the Irish and the Italians in America, suggesting that over time they "became" white. However, there is a counter-argument developed by some historians such as Eric Arnesen (2001) and Tom Guglielmo (2003) that European immigrants did not actually have to "become" white, relative to Blacks and Mexicans, for example, and that the "inbetween people" theory does not withstand scrutiny. I think the key to unravelling this knot are reasonably straightforward. They are to do with understanding the priorities and assumptions of the protagonists. The first thing to realize is that the "inbetween people" thesis does not claim that Irish, Italian and other European immigrants were really "black," but that they were literally "denigrated," that is, likened to black Americans (in terms of civilization and social status), and they temporarily occupied the lowest positions on the economic and social ladder of free labor. This social, occupational and often geographical proximity to Free Blacks gave rise to the imperative for these migrant groups to distance themselves from them. The further they moved from blackness, the closer they got to whiteness. This strategy was executed in some cases through the urban equivalent of ethnic cleansing (Bernstein, 1990; Ignatiev, 1996).

So the point is not to suggest that certain groups of immigrants were not phenotypically white, which is why Tom Guglielmo (2003) correctly identifies "race" and color as often separate but overlapping criteria in late nineteenth- and early twentieth-century American institutional definitions, but that ideologically and culturally they were indeed considered different and lesser "white races." The corollaries of this categorization were not a set of life chances equivalent to those of Blacks, Native Americans or Hispanics, rather the obligation to define themselves as "white" in a society where that mattered a great deal, whereas in their countries of origin, it had mattered scarcely at all. European immigrants thus "became" white on arrival in the New World, runs the argument, because they disembarked into a new set of social identities that articulated with those they had brought with them, and one overarching identity was whiteness.

I think this conclusion needs qualification. Not being white, and being black, are two very different things: the Catholic Irish were always salvageable for whiteness in a way that African, Mexican, Asian and Native Americans were not (Garner 2003). This is because legally they were definitely white, in as far as they could become naturalized citizens, and were not treated as imports (Haney-López 1996, Jacobson 1998). The second problem is an interesting one that illustrates a divergence of interpretations of identical material. The protagonists in this debate prioritize different arenas as the source of their claims. On one side, Barrett and Roediger see the cultural domain as the one in which perceptions of "inbetweenness" are made explicit, while Arnesen and Guglielmo pragmatically see the legal domain as predominant. Whatever people said or did, argue the latter, in law all white people were white. However, this reasoning is open to the criticism that in sociological terms, the law can just as easily be deconstructed as can popular culture: it is not a superior level of discourse. The legal domain, argues Cheryl Harris (1993), was utilized from the nineteenth century to inject scientific rationality into decisions about who belonged to which race: and these decisions had material impacts. Yet the basis of the law was spurious, reliant as it was on unfeasibly accurate records about people's ancestry, and understandings of definitions of "race" that were not empirically provable. The result of this was that the legal concept of "blood" was no more objective than that which the law dismissed as subjective and unreliable (Harris 1993: 1740). Guglielmo (2003), for example, refers to material suggesting that Italians (especially from the South) were subject to the same kind of racializing discourses, placing them at a lower level of civilization vis-à-vis Anglo-Saxons, as were the Irish. Yet it is worth reiterating that "not white" does not mean "black." Even if it did, how can we explain the court ruling referred to by Jacobson (1998: 4) in which an Alabama court found that the State had not proved beyond doubt that a Sicilian woman was white?

Used sociologically, the term "white" can be interpreted as encompassing non-material and fluid dominant norms and boundaries. Within the white racialized hierarchy were, as Guglielmo rightly points out, a number of "races." Indeed, using the distinction between "white" and "non white" as a starting point is a legitimate historical argument. In the USA, white migrants were people with rights, while Blacks were property without rights, for example. Yet this approach regards the terms "white" and "black" themselves as natural entities or givens, whose existence is then transposed into law. A sociologist however, ought to view these terms and the social relations they cover as part of the puzzle itself, that is, as products of the processes of racialization.

What emerges from this is that there are various contexts: economic, social, legal, cultural, for example, in which meaning is attributed to types of difference. In practice, it is impossible to completely separate these dimensions, but it is useful to start from this basis as a way of thinking through these issues. Moreover, the period covered, around 70 years from the mid nineteenth century to the First World War, enables us to see that understandings of who fits where in the social hierarchies can change. Why this happens when it happens can only be answered by reference to the historical record. We might put forward a few important structural items here, such as the Irish Famine, which altered the complexion of Irish migration to America; the Civil War, Reconstruction and after, which provided the framework both for black/white relations and for the formation of a "white vote" in American politics; the development of the U.S. economy to a stage which required so many manual workers that the labor supply was exhausted within the country and meant that there was plentiful work available for migrants; the consequent slump at the end of the nineteenth century experienced by Western Europe, which meant that the availability of employment that had absorbed some of the workers from Southern and Eastern Europe was diminished. Place all these together with the framework for understanding difference established by racial science in the nineteenth century, and outlines of the problem we have seen conceptualized, using the shorthand "inbetween peoples," or the process of "becoming white," emerge more clearly. Bear in mind that being white was not just about a certain range of phenotypes, but also about claims on culture and values.

## CASE STUDY 2: "WHITE AUSTRALIA"

The Australian colonies were founded, much like the American colonies, as separate entities. Their foundation at the end of the eighteenth century, under the British Crown, proceeded on the legal principle that Australia was empty, uninhabited and unsettled land (*terra nullius*). Thus the white European settlers founded the colonies on the contradictory basis that the Aboriginal populations (now referred to as "First Australians") did not exist, yet their collective relations with them were, as for the European settlers in North America, frequent and necessary. By the mid nineteenth century, the Australian colonies were absorbing migrant labor from the Pacific Islands, China and India. Between 1901 (when the Commonwealth of Australia became a dominion, with its own federal government) until 1972, Australia's immigration policy was based on the objectives of:

1. Protecting indigenous (i.e. white) labor from competition with Asian and Pacific Island labor, and
2. Preserving an Anglo-Celtic majority in the country.

The term "White Australia" was coined in 1906, as an assertion of these twin objectives. The point of looking at this policy and the problems it ran into later in the twentieth century is firstly, to highlight both the haziness around who is considered white at a given moment and why; and secondly, to give an idea of some of the contextual, structural considerations that frame such changes within a hierarchy.

"White Australia" then was not a single piece of legislation, but a doctrine underlying an accumulation of laws and practices that restricted immigration from outside the country (except Europe) and excluded foreign nationals within Australia from various benefits and elements of citizenship. The 1901 Commonwealth Immigration Restriction Act (I.R.A) was the first piece of legislation passed by the new Federal Government. Its most well-known features were its provision for a written test in any European language, at the discretion of an immigration officer, to determine a prospective immigrant's fitness for approval; and the categories of person whose entry was prohibited. These were: the physically or mentally ill, categories of criminal other than political prisoner, prostitutes, those living on prostitutes' earnings, and those likely to be a charge on the communal purse (Tavan 2005: 7–8). In addition, various other laws provided for the repatriation of foreigners (Pacific Island Labourers Act 1901), excluded foreigners from voting (Commonwealth Franchise Act 1902; Naturalization Act 1903) and from benefits like pensions (Old-Age and Invalid Pensions Act 1908) and the Commonwealth maternity bonus (1912).

However, to properly understand the compound anxieties about being usurped by foreign labor and facing "racial contamination," as Labor Party leader John Christian Watson put it during parliamentary debate in 1901, it should be noted that blueprints of White Australia were already embodied in the legislation of the various Australian colonies before they combined to form the Commonwealth of Australia in 1900. Asian and Pacific Islanders had been working in Australia since the first half of the nineteenth century, primarily in the mining and sugar industries respectively. Hostile political agitation as a response to the migration of Indian, Chinese and Pacific Islanders into various parts of the country had led to state governments passing restrictions in a number of waves during the second half of the century. This became particularly intense in the late 1880s. By the end of the century, a model of indirectly discriminatory policies had been introduced. The 1901 I.R.A was therefore the endorsement, on a national level, of a set of practices ongoing across Australia. What was at stake was a conception of Australia as a unique civilization of Europeans encountering and overcoming a natural environment that other Europeans did not have to tame. The combination of whiteness, Britishness and embryonic Australianness that this embodied was most clearly defined in its dealings with First Australians and with the Chinese, not only through the physical differences shorthanded as racial, but the underlying values that Australians saw themselves as having and the other groups as lacking: vitality, industriousness, purity, cleanliness. The idea of geographical vulnerability added urgency to turn-of-the-century Australians' view of themselves as the pioneers of civilization surrounded by potential adversaries. In the prevailing social Darwinist ideological context, they were the spearhead of the white race forced into proximity with lesser races. In the ensuing struggle, they would prevail as the stronger, fitter race[4]. This is why although non-Europeans had their uses, mixing with them and allowing them citizenship was seen as counter-productive. Governments did not attempt the mass deportations provided for in the IRA, and particular industries such as pearl diving enjoyed, de facto, special dispensation to employ Pacific Islanders and Chinese, who were seen as "naturally" more suited to this work. Gwenda Tavan (2005: 15) interprets White Australia as a populist and popular device for generating nationalism in a fledgling society. It garnered support from all interest groups despite tensions of gender, class and religion. She goes on to contextualize it as central to the specific form of social liberalism that was the national ideology of the emergent State. This required state intervention to mitigate the excesses of the market, ensure fairer distribution of wealth, and provide minimum living conditions. The cultural homogeneity putatively anchoring this set of values was seen as essential to successfully building a civilization geographically remote from the epicenter of world civilization (Europe). Within this, the labor movement's opposition to the conditions of Kanaka (Pacific Island) workers in the sugar industry, on the grounds of their virtual slavery, was not viewed as contradictory to its support for repatriation of the foreign element of the workforce.

Indeed, it was the tropical part of Australia, the Northern Territories, that most exercised elite Australians' minds in the first half of the twentieth century. While the baseline for Australian immigration was to build on British and, to a lesser extent, Irish stock, the idea of "race" and its relationship to climate and space proved problematic. Simply put, the association of different "races" with particular types of climate, and with innate characteristics militated against Northern Europeans flourishing in this tropical environment (Anderson 2006). Yet with the departure of the Pacific Islanders in the first decades of the twentieth century, the North required a substitute labor force. The settlement of the North needed not just white supervisors, as had been the case in other tropical areas of colonial expansion, but a tropical white male laboring workforce. Was this a contradiction in terms? Alison Bashford (2000: 255) argues that tropical medicine debated the question, "Is White Australia possible?" between 1900 and the 1930s. The problem revolved not around white men colonizing other people in the tropics, but "as colonizers of a difficult and resilient space" (2000: 258). In this debate, First Australians had again been made invisible. The focus was on how whiteness could be adapted to overcome the tropical environment. Indeed, suggestions of how to accomplish this contributed, maintains Bashford, to producing "an idea that whiteness was not only a characteristic of skin and color, but was also about how one lived, how one arranged one's moment by moment existence in space and time […] the capacity to live in the tropics had to be learnt in minute, detailed and constant ways" (2000: 266).

At least for those engaged in the public health discourse, the solution was to apply science and rationality to impose order on the environment (Anderson 2006). A more pressing problem for employers in the Queensland and Northern Territories sugar plantations was to remain economically viable. Here, the niceties of the public health debate were ignored by workers intent on retaining a standard of living promised by the dismissal of competition in the form of Pacific Island labor. Yet in the mid 1920s, migrants from Italy began arriving in their thousands to work on the estates. This triggered a hostile campaign led by the Brisbane-based *Worker* newspaper against Italian immigration (Sheills 2006). The Italians occupied a position straddling the lines of whiteness. Officially categorized as "white aliens," they became the object of a discourse aimed at presenting them as a threat not just to jobs, but to living standards (being willing to work for lower wages) and the cultural future of Australia (due to their clannishness, corruption, backward civilization and unfitness for vigorous pioneer activity required to settle and develop empty land). By 1925, the Queensland government had set up a Royal Commission to investigate the impact of the increased number of aliens in North Queensland. The Commissioner charged with producing a report made a sharp distinction between Northern and Southern Italians, castigating the latter vis-à-vis their Northern counterparts, for their clannishness, resistance to assimilation and propensity towards crime and violence. He was not alone in thinking this, either in Australia or elsewhere. Italians themselves debated the North–South divide in terms of culture and civilization (Verdicchio 1997), and the characterization of the Sicilians as "inferior types" represented a boundary line between white and less white aliens.

Indeed, while the 1901 Immigration Act had been primarily aimed at keeping out the Chinese, the second- and third-largest groups of "prohibited" immigrants (i.e. those refused the right to land in Australia) were Southern Europeans: Maltese and Italians. Distinctions within the "white race" meant that Latins were lower down the racial pecking order than Anglo-Saxons, Alpines and Nordic peoples. Added to this complication was the reclassification of Axis member nationals (from Bulgaria, the Austro-Hungarian Empire, Germany and Turkey) during World War I as hostile aliens. There was even a temporary internment camp in New South Wales, and bans continued until at least 1923. Between 1912 and 1946 (the period when separate figures on the Maltese were kept), the prevailing practice of immigration officers was to question the right of Southern Europeans to land, even if, as in the case of the Maltese, they had British passports. Perceived racial difference here overrode nationality. In the most well-known case, 208 Maltese were kept out of Australia in 1916 (York 1990) by Melbourne immigration officials who gave them the dictation test in Dutch: all failed.

What this reveals about the workings of whiteness is its lack of solidity and stability. Even the taken-for-granted visible signs can be misleading, or be irrelevant to those wielding power in precise situations. Cultural and political factors can override the phenotypical ones. Moreover, the capacity to centre problems around whiteness per se can make other people invisible. Despite First Australians living in Northern Territories and Northern Queensland for millennia, public discourse obliterated them from the picture. The land was read through white eyes as "empty" because it was neither owned according to private land-ownership laws, nor cultivated in ways that made sense in agrarian norms (planting, cultivation and harvest).

The basis for anxiety about shades of whiteness is expressed again through competition, or at least perceived competition, for work and conditions within international labor markets. It is not feasible to extricate the material from the cultural aspects of whiteness if we seek to understand it in its lived context.

## CASE STUDY 3: THE RACIALIZATION OF WORKING-CLASS CULTURES

### "Abject Whites" in the U.K.

Ethnographic writing on white racialized identities in the U.K. has focused disproportionately, as has much of the academic work on class, on working-class men. This can be seen as a reflection of the academy's middle-class composition and of ethnography's colonial heritage. Since Victorian times, middle-class academics and philanthropists have conducted surveys of the poor, the work of Friedrich Engels (1969[1844]), Henry Mayhew (1967[1861]) and Charles Booth (1902) being the best-known examples. The objective of such projects may have been to reform, politicize or evangelize the working classes, but the common strands were the revelation of their failings, and the creation of an inventory of what they did not have. In describing them, researchers drew parallels between them and colonized peoples. Anthony Wohl, on the web resource "Victorian Web"[5] notes that a number of characteristics were applied by British commentators to the nineteenth-century working classes, Irish immigrants and colonial subjects. They were: unreasonable, irrational, and easily excited, childlike, superstitious (not religious), criminal (with neither respect for private property, nor notions of property), excessively sexual, filthy, inhabited unknown dark lands or territories and shared physical qualities. Wohl has clearly identified an overlap between the language of "race" and that of class, locating both as being fixed on the body and culture.

The key point to grasp in the discourse on whiteness is that behavior, appearance and culture are linked. There has to be an explanation for why some of the "race" placed at the top of the hierarchy clearly do not match the criteria established for superiority: bad genes and dysfunctional culture. From this viewpoint, the language and frames used in order to discursively distinguish (or make) classes, class fractions and "races," are very similar.

This process of negatively evaluating working-class habitus and behavior has become so dominant a discourse that in the post-industrial era of structural un- and underemployment, studies demonstrate that such values have to some extent become internalized. Bev Skeggs (1997) observes that the working-class women she interviews themselves often dis-identify from the working class. They define "working class" by reference to values they personally do not or no longer have, or to economic predicaments they do not face. Indeed, the age of readily-sanctioned reference to a working-class "us" appears, outside particular work milieux, to have disappeared from their social world. The anxiety around owning white working-class subject positions can be read as a reflection of white middle- and ruling-class attempts to pathologize and racialize them as an "underclass." Although the "underclass" is rarely used as a sociological term in twenty-first century British scholarship (after intensive use in the late 80s and 90s), parts of the underclass debate map onto groups within the working class who are perceived as lacking in respectability: in the contemporary period these are "Chavs" (Haywood and Yar, 2005; Nayak, 2003), or more abstractly, in Chris Haylett's (2001) argument, "abject whites."

She contends that sections of a white "underclass" are constructed in turn-of-the-century Britain as "people who are outside/beyond/beneath the nation" (2001: 358). This process involves devaluing social actions carried out by them. The protagonists in the Autumn 1993 "white" riots (in Oxford, Cardiff and Newcastle) "were not hailed as class revolutionaries or even righteously angered disenfranchised minorities, rather they were an embarrassing sign of what the white working-class poor had become—a disorganized, racist and sexist detritus" (ibid.: 358). Indeed, in the de-unionized post-Fordist landscape, blame for this "decline" in the working class, is placed on the working class themselves, or at least the poorest sections of it. Over time, argues Haylett, explanations of decline have become increasingly less structural, and more individual, and fixed around pathological working-class masculinities, and backwardness. In short the poor emerge as the exact opposite of the expanding multicultural, cosmopolitan middle classes. Indeed, Haylett stresses that the identity work accomplished in this discourse is relational, that is the multicultural modern group (the British middle classes) depend on the "abject unmodern" white working class (ibid.: 365) for their own identity.

This "power-evasive discourse" (Frankenberg, 1994) is picked up in specific relation to "race," in for example the work on "color-blind racism" (Bonilla-Silva, 2002) in the USA. Like minorities, with whom they are often compared, working-class Whites in these narratives are culturally disposed to degeneracy, crime, over-fecundity, feckless-ness, etc.

### "White Trash" in the USA

Similar themes resonate throughout the new studies and problematization of "white trash" in the USA (Wray and Newitz 1997, Hartigan 2005, 1999, 1997a, b, Wray 2006). In these accounts, whiteness is significantly mediated by class (Bettie 2000, Gibbons 2004, Morris 2005). The polarized pairing of productiveness–unproductiveness is also central. Hartigan's tracing of the development of the phenomenon of "white trash" in the USA (2005) demonstrates some interesting points of comparison between "race" and class on one hand, and the U.K. and the USA on the other. Using the conclusion of nineteenth-century travel writer James Gilmore[6] he distinguishes between elements of the working class: "The *poor* white man labors, the *mean* white man does not labor: and labor makes the distinction between them."

Again, echoes of the underclass debate resonate loudly, with a moral categorization of the working class into productive and unproductive groups: the deserving and un-deserving poor. Writing from the 1860s, says Hartigan, evidenced the struggle between those for whom such "meanness" was in the blood and those who recognized a degree of environmental input. These competing logics developed into the twentieth century. Racial theorist Madison Grant, for example, understood "white trash" as a combination of natural habitat and bloodlines: to do with sexuality, urbanization and crime, rather than just immigration (Grant 1916). Eugenics discourse stressed the perils of mixing good with bad genes, and responsibility for policing the genetic border. It argued that a host of antisocial and expensive behavior derived from poor family etiquette and prac-tices. The result of this discourse in popular outlets, contends Hartigan, was heightened middle-class awareness of their racial selves, and of threat from below. In the scenarios popularized in the press, the idea of "racial poisons" dominated discourse, with the weaker blood multiplying faster than the stronger. Gertrude Davenport (the wife of leading eugenicist Charles Davenport) wrote in a popular magazine in April 1914 that "the greatest menace of imbecility is not that the imbecile may break into our house and steal our silver, or that he might set fire to our barn, but that he may be born of our flesh" (Hartigan 2005: 95).

Similarly, in Winthrop Stoddard's (1922) Freudian fight for civilization taking place within the Self, class status coincides with racial value:

> Let us understand once and for all [he warns] that we have among us a rebel army—the vast host of the inadaptable, the incapable, the envious, the discontented, filled with instinctive hatred of civilization and progress, and ready on the instant to rise in revolt. Here are foes that need watching. Let us watch them (1922: 87).

The overlap with contemporaneous American eugenics discourse on immigrants from Southern and Eastern Europe is very similar to Stoddard's comments here, and underscores the idea that "race" and class are intimately connected in discourse of hierarchization. People's culture and behavior is in the blood, these theories argue, and within the dominant "race" there are those whose culture and behavior is more like those of subordinate races than those of the dominant. The struggle is for the dominant to remain pure and unpolluted, a theme pivotal to discourse on "race." The white trash figure then is marked as an excessive body that pollutes others. It displays the innate behavior that both confirms the depths to which the working class has collapsed (so far from work, so far from respectability), and at the same time emphasizes the industriousness and respectability of the middle-class subjects that fill the signifier "white trash," with meaning.

## PLURAL TRAJECTORIES OF WHITENESS

I began this chapter by floating the idea that there are a set of internal borders within the ostensibly homogenous "white" group, and that these borders are contingent on political, economic and social factors that make them more or less relevant. In this final section, I want to draw out some of the complexity involved in the social relations that white working-class people maintain with minorities in Britain, as illustrated through empirical fieldwork.

Ethnographic fieldwork has illuminated what we could call the "plural trajectories" of whiteness. In other words, how white people in broadly similar class positions make sense of the social material used to understand "race" in differing ways. We are going to look briefly at two pieces of British ethnographic fieldwork to demonstrate some aspects of these "plural trajectories": Katherine Tyler's discussions with residents of a former mining town in the English Midlands (2004), and Les Back's study of young people on the "Riverview" estate in South London (1996).

Tyler's (2004) inter-generational dialogue among small-town Leicestershire inhabitants shows how personal biographies profoundly shape the ways in which people perceive "Others." Among the interviewees, no homogenous representative voice is expressed: white superiority is contested by some, just as it is accepted unthinkingly by more. Identification can take the form of empathy. "Sarah's" experience of growing up working in her Czech immigrant father's shop gives her empathy with the people working in family-run Asian businesses when she hears criticisms of Asian corner shops, for example (Tyler 2004: 304). Moreover, a person may develop a critical angle through mobility and return. Another of Tyler's respondents, "Jim," returns to the town after three years at university in a small, more multicultural city. He reports that his recognition and awareness of racism increased dramatically after he was reabsorbed into family circles and heard the types of discourse that he previously listened to uncritically. He can now reflect on the older generation's assumptions and dissect them. When his grandmother died, the house she had lived in was bought by an Asian family, something that his uncles were unhappy about. "The presence of Asians in the home where they were brought up," paraphrases Tyler (2004: 299), "signifies an intolerable and unacceptable transformation." Here we see a crucial element of the mechanism of enacting whiteness. A perceived negative change (in this case the retrospective tainting of the family) is attached to an effect (the Asian buyer) rather than a cause (the grandmother's death, the psychological toll of memories of childhood in that home, the broader global changes that brought the family in question from Asia to Britain).

Inter-generational and gendered differences are also revealed by this study. The older people are generally less reflexive about whiteness and quicker to deploy racialized discourse, as are men as compared to women, many of whom see more positives where the men see only negatives.

There are clearly a number of places to be located ideologically in the racialization process, which becomes even more evident in the London housing estates where Les Back worked in the early 1990s. Back's (1996) ethnography of youth culture on South London estates suggests that values determine the salient borders of identity, and that culture becomes the "modality" (following Stuart Hall) through which they are racialized. Black and white youths there put aside sporadic but real differences in order to ally against Vietnamese and Bangladeshi newcomers (1996: 240–241) in what Back terms "neighborhood nationalism." This alliance assumes the form of verbal and occasionally physical attacks. While the black youths are well aware that in other circumstances they could, and indeed have been, the victims of such aggression from their white counterparts, in the context of defining membership of the estate, their secular, linguistic and music-based coalition with white youth in "Riverview" estate appears to predominate. They thus become what Back terms "contingent insiders" (1996: 240), while their counterparts in "Southgate" estate seemed to enjoy a qualitatively different relationship with their white peers, who had "vacated concepts of whiteness and Englishness … in favor of a mixed ethnicity that was shared" (ibid.: 241). So while there is frequently tension, there is also often alliance, through personal relationships drawing on shared knowledge and experiences.

Indeed, a recurrent topic in British ethnographic studies is the heterogeneity and elasticity of the category "white" in its members' affiliations with black and Asian cultures, to the point where, in some specific contexts, terms such as "black" or "white" culture become almost ideal-types.[7]

These groups of young people illustrate a paradox that resurfaces elsewhere in British fieldwork. In their survey of shopkeepers in a London borough, Wells and Watson (2005) find that not all those championing "white values" are white, while some champions of white rights include their black neighbors in their embattled and beleaguered "we." In these cases the "Other" is usually Muslim. Clearly, the power relationships at a personal and local level allow for whiteness to be expanded to incorporate those not phenotypically white beneath its cultural canopy for the enactment of both rhetorical and physical violence. People who are not white can be absorbed into honorary whiteness in particular circumstances, yet this invariably involves othering different groups. In fact this othering appears constitutive of the process of redrawing the boundary of whiteness in terms of values, so that it embraces British black or Asian people, depending on the context. In confirming shared values, the groups that share and do not share them are defined.

## CONCLUSIONS

### Overlapping Hierarchies of Class and Whiteness

In previous chapters, I focused on the borders between white and non-white. Here, the concentration has been on the other end of whiteness, between the constituent groups of the white whole. I want to emphasize that these latter borders are contingent, that is, open to political and social change. A group might be considered unproblematically white at one stage in one place, but not in another place at another time. Or, this might change for a specific group in the same place over different periods. Changing economic and social conditions led to different appraisals of who was allowed into Australia and why: what were the criteria? The design and application of the White Australia strategy, as well as the example of the "inbetween peoples" thesis, are clearly about the parallel boundaries of whiteness; the one separating white from its non-white Other, and those separating the really white from the less so.

While groups such as Jews, Gypsies and immigrants frequently find themselves marginalized within the social relations of "race," I want to encourage you to think of how the process works in relation to class. We have already noted that for a long time, the way in which membership of classes and "races" was conceptualized was very similar. One function of the internal borders of whiteness is to isolate a group of Whites as being the sole agents of negative and un-modern behaviors and attitudes, thus removing responsibility for discrimination from the others. As Hartigan concludes:

> "Part of what the epithet white trash expresses is the general view held by whites that there are only a few extreme, dangerous whites who are really racist or violently misguided, as opposed to recognizing that racism is an institutional problem pervading the nation and implicating all whites in its operation" (Hartigan 2005: 118–119).

I am tempted here to paraphrase Orwell, and suggest that in the process of racialization, all Whites are nominally equal, but some are more equal than others. This is true not only of how people express racism, but in the representations of how racism is expressed. The idea of portraying, or representing some groups as not-quite-white is part of the same power imbalance as the one that enables racism to function at a collective level. The discourse of "race" and class are intimately connected.

Indeed, while racist ideas do abound in the working-class communities studied—although this label is contested in Chicago's Midtown (Kefalas 2003), and Detroit's Corktown and Warrendale (Hartigan 1999)—academics and media professionals play a significant role in creating a selective picture in which only the working class express such ideas and live in segregated neighborhoods. This is not borne out, even by the often questionable opinion poll results. Studies of whiteness in middle-class circles, residential areas or workplaces, or at all, are unfortunately few and far between[8]. Whiteness is neither just for the wealthy, nor just the poor. Yet the people who have engaged in defining the desirability of including particular segments of their compatriots in the civilized, right-thinking mainstream have been middle- and upper-class British and Americans.

Moreover, under certain conditions, whiteness (as a dominant set of values and assumptions that make various groups problematic) is not even always only for white people. It is clear from survey research that minorities generally have more sympathy for immigrants and asylum seekers, and more of them tend to understand racism as structural rather than individually generated (Lamont 2000, Weis and Fine 1996), yet from the examples of Back (1996), Wells and Watson (2005) and Hoggett *et al.* (1992, 1996) there is enough to suggest that there might occasionally be a strategic overlap of values between white and black people that coalesce around defending neighborhoods, and possibly jobs. Moreover, minorities do engage to a degree with power-evasive discourse such as color-blind racism (Bonilla-Silva, 2002), just as many of Skeggs' respondents defined "working class" as not them, but somebody else. There is a great deal of complexity on view in the fieldwork done on white working-class communities, and a number of individual biographical pathways that lead people also to be anti-racist. If this work teaches us anything, it is that attitudes cannot be read off simplistically from class positions.

We should recognize throughout that hierarchies are always in the process of construction, deconstruction and reconstruction: nothing is fixed, not even racialized boundaries. The hierarchies I refer to are expressed in terms of patterns of power relations; that is, the power to name, the power to control and distribute resources. While the group defined as "white" has historically monopolized this sort of power, who counts as "white" at a given moment and at a given time is far less certain. This requires us to understand political, social, cultural and economic factors as a messy whole, rather than as easily distinguishable and analyzable components: a challenge, but a worthwhile one.

## DISCUSSION QUESTIONS

1. What do class and racial identities have in common and what distinguishes them?
2. What role do specific national contexts play in the way class and race get linked and unlinked?
3. When we define our own group, we define another implicitly. What evidence of this emerges from the discussion of class and "race" here?
4. What does the author mean by "… in the process of racialization, all Whites are nominally equal, but some are more equal than others" in this context?

## NOTES

1. Indenture was a form of labor whereby the worker generally signed up to work for a specified period without pay on the basis that s(he) would receive a lump sum or a parcel of land at the expiry of the contract. However, political and other types of prisoner were also made into indentured laborers in the British Empire, particularly in the seventeenth century.
2. Scottish surgeon Robert Knox's *The Races of Men* (1850), and French aristocrat de Gobineau's *Essai sur l"inégalité des races humaines* (1853–55) are key works in this regard.

3. W.E.B Du Bois' much referred to passage in *Black Reconstruction* (1998: 700), his history of class and race relations in post-bellum America, attempts to find a reason why otherwise poor and oppressed white Southerners sided with the landed elite against the freed slave population in the 1870s. His answer is that it was not merely a question of economics, but of psychology. The status effect of feeling racially superior was equivalent to a "public and psychological wage" (of whiteness) that they were paid in excess of their meager financial rewards. Barrett and Roediger are not alone in positing whiteness as an overarching mainstream value of Americanness; Horsman (1981), Saxton (1990), Bernstein (1990), Almaguer (1994), Allen (1994), Ignatiev (1996) and Jacobson (1998) all suggest this.

4. "Social Darwinism" was a framework for understanding the social world, developed from Darwin's research into plants and animals and particularly popular during the last quarter of the nineteenth century. Evolution is cast in social Darwinism as an ongoing struggle for survival with the best-adapted and powerful species surviving at the cost of the weaker ones. It was used to justify imperialism, the class order of society and gender inequalities among other things.

5. "Victorian Web" is accessible at: <http://victorianweb.org/history/race/rcov. html>. On the overlap of "race" and class, see also Lorimer (1978).

6. Gilmore, J. *Down in Tennessee*, 1864: 188–89.

7. In their study of the East End of London, Paul Hoggett *et al.* (1996: 113) remark on a similar set of provisional allegiances, noting the large Afro-Caribbean presence in a demonstration following the fatal stabbing of a white schoolboy by a Bangladeshi boy:

> "The paradox is that whilst Afro-Caribbean soccer players can still be the object of crude racial abuse at nearby Millwall Football Club, Afro-Caribbeans can nevertheless also be included in an imaginary community of English-speaking Christian Eastenders which stands opposed to the alien Muslim threat."

8. Hall 1992; Ware 1992; Pierce 2003; Johnson and Shapiro 2003; Hartigan (1999); Forman and Lewis, 2006); Reay *et al.*, 2007; Clarke and Garner (forthcoming).

## REFERENCES

Allen, T. (1994) *The Invention of the White Race (Vol. 2)* New York: Verso.

Almaguer, T. (1994) *Racial Fault Lines: the origins of white supremacy in California* Berkeley: University of California Press.

Anderson, W. (2006) *Cultivating Whiteness: Science, Health and Racial Destiny in Australia* Cambridge: Cambridge University Press.

Arnesen, E. (2001) "Whiteness and the Historians' Imagination" *International Labor and Working Class History* 60:3–32.

Back, L. (1996) *New Ethnicities and Urban Culture: Social Identity and Racism in the Lives of Young People* London: UCL Press.

Barrett, J. and Roediger, D. (2005) "The Irish and the 'Americanization' of the 'New Immigrants' in the Streets and in the Churches of the Urban United States, 1900–1930" *Journal of American Ethnic History* 24(4): 4–33.

—— (2004) "Making new immigrants inbetween: Irish hosts and white pan-ethnicity, 1890–1930" in Foner, N. and Frederickson, G. (eds) *Not Just Black and White: Immigration and Race, Then and Now* New York: Russell Sage Foundation Press, pp. 167–196.

—— (1997) "Inbetween Peoples: Race, Nationality and the 'New Immigrant' Working Class" *Journal of American Ethnic History* Spring, 1997:3–44.

Bashford, A. (2000) ""Is White Australia possible"? Race, colonialism and tropical medicine *Ethnic and Racial Studies* 23(2): 248–71.

Bernstein, I. (1990) *The New York Draft Riots of 1863: their Significance for American Society in the Civil War Period* New York: Oxford University Press

Bettie, J. (2000) "Women without Class: Chicas, Cholas, Trash, and the Presence/Absence of Class Identity" *Signs* 26(1): 1–35

Bonilla-Silva, (2002).

Booth, C. (1902) *Labour and life of the people of London* London: MacMillan

Brodkin, K. (1994) "How Did Jews Become White Folks?" in Gregory, S. and Sanjck, R. (eds) *Race* New Brunswick, NJ: Rutgers University Press.

—— (1998) *How Jews became White Folks: and What That Says About Race in America* New Brunswick, NJ: Rutgers University Press.

Clarke, S. and Garner, S. (forthcoming) White Identities London: Pluto.

Daniels, J. (1997) *White Lies: race, class, gender, and sexuality in white supremacist discourse* New York, Routledge.

Du Bois, W. E. B. (1998 [1935]) *Black Reconstruction in the United States, 1860–1880* New York: Free Press.

Engels, F. (1969 [1844]) *The Condition of the Working Class in England: From Personal Observation and Authentic Sources* St.Albans: Panther.

Eze, E (1997) *Race and the Enlightenment: a Reader* Boston: Blackwell.

Forman, T. and Lewis, A. (2006) "Racial Apathy and Hurricane Katrina: the Social Anatomy of Prejudice in the Post-Civil Rights Era," *Du Bois Review: Social Science Research on Race,* 3: 175–202.

Frankenberg, R. (1994) White Women, Race Matters Madison: University of Wisconsin Press.

Frederickson, G. (1988) *The Arrogance of Race: historical perspectives on slavery, racism and social inequality* Hanover NH: Wesleyan University Press.

Garner, S. (2003) *Racism in the Irish Experience* London: Pluto.

Gibbons, M. (2004) "White Trash: A Class Relevant Scapegoat for the Cultural Elite" *Journal of Mundane Behaviour* 5(1). Online <http://www.mundanebehavior.org/issues/v5n1/gibbons.htm> Accessed on 25 June 2008.

Grant, M. (1916) *The Passing of The Great Race; or, The racial basis of European history The Passing of The Great Race; or, The racial basis of European history* New York: Charles Scribner and Sons.

Guglielmo, T. (2003) "Rethinking Whiteness Historiography: the Case of Italians in Chicago, 1890–1945" in Doane and Bonilla-Silva (eds), pp.49–61.

Guglielmo, J. and Salerno, S. (2003) *Are Italians white? How race is made in America* New York: Routledge.

Hall, C. (1992) *White, Male and Middle Class: explorations in feminism and history* Cambridge: Cambridge University Press.

Haney-López, I. (1996) *White by Law: The Legal Construction of Race* New York: New York University Press.

Harris, C. (1993) "Whiteness as Property" *Harvard Law Review* 106(8): 1707–93.

Hartigan, J. (2005) *Odd Tribes: toward a cultural analysis of white people* Durham, NC: Duke University Press.

—— (1999) *Racial Situations: class predicaments of whiteness in Detroit* Princeton NJ: Princeton University Press.

—— (1997a) "Locating White Detroit in Frankenberg (ed) pp.180–213.

—— (1997b) "Name Calling: Objectifying 'Poor Whites' and 'White Trash' in Detroit" in Wray and Newitz (eds), pp.41–56.

Haylett C. (2001) "Illegitimate Subjects?: Abject Whites, Neo-Liberal Modernization and Middle Class Multiculturalism" *Environment and Planning D: Society and Space* 19 (3): 351–70.

Hayward, K. and Yar, M. (2005) "The "chav" phenomenon: consumption, media and the construction of a new underclass," *Crime, Media and Society* 2(1): 9–28.

Hoggett, P. (1992) "A place for experience: a psychoanalytic perspective on boundary, identity and culture" *Environment and Planning D: Society and Space* 10:345–356.

Hoggett, P., Jeffers, S., and Harrison, L. (1996) "Race, ethnicity and community in three localities," *New Community* 22(10):111–125.

Horsman, R. (1981) *Race and Manifest Destiny: the Origins of American Anglo-Saxonism* Cambridge: CUP.

Ignatiev, N. (1996) *How the Irish Became White* New York: Routledge.

Jacobson, M. (1998) *Whiteness of a Different Colour: European Immigrants and the Alchemy of Race* Cambridge, MA: Harvard University Press.

Johnson, H., and Shapiro, T. (2003) "Good Neighborhoods, Good Schools: Race and the 'Good Choices' of White Families in Doane and Bonilla-Silva (eds), *White Out: the continuing significance of racism* New York: Routledge, pp. 173–88.

Jordan, W. (1968) *White over Black: American Attitudes Toward the Negro, 1550–1812* Chapel Hill: University of North Carolina Press.

Kefalas, M. (2003) *Working-class Heroes: Protecting Home, Community and Nation in a Chicago Neighborhood* Berkeley: UCLA Press.

Lamont, M. (2000) *The Dignity of Working Men* Cambridge, MA: Harvard University Press.

Lorimer, D. (1978) *Color, Class, and the Victorians: English Attitudes to the Negro in the Mid-Nineteenth Century.* Leicester: Leicester University Press.

Mayhew, H. (1967 [1861]) *London Labour and the London Poor: A Cyclopaedia of the Condition and Earnings of Those That Will Work, Those That Cannot Work, and Those That Will Not Work* New York: A.M. Kelley.

Morris, E. (2005) "From 'Middle Class' to 'Trailer Trash': Teachers' Perceptions of White Students in a Predominantly Minority School" *Sociology of Education* 78: 99–121.

Naipaul, V.S. (1969) *The Middle Passage* London: Penguin.

Nayak, A. (2003) "Ivory Lives: Economic Restructuring and the Making of Whiteness in a Post-industrial Youth Community" *European Journal of Cultural Studies* 6(3): 305–25.

Pierce, J. (2003) "Racing for Innocence": Whiteness, Corporate Culture and the Backlash against Affirmative Action" in Doane and Bonilla-Silva (eds), pp.199–214.

Reay, D., Hollingworth, S., Williams, K., Crozier, G., Jamieson, F., James, D., and Beedell, P. (2007). "A Darker Shade of Pale?" Whiteness, the Middle Classes and Multi-Ethnic Inner City Schooling," *Sociology*, 41(6): 1041–1060.

Roediger, D. (1991) *The Wages of Whiteness: race and the making of the American working class* London: Verso.

Saxton, A. (1990) *The Rise and Fall of the White Republic: Class Politics and Mass Culture in Nineteenth Century America* New York: Verso.

Shiells, G. (2006) "A Different Shade of White" *National Library of Australia News*, August. Online: <http://www.nla.gov.au/pub/nlanews/2006/aug06/article4.html> (Accessed on 25 June 2008).

Skeggs, B. (1997) *Formations of Class and Gender: Becoming Respectable* London: Routledge.

Stoddard, W. (1922) *Revolt Against Civilization* New York: Scribner.

Tavan, G. (2005) *The Long Slow Death of White Australia* Carlton, VA: Scribe.

Tyler, K. (2004) "Reflexivity, tradition and racism in a former mining town" *Ethnic and Racial Studies* 27(2): 290–302.

Verdicchio, P. (1997) *Bound by Distance: Rethinking Nationalism Through the Italian Diaspora* Madison, NJ: Fairleigh Dickinson University Press.

Ware, V. (1992) *Beyond the Pale: White Women, Racism and History* Verso: London.

Weis, L. and Fine, M. (1996) "Narrating the 1980s and 1990s: Voices of Poor and Working-Class White and African-American Men" *Anthropology and Education Quarterly* 27(4): 493–516.

Wells, K. and Watson, S. (2005) "A Politics of Resentment: Shopkeepers in a London Neighbourhood" *Ethnic and Racial Studies* 28(2): 261–77.

Wohl, A. (187) "Race and Class Overview: Parallels in Racism and Class Prejudice," <http://www.victorianweb.org/history/race/rcov.html>.

Wray, M. (2006) *Not Quite White: White Trash and the Boundaries of Whiteness* Durham, NC: Duke University Press.

Wray, M. and Newitz, A. (1997) (eds) *White Trash: race and class in America* New York: Routledge.

York, B (1990) *Empire and Race: the Maltese in Australia, 1881–1949* Kensington, NSW: University of New South Wales Press.

# Becoming Hispanic

## Becoming Hispanic: Mexican American and the Faustian Pact with Whiteness

### Neil Foley

IN 1980 THE U.S. Bureau of the Census created two new ethnic categories of Whites: "Hispanic" and "non-Hispanic." The Hispanic category, an ethnic rather than racial label, comprised Mexicans, Puerto Ricans, Cubans, Panamanians, and other ethnic groups of Latin American descent. Creating a separate ethnic category within the racial category of White seemed to solve the problem of how to count Hispanics without racializing them as non-Whites, as it had done in 1930. To identify oneself today as a "Hispanic" is partially to acknowledge one's ethnic heritage without surrendering one's "whiteness." Hispanic identity thus implies a kind of "separate but equal" whiteness—whiteness with a twist of salsa, enough to make one ethnically flavorful and culturally exotic without, however, compromising one's racial privilege as a White person. The history of Mexican Americans in the Southwest is thus more than the history of their "becoming" Mexican American or Hispanic; for many, especially those of the middle class, it is also the history of their becoming White.

Unlike Black Americans, who experienced de jure segregation throughout the South before 1960, Mexican Americans in the Southwest experienced de facto segregation based on custom rather than statutory authority. Legally, Mexican Americans were accorded the racial status of White people; socially, politically, and economically, however, they were treated as non-Whites. With the rise of the so-called Mexican American generation of the 1930s, '40s, and '50s, Mexican Americans began insisting on their status as Whites in order to overcome the worst features of Jim Crow segregation, restrictive housing covenants, employment discrimination, and the social stigma of being "Mexican," a label that, in the eyes of Anglos, designated race rather than one's citizenship status.

Many middle-class Mexican Americans did not object to the segregation of Blacks or challenge the assumptions of White supremacy. On the contrary, they supported strict segregation of Whites and Blacks in the schools and in public facilities. The basis for their claim for social equality was that they were also White, that some unfortunate mistake had been made in regarding persons of Mexican descent as non-Whites.

A group of Mexican Americans, mostly urban and middle class, founded their own organization in 1929 in Corpus Christi, the League of United Latin American Citizens (LULAC), to foster the goals of Americanization in Texas and other states of the Southwest, restricting membership to U.S. citizens and emphasizing English language skills and loyalty to the Constitution of the United States. LULAC members sought to set the racial record straight. In a 1932 article in the *LULAC News* titled "Are Texas-Mexicans 'Americans'?" the author asserted that Mexican Americans were "the first white race to inhabit this vast empire of ours." Another member of LULAC boasted that Mexican Americans were "not only a part and parcel but as well the sum and substance of the white race." As self-constituted Whites, LULAC members considered it "an insult" to be associated with Blacks or other "colored" races.[1] In 1936 a LULAC official deplored the practice of hiring "Negro musicians" to play at Mexican *bailes* (dances) because it led to "illicit relations" between Black men and "ill-informed Mexican girls." He urged fellow LULAC members to "tell these Negroes that we are not going to permit our manhood and womanhood to mingle with them on an equal social basis."[2] Not surprisingly, therefore, LULAC, the premiere civil rights group for Mexican Americans, turned its back on opportunities to forge ties with the NAACP during its own civil rights battles in the 1940s and 1950s. The African American author and Nobel Prize winner Toni Morrison deserves credit for stating bluntly what many Mexican Americans have been slow to acknowledge: "In race talk the move into mainstream America always means buying into the notion of American blacks as the real aliens."[3]

Of course, African Americans are not "aliens" in any legal or cultural sense; they are natives of the United States, share in intimate ways the culture and history of the United States, and in many important respects have shaped White culture. W. E. B. Du Bois wrote that he saw through the "souls of white folks": "Not as a foreigner do I come, for I am native, not foreign. ... I see the working of their entrails. I know their thoughts and they know that I know."[4] Blacks are inside American culture, but Morrison's point is that they remain alienated and estranged from the domain of White power and privilege. Mexican immigrants may begin as racial outsiders and "illegal aliens," but their U.S.-born offspring are sometimes able to forge identities as ethnically White Hispanics.

Unlike the experience of most immigrants, however, discrimination against Mexicans in the United States has been continuous, pervasive, and systemic. After Mexican Americans established LULAC and the G.I. Forum (founded in 1948), they challenged school segregation and other forms of discrimination in state and federal courts. While these organizations and their middle-class Mexican American leaders sought equality based on their constitutional rights as U.S. citizens, increasingly they came to the realization that race—specifically, being White—mattered far more than U.S. citizenship in the course of everyday life. The majority of people of African descent in the United States were citizens, but that fact did not enable them to sit in the front of the bus or attend White schools. As sociologist Mary Waters observed, "If the Irish had to sit at the back of the bus sometime in the past, and now being Irish just means having fun at funerals, then there is hope for all groups facing discrimination now."[5] The assumption here is that most immigrant groups, including Mexicans, have had the "option," unlike Blacks, of becoming White and thus benefiting from what historian George Lipsitz has called the "possessive investment in whiteness."[6] Choosing the Caucasian option, as had the Irish before them, enabled some Mexican Americans to forge White racial identities that were constructed, as Toni Morrison has accurately observed, "on the backs of blacks."[7]

Having failed to convince Anglos that the word "Mexican" denoted nationality rather than a separate race, LULAC members and other urban Mexican Americans constructed new identities as "Spanish American" or "Latin American" in order to arrogate to themselves the privileges of whiteness routinely denied to Mexicans, Blacks, Chinese, and Indians. Becoming Spanish or Latin American also enabled Mexican Americans to distance themselves from recently arrived Mexican immigrants who were often illiterate, poor, non-English speaking, and dark skinned. Mexican Americans thus began to object strenuously to being labeled as "colored" or forced to share facilities with Black Americans. Increasingly, middle-class Mexican Americans during the thirties and forties began to call themselves "Spanish" and insist on their whiteness. ...

Many Mexicans had learned whiteness and "whitening" *(blanqueamiento)* before coming to the United States. Long-term interaction among African, indigenous, and Spanish peoples had led to the formation of a complex, hierarchical racial system in Mexico. After centuries of *mestizaje,* or race-mixing, society in colonial New Spain was composed of multiple ethnoracial groups. By the early twentieth century, the Mexican government had created census categories for three racial groups: Whites, Indians, and mestizos. The population of Mexico in 1920 consisted of about 14 million: 10 percent were classified as *raza blanca* (Whites), 30 percent as *raza indígena* (Indians), and about 60 percent as *raza mezclada* (mestizos).[8] Mestizos had occupied an awkward position in this racial hierarchy, often hated by the Spanish for being part Indian and shunned by the Indians for being part Spanish. Those able to construct identities as Spaniards often regarded mestizos, Indians, and Africans with racial contempt. By the end of the nineteenth century, however, many urban mestizo elites claimed to be Spanish, or mostly Spanish, in order to establish racial and cultural distance between themselves and Indians. …

Some Mexican Americans were therefore mortified when Anglo Americans made no effort to distinguish between "Spanish" or "White" Mexicans and "Indian" Mexicans, which also became a source of irritation to the Mexican government. Mexican consuls frequently complained that Mexican citizens were not being treated like White people in the United States. In 1933 the Mexican consul in Dallas wrote a county sheriff to protest that a Mexican citizen had been jailed "with the negro prisoners" instead of with the Anglos. "It is my opinion," the Mexican consul general wrote to the sheriff, "that there is no reason for segregating Mexicans from white Americans, inasmuch as they are both of the white race."[9]

The different views of the Texas sheriff and the Mexican consul over the racial status of Mexicans in the United States reflected their countries' legal and cultural perspectives on the issue of race mixing. For Mexicans, theoretically at least, *mestizaje* produced racial strength. The fusion of Spanish, Indian, and African created a race of people that was greater than the sum of its parts, what the Mexican philosopher José Vasconcelos called the "cosmic race." To the Texas sheriff and the average White person in America, however, race mixing was a menace to the purity of the Nordic race that, unchecked, would lead to the demise of White civilization. When Spaniards mixed their blood with Indians and Africans, White Americans believed, they removed themselves from the domain of whiteness. This "dark stream" of "peon blood" was inferior to even that of southern European Jews and Slavs whom the eugenicist Madison Grant accused of producing "race bastards" and other "amazing racial hybrids" and "ethnic horrors that will be beyond the powers of future anthropologists to unravel."[10]

The history of discrimination against Mexican Americans in the Southwest is a thrice-told tale and does not bear repetition here. What is key, however, is the way in which the courts and the census constructed whiteness and the often conflicting and contradictory way in which Whites themselves constructed it. Historically, if not legally, Mexicans had been regarded as non-White and denied most of the rights and privileges that whiteness bestowed. In school segregation cases, however, the courts uniformly ruled that Mexicans belonged to the White race; and in the one naturalization case concerning a Mexican American, the court ruled that Mexican citizens, regardless of race, were entitled to become U.S. citizens as a result of treaty agreements. Mexican Americans reasoned that if the law said they were White, then Anglos broke the law by discriminating against them as non-Whites. …

The Supreme Court acknowledged that many immigrants from eastern and southern Europe who were considered White in the 1920s—Italians, Greeks, Slavs, and Jews, for example—were outside the bounds of whiteness in 1790 and had only later been granted status as Whites. The courts, especially those adjudicating whiteness for the purpose of naturalization, often relied on "common knowledge," or how the average White person viewed the whiteness of a person. Between 1878 and 1909 the courts heard twelve prerequisite or naturalization cases to determine whether a person seeking U.S. citizenship was White or not. In eleven of the cases, the courts barred the naturalization of applicants from China, Japan, Burma, and Hawaii, as well as that of two mixed-race applicants. As in other prerequisite cases, the applicants sought to convince the court that they met the racial criteria of whiteness by either scientific evidence (the division of humans into five racial groups: Mongolian, Negro, Caucasian, Indian, and Malay) or "common knowledge." The courts used either or both of these criteria to decide who was White and who was not. Takao Ozawa, a Japanese citizen educated at the University of California at Berkeley and resident of the United States for twenty-eight years, petitioned the court to become a citizen on the grounds that his skin color made him a "white person." The court disagreed with this literal interpretation of whiteness and in 1923 denied him citizenship on the grounds that he was of the Mongolian, not the Caucasian, race. White skin, by itself, did not guarantee one's "property right" in whiteness."

Three months after ruling that Japanese were not Caucasian and therefore not White, the Supreme Court in *United States v. Thind* (1923) rejected its own equation that, only Caucasians were White. Bhagat Singh Thind, one of approximately 6,400 Asian Indians in the United States by 1920, applied for citizenship on the grounds that Asian Indians were Caucasian and not. Mongolian, were therefore White, and were therefore eligible for citizenship. The court did not dispute that Thind was a Caucasian but ruled that not all Caucasians were White despite the technical link between Europeans and South Asians. "It may be true," the court ruled, "that the blond Scandinavian and the brown Hindu have a common ancestor in the dim reaches of antiquity, but the average man knows perfectly well that there are unmistakable and profound differences between them today."[12] The Supreme Court thus ruled in the same year that Takao Ozawa was not White because, although he had white skin, he was not of the Caucasian race, whereas Bhagat Singh Thind was denied citizenship on the grounds that, although he was a Caucasian, he was not White. Whiteness, the courts increasingly ruled, was whatever they said it was. The Thind ruling was the Supreme Court's final concession to the subjective, cultural construction of whiteness. …

To many Whites it must have seemed long overdue when the census bureau announced in 1930 that it had created a separate category for Mexicans. For the first time in census history, Mexicans had become racialized as a non-White group. The absence of a separate classification for persons of Mexican descent before 1930 had prevented immigration restrictionists and antirestrictionists alike from knowing the demographic dimensions of the "Mexican problem" during the 1920s when immigration restriction was hotly debated in Congress.[13] Accordingly, the instructions to the enumerators for the 1930 census stated: "Practically all Mexican laborers are of a racial mixture difficult to classify, though usually well recognized in the localities where they are found. In order to obtain separate figures for this racial group, it has been decided that all persons born in Mexico, or having parents born in Mexico, *who are not definitely white,* negro, Indian, Chinese, or Japanese, should be returned as Mexican.[14] Unlike census instructions before and after 1930, the 1930 census presumed Mexicans to be non-White unless "definitely white." Although no instructions were given to determine who was and who was not "definitely white," enumerators had to decide which Mexicans to count as Whites and which to enter in the non-White "Mexican" column. The outcome, not surprisingly, was that over 1.4 million persons were returned as "Mexicans" and therefore non-White, while only 65,986 (4 percent) of persons of Mexican descent were listed as White.[15] The majority of Mexicans in the United States were therefore recognized by the census, if not the courts, as non-Whites. Both the Mexican government and many Mexican Americans objected strenuously to the new classification scheme, and much to the dismay of eugenicists and assorted nativists, the census abandoned the category in subsequent censuses. Although having their whiteness restored did not lessen discrimination, the Mexican government and Mexican Americans fully understood the implications of being officially or legally recognized as a non-White group.

Segregation statutes consistently defined all those without African ancestry as "whites." Texas, for example, defined "colored children" as persons of mixed blood descended from "negro ancestry" for purposes of its school segregation laws and defined all persons besides those of African descent as White for purposes of its antimiscegenation and Jim Crow laws.[16] Chinese and Mexicans in Texas were thus White under state laws governing the segregation of the races, although in practice Mexicans were segregated into "Mexican schools" on the grounds that they needed special language instruction, were "dirty," or had fallen too far behind to be educated with Anglos of the same age.

In Texas the line between de jure and de facto segregation became increasingly blurred as school officials made decisions about district boundaries, school construction, transportation, and so forth that resulted in segregation of Mexican children from White schools. In the absence of statutory segregation that existed in the South between whites and blacks, Mexican Americans first challenged school segregation in 1930, the same year in which they achieved segregated status in the census. In *Independent School District v. Salvatierra* (1930), the Mexican American plaintiffs of Del Rio, Texas, sought to prove that the actions taken by school officials were designed to accomplish "the complete segregation of the school children of Mexican and Spanish descent ...

from the school children of *all other white races* in the same grade." This clever word-
ing recognized that Mexicans were not White in the sense that Anglos were, but that
they belonged to a parallel universe of whiteness. The Texas Court of Civil Appeals
agreed with the plaintiffs and ruled that "school authorities have no power to arbitrarily
segregate Mexican children, assign them to separate schools, and exclude them from
schools maintained for children of *other white races,* merely or solely because they are
Mexicans."[17] However, it was a Pyrrhic victory for Mexicans because the court also affirmed the principle that children could be segregated if they had language difficulties
or if as migrant workers they started school late. School officials were barred only from
segregating Mexican children arbitrarily.

Mexican Americans had learned that the courts ended officially sanctioned segregation of Mexicans only when they insisted on their status as Whites, But how was one to
become de facto White as well as de jure White? LULAC members had tried just about
everything they could to prove how Americanized they were: they spoke English, voted,
used the court systems, got elected to office, actively opposed Mexican immigration,
and excluded Mexican citizens from membership in LULAC. They organized baseball
teams and ate quantities of hot dogs. What more could they do to assimilate whiteness?
Assimilation, however, is not only about what one leaves behind; it is also about what
one is moving toward, what one acquires in the process of cultural exchange and fusion.

For many immigrant groups, assimilation, in part, meant becoming "American,"
which is also to say, becoming White, And becoming White, Toni Morrison has
written, means that "A hostile posture toward resident blacks must be struck at the
Americanizing door before it will open," adding that African Americans have historically served the "less than covert function of defining whites as the 'true' Americans."[18]
As with other ethnic groups in the past—Italians, Poles, and Irish, for example—for
Mexican Americans the path to whiteness involved not so much losing one's culture
as becoming wedded to the notion that people of African descent were culturally and
biologically inferior to Whites. "Only when the lesson of racial estrangement is learned,"
Toni Morrison reminds us, "is assimilation complete."[19]

Growing numbers of middle-class Mexican Americans thus made Faustian bargains
that offered them inclusion within whiteness provided that they subsumed their ethnic
identities under their newly acquired White racial identity and its core value of White
supremacy. ...

Not all Mexican Americans, of course, sought to define themselves as Caucasian or
to achieve equality with Anglos on "the backs of blacks." One member of the Mexican
American generation who resisted the lure of whiteness was Emma Tenayuca, a labor
organizer and leader of the Pecan Shelters Strike in San Antonio, Texas, during the 1930s.
As a woman Tenayuca defied the gendered boundaries of both Anglo and Mexican

culture when she assumed the role of labor activist; she also crossed the ideological divide between "patriotic Americans" and "traitors" when she joined the Communist Party.[20] While Anglos probably regarded Tenayuca as a stereotypical Mexican who had suddenly gone "loca," the largely Catholic, anti-Communist, and middle-class Mexican American community of San Antonio, which included LULAC leaders and the Catholic Church, opposed Tenayuca along ethnoracial fault lines as well as those of religion, gender, and politics. Tenayuca identified herself as an "Indian" like her father and was fond of saying that she did not have a "fashionable Spanish name like Garcia or Sanchez."[21]

Despite numerous examples of those who, like Emma Tenayuca, rejected whiteness and White privilege, many Mexican Americans must nevertheless acknowledge their complicity in maintaining boundaries around "blackness" in order to claim the privileges of whiteness. By embracing whiteness, Mexican Americans have reinforced the color line that has denied people of African descent full participation in American democracy. In pursuing White rights, Mexican Americans combined Latin American racialism with Anglo racism, and in the process separated themselves and their political agenda from the Black civil rights struggles of the forties and fifties.

After 1960 a new generation of Mexican Americans, Chicanos and Chicanas, rejected the accommodationist strategies of the Mexican American generation and sought empowerment through "brownness" and the return, symbolically at least, to Aztlán, the heritage of their Indian past. Chicanos, many who were themselves middle class and college educated, were ridiculed for wearing serapes and resurrecting their Indian heritage, about which they knew very little, but these criticisms have largely missed the mark: in rejecting whiteness, Chicanos found common cause with all oppressed groups—Blacks, Indians, Chinese, and Vietnamese, as well as Mexican immigrants. They rejected the "wages of whiteness" as the "wages of sin" and celebrated their exclusion from and opposition to White America. The White response, about 150 years too late, was: "Why do you insist on being different, on being Chicano or Mexican? Why can't you just be American?" Chicanos rejected being "American" on the historically accurate grounds that being American had always meant being White. But as they accused LULAC members and conservative Mexican Americans of running from their brownness, it was also the case that many Chicanos were trying to escape from their whiteness. Many still are.

Today many Hispanics enjoy the "wages of whiteness" as a result of a complex matrix of phenotype, class position, culture, and citizenship status, as well as the willingness of many Anglos to make room for yet another group of off-white Hispanics. Still, many persons of Mexican descent, especially recent immigrants, are excluded from the domain of whiteness. A dark-skinned non-English-speaking Mexican immigrant doing lawn and garden work does not share the same class and ethnoracial status as acculturated, educated Hispanics. Hispanicized Mexican Americans themselves often construct a "racial" gulf between themselves and "illegal aliens" and "wetbacks."

The lure of whiteness continues to divide various Mexican constituencies along both race and class lines in their fractured, and often fractious, struggles for civil rights. Research on the various paths by which Mexican Americans sought to achieve their own civil rights goals since World War II has the potential to alter significantly our understanding of the complexity and confusion surrounding the ethnoracial identity of Mexican Americans and the process by which many became Hispanic, an identity given official sanction by the U.S. government, business, and academic communities. By examining how law (naturalization, segregation, and miscegenation), comparative civil rights politics (e.g., LULAC and NAACP), labor disputes, culture (e.g., "hispanismo"), religion (e.g., evangelical Protestantism), and literary works have constructed whiteness, often in conflicting and contradictory ways, such a study can illuminate the peculiarly hybrid identities of Mexican Americans and explore the historical roots of the tension that exists between the Hispanic and African American communities, analogous to the tension that has developed between Jews and Blacks, in the context of these groups' particular orientations toward whiteness.

## DISCUSSION QUESTIONS

1. Why did Mexican Americans seek recognition as White people?
2. What rationale did Mexican Americans use to distinguish their civil rights claims from those of African Americans?
3. What changes have Mexican Americans gone through under census bureau racial categories? Why are these changes important?

## NOTES

1. *LULAC* News 1 (1932) and 4 (1937), LULAC Collection, Benson Latin American Collection, University of Texas at Austin; and Benjamin Marquez, *LULAC: The Evolution of a Mexican American Political Association* (Austin: University of Texas Press, 1993), 32–33.
2. Márquez, *LULAC,* 33.
3. Toni Morrison, "On the Backs of Blacks," *Time* 142 (Fall 1993): 57.
4. Quoted in *Off White: Readings on Race, Power, and Society,* ed. Michelle Fine et al. (New York and London: Routledge, 1997), vii.
5. Mary Waters, *Ethnic Options: Choosing Identities in America* (Berkeley: University of California Press, 1990), 162.

6. George Lipsitz, "The Possessive Investment in Whiteness: Racialized Social Democracy and the 'White' Problem in American Studies," *American Quarterly* 47 (September 1995): 369–387. For the historical literature on whiteness, see David Roediger, *The Wages of Whiteness: Race and the Making of the American Working Class* (London: Verso, 1991); and his *Towards the Abolition of Whiteness: Essays on Race, Politics, and Working Class History* (London: Verso, 1994); Eric Lott, *Love and Theft: Blackface Minstrelsy and the American Working Class* (New York: Oxford University Press, 1993); Theodore W. Allen, *The Invention of the White Race,* vol. 1: *Racial Oppression and Social Control* (London: Verso, 1994); Alexander Saxton, *The Rise and Fall of the White Republic: Class Politics and Mass Culture in Nineteenth-Century America* (London: Verso, 1990); and Neil Foley, *The White Scourge: Mexicans, Blacks, and Poor Whites in Texas Cotton Culture* (Berkeley: University of California Press, 1997). On the legal construction of whiteness, see Ian F. Haney Lopez, *White by Law: The Legal Construction of Race* (New York: New York University Press, 1996); and Cheryl I, Harris, "Whiteness as Property," *Harvard Law Review* 106 (June 1993): 1709–1771. On racial formation and the gendered construction of racial ideologies, see Howard Winant, *Racial Conditions: Politics, Theory, Comparisons* (Minneapolis: University of Minnesota Press, 1994); Evelyn Brooks Higginbotham, "African-American Women's History and the Metalanguage of Race," *Signs* 17 (Winter 1992): 251–274; Peggy Pascoe, "Miscegenation Law, Court Cases, and Ideologies of 'Race' in Twentieth-Century America," *Journal of American History* 83 (June 1996): 44–69; Ruth Frankenberg, *White Women, Race Matters: The Social Construction of Whiteness* (Minneapolis: University of Minnesota Press, 1993); and Vron Ware, *Beyond the Pale: White Women, Racism, and History* (London: Verso, 1992). See also Barbara J. Fields, "Ideology and Race in America," in *Region, Race, and Reconstruction: Essays in Honor of C. Vann Woodward,* ed. J, Morgan Kousser and James M. McPherson (New York: Oxford University Press, 1982), 143–177; Thomas C. Holt, "Marking: Race, Race-Making, and the Writing of History," *American Historical Review* 100 (February 1995), 1–20; Toni Morrison, *Playing in the Dark: Whiteness and the Literary Imagination* (New York: Vintage Books, 1993); and Ronald Takaki, *Iron Cages: Race and Culture in 19th-century America* (Seattle: University of Washington Press, 1979).

7. Morrison, "On the Backs of Blacks," 57.

8. Douglas R. Cope, *The Limits of Racial Domination in Mexico: Plebeian Society in Colonial Mexico City, 1600–1720* (Madison: University of Wisconsin Press, 1994);and Patricia Seed, "Social Dimensions of Race: Mexico City, 1753,"

*Hispanic American Historical Review* 62 (1982): 559–606. See also Michael C. Meyer and William L, Sherman, *The Course of Mexican History,* 5th ed. (New York; Oxford University Press, 1995), 214–215; and Magnus Mörner, *Race Mixture in the History of Latin America* (Boston: Little, Brown, 1967), 9–19

9. Raul G. Domínguez to J. B. Davis, June 1, 1933, folder "Mexican Affairs," box 301–495, Miriam A. Ferguson Papers, Archives Division, Texas State Library, Austin, Texas. In another case the Mexican consul general in San Antonio wrote to the governor of Texas to protest the policy of Brackenridge Hospital in Austin, where Mexicans "are placed in the same ward with colored people, and treated as such." Ricardo G. Hill to James V. Allred, May 13, 1937, folder "Mexican Affairs," box 4–14/260, James Allred Papers, Texas State Library.

10. Jose Vasconcelos, *The Cosmic Race* (1925; reprint, Baltimore: Johns Hopkins University Press, 1997); Madison Grant, *The Passing of the Great Race, Or the Racial Basis of European History* (New York: Charles Scribner's Sons, 1916), 69, 81; and C. M. Goethe, "Peons Need Not Apply," *World's Work* 59 (November 1930): 47–48.

11. See Haney Lopez, *White by Law;* and Harris, "Whiteness as Property.

12. Haney Lopez, *White by Law,* 89.

13. The debate can be traced through the numerous congressional hearings by the Immigration and Naturalization Committee during the 1920s. See, for example, United States Congress, House, Committee on Immigration and Naturalization, *Immigration from Countries of the Western Hemisphere,* 70th Cong., 2nd sess. 1930; idem, *Immigration from Countries of the Western Hemisphere,* 70th Cong., 1st sess., Hearing No. 70.1.5 (Washington, D.C.: Government Printing Office, 1928); idem, *Immigration from Mexico,* 71st Cong., 2nd sess. 1930; idem, *Naturalization,* 71st Cong., 2nd sess. 1930; idem, *Restriction of Immigration,* 68th Cong,, 1st sess., serial 1~A. 1924; idem, *Seasonal Agricultural Laborers from Mexico,* 69th Cong., 1st sess. 1926; idem, *Temporary Admission of Illiterate Mexican Laborers,* 66th Cong., 2nd sess. 1920; idem, *Western Hemisphere Immigration,* 71st Cong., 2nd sess. 1930. For a scholarly treatment and analysis of the immigration debate, see Mark Reisler, *By the Sweat of Their Brow; Mexican Immigrant Labor in the United States, 1900–1940* (Westport, Conn,: Greenwood Press, 1976); and David G. Gutierrez, ed., *Between Two Worlds: Mexican Immigrants in the United States* (Wilmington, Del.: Scholarly Resources, 1996).

14. Quoted in Gary A. Greenfield and Don B. Kates Jr., "Mexican Americans, Racial Discrimination, and the Civil Rights Act of 1866," *California Law Review* 63(January 1975), 700.

15. T.J. Woofter Jr., *Races and Ethnic Groups in American Life* (New York: McGraw-Hill, 1933), 57; Greenfield and Kates, "Mexican Americans and the Civil Rights Act of 1866," *California Law Review* 63 (January 1975), 700.

16. Jorge C. Rangel and Carlos M. Alcalá, "Project Report: De Jure Segregation of Chicanos in Texas Schools," *Harvard Civil Rights-Civil Liberties Law Review* 7(March 1972), 311–312, 332–333; Greenfield and Rates, "Mexican Americans and the Civil Rights Act of 1866," 682.

17. Quoted in Rangel and Alcalá, "De Jure Segregation of Chicanos in Texas Schools," 334. See also Guadalupe San Miguel, Jr., *"Let All of Them Take Heed" Mexican Americans and the Campaign for Educational Equality in Texas, 1910–1981*(Austin: University of Texas Press, 1987), 78–81.

18. Morrison, "On the Backs of Blacks," 57.

19. Morrison, "On the Backs of Blacks," 57.

20. Teresa Córdova et al., eds., *Chicana Voices: Intersections of Class, Race, and Gender* (Austin: Center for Mexican American Studies Publications, University of Texas at Austin, 1986), 38. See also Zaragosa Vargas, "Tejana Radical: Emma Tenayuca and the San Antonio Labor Movement," *Pacific Historical Review* (1997).

21. Cordova, *Chicana Voices*, 38.

# CHAPTER 4
# Institutional Racism

# Housing and Education
## *The Inextricable Link*

### Deborah L. McKoy and Jeffrey M. Vincent

As researchers begin to explore the impacts of nonschool factors on educational quality and student achievement, evidence suggests that housing issues play a key role. For several decades, metropolitan areas have experienced changes in residential housing patterns. At the same time, the quality of urban public schools has become increasingly problematic, suggesting a possible connection between residential trends and educational quality. However, knowledge about the specific impacts of housing on education remains limited. Most often, planning and redevelopment efforts are undertaken with little consideration for their potential impacts on local schools, while educational reforms and school facility construction rarely relate to broader urban revitalization activities. Government actions often exacerbate the problem, for example, by failing to promote mixed-income and affordable family housing such that both schools and neighborhoods can become more socioeconomically integrated. This chapter seeks to describe several major connections between housing and schools, identify specific school and housing initiatives that have tried to leverage the connections between the two to improve both, and to identify some of the challenges in integrating housing and educational policy, research, and development.

The complex relationship between housing and education—the "housing–schools nexus"—is found across the United States in varying degrees. As increasing evidence reveals that housing values rise and fall with test scores, real estate agents say that the quality of schools is now a central driving force behind the country's most expensive housing markets.[1] As a result, families with the resources to consider the many housing and school options available have been moving into newer suburbs where recent development provides access to higher-quality housing and good schools. Or, if families remain in older neighborhoods, they often opt out of the public system for private or alternative schools. As middle- and high-income families leave for the suburbs, urban neighborhoods deteriorate.[2] Areas of increasing poverty develop, where residents too poor to leave—the majority being black and Latino—send their children to local, poverty-concentrated schools. In addition, the recent National Fair Housing Alliance Study revealed continued racial discrimination against blacks and Latinos in the rental and sales markets, steering families toward neighbors with poverty-concentrated schools.[3]

What does this situation mean for those schools? The departure of middle-income residents erodes the tax base of cities and inner-ring suburbs, leaving them with fewer resources and greater challenges, including aging school buildings, students whose social and educational needs are greater owing to the environment of poverty, and often a rising population of new immigrants with limited English proficiency. As a result, urban and increasingly inner-ring suburban school districts are left to cope with a complex set of issues that they are often ill equipped to handle. As has been repeatedly pointed out, "bad schools and decaying neighborhoods are a familiar and disheartening combination seemingly locked together."[4] One consistent finding in educational research is that socioeconomic conditions largely predict student achievement and that poverty concentration is correlated highly with school and student failure.[5] Despite this evidence, little research has been directed at the question: What impact do residential patterns and housing trends have on education?

Two interrelated trends are particularly noteworthy in understanding the housing–schools nexus. First, on a regional level, decades of metropolitan expansion and demographic change have led to increasing racial and economic segregation in both older neighborhoods and their schools, with a bifurcated public education system of "good" suburban schools and "failing" city schools. However, more recently the situation continues to change; the conventional "city versus suburb" dichotomy is less the case. The proportion of high-poverty census tracts in the suburbs rose from 11 percent in 1980 to 15 percent in 2000.[6] By 2002 about the same number of low-income people lived in suburban cities as lived in central cities.[7] Still, higher-income families continue to move to suburbs farther out. Public schools are feeling this impact. The problems typically associated with urban schools—racial tension, violence, economic disparities, new immigrants—are an increasing reality for some suburban communities.

Second, affordable housing, even in inner cities and first-ring suburbs, is becoming scarce, often because of rising housing costs, new immigration, and/or gentrification. As a result, residential mobility rates often increase for low-income families when they find themselves priced out of the markets where they live.[8] This means that many low-income students move frequently, and the disruption of their academic experience plays a major role in low achievement levels and high dropout rates; the impact is felt not only on their education, but on the experience of their classmates.

## THE HOUSING–SCHOOLS NEXUS

### Neighborhoods and School Change

The effects of a half-century of metropolitan expansion and demographic change have been increasing racial and economic segregation, with poverty concentrated in older neighborhoods and their schools. On the housing side of the equation, although more neighborhoods now are considered racially integrated than a decade ago, many communities remain almost exclusively composed of households of one race or ethnicity. Neighborhoods that had black majorities in 1990 were more likely to gain black residents than to become more racially integrated by 2000. More than half of all people living in concentrated poverty are black, and concentrated suburban poverty is increasing. In terms of public schools, a January 2005 report titled *Brown At 50: King's Dream or Plessy's Nightmare* concludes that fifty years after the Supreme Court's *Brown v. Board of Education of Topeka* (1954) ruling made legally sanctioned racial segregation in public schools unconstitutional, "desegregation efforts are largely failing and … the nation's public schools are actually re-segregating."[9] Between 1992 and 2002 the number of minority students attending majority-minority schools increased. During the same time, the proportion of minority students attending public schools with white students declined. Thus, by 2000, minorities, particularly Latino and black students, were in schools with substantially fewer white students than was the case in 1990.[10]

Efforts to dismantle segregation were hampered by the Supreme Court's 1974 *Milliken v. Bradley* ruling, which found that suburban districts were not legally mandated to take part in cross-district desegregation efforts. School district boundaries, along with the traditional assignment of students to schools in their neighborhood, are the mechanism by which neighborhood demographics are translated into school demographics.[11] As a result, separate suburban school districts have been created within virtually all metropolitan regions. Homebuyers have access to a wealth of data about public schools; through their housing decisions, they sort themselves into school districts they view as acceptable, and the most commonly researched factors are test scores and racial and economic composition of the student body.[12] Middle- and higher-income households move out of urban districts, where the quality of schools continues to decline, contributing to deteriorating neighborhoods.[13] Since many families, especially middle- and higher-income families, use educational quality as a key factor in choosing where to live, entire communities have developed around demand for high-quality public schools. When the American Planning Association/American Institute of Certified Planners (APA/AICP) 2000 Millennium Survey asked voters in suburbs and small to medium cities what might lead them to live in a more urban setting, better schools ranked first.[14] Also, the 2002 Public Policy Institute of California Statewide Survey on Land Use found schools to be the third most important factor Californians considered in choosing neighborhoods to live in.[15]

Parents who have the resources are willing to pay for better schools by paying more for housing. One study found that parents will pay an additional 2.5 percent in housing costs for a 5 percent increase in test scores at the local public school,[16] whereas another study found that the distinction between an A and a B on a school report card is valued in the housing market at 7 percent.[17] School closures can also impact real estate: the loss of a neighborhood school can reduce home values by nearly 10 percent.[18] Thus, schools and their quality—both real and perceived—greatly impact residential choices and the housing market.

Community and school desegregation efforts are further hampered by discrimination in the real estate market. The National Fair Housing Alliance (NFHA) estimates that at least 3.7 million instances of housing discrimination occur annually against blacks and Latinos in the rental and sales markets.[19] The NFHA study also provides evidence of the education connection, finding that schools are being used as a proxy for the racial or ethnic composition of neighborhoods. Generally, white testers were asked whether they had children, and if they said yes, most agents discussed the importance of schools and selected homes to show them on the basis of schools—schools in districts that were overwhelmingly white. Agents rarely brought up the issue of schools with black and Latino testers who had children. In fact, the white testers were told to avoid the same schools that served the homes selected for black and Latino testers, schools predominantly composed of children of color.

Discriminatory practices like these have a range of consequences for public schools. By 2050, public school enrollment is expected to reach nearly 60 percent nonwhite (from 36 percent in 1996).[20] Between 1992 and 2002 the likelihood increased that black and Latino students would be enrolled in schools with fewer white students.[21] Whereas geographic concentrations of poverty decreased in the past decade,[22] the level of concentrated poverty in public schools grew.[23] Among the public school student population, race and income are closely linked, as are race and the likelihood of being enrolled in a high-poverty school.[24] More than 60 percent of black and Latino students attend high-poverty schools (in which more than half the families are below the poverty line), compared with 30 percent of Asian students and only 18 percent of whites. Most white and Asian students attend schools where less than 30 percent of families are below the poverty line. Additionally, the spectrum of languages spoken constitutes one of the greatest pressures on urban systems. In 1979 only 9 percent of schoolchildren came from homes where English was not spoken, but today around 20 percent of children do so, largely as a result of Latino population increases throughout the country.[25] The share of school-age children with immigrant parents rose from 6 percent in 1970 to nearly 20 percent by 2000.[26]

Schools in low-income communities are left with the difficult and unfair task of overcoming the obstacles of poverty. This places enormous pressure on schools not only to educate children but also to battle symptoms of poverty such as the lack of health care, nutrition, and quality housing for their students. Further, when low-income children are concentrated and isolated, they are denied not only school resources but also connections to social networks that can help them escape poverty by linking to the world of economic and social success.[27] The racial isolation in schools stems from the prevailing history of urban policies and residential preference linked to family income.[28] As one author notes, "What we may actually be seeing is not racial and ethnic separation but economic sorting."[29]

Concentrations of race and poverty found in neighborhoods manifest themselves in schools and classrooms. Richard Rothstein, in *Class and Schools*, argues that because minorities are more likely to be segregated into areas of concentrated poverty,

> their communities usually reflect conditions of distress—housing inadequacy and decay, weak and failing infrastructure, and critical lack of mentors and jobs—all of which adversely affect school resources but also connections to networks that can help them out of the neighborhood of poverty into the world of economic and social success.[30]

As two prominent researchers note, "Socio-economic segregation is a stubborn, multi-dimensional and deeply important cause of educational inequality."[31]

## Impacts on Students And Families

Educational achievement is strongly impacted by the racial and income composition of the student body. Majority-white schools have high graduation rates, whereas schools with large minority and low-income populations tend to have high dropout rates. In 2002, for example, one-third of high schools that were 50 percent or more minority graduated less than half their class, while only 2 percent of schools that were less than 10 percent minority did.[32] Two-thirds of schools that were 90 percent or more minority had a dropout rate of 40 percent or greater.

The average black or Latino student in elementary, middle, or high school currently achieves at about the same level as a white student in the lowest quartile of white achievement.[33] Gains made by black and Latino students from the late 1970s to the late 1980s on national measures eroded in the 1990s. These declines occurred despite aggressive school reform. It is also significant that black students are much less likely than white students to graduate from high school, acquire a college or advanced degree, or earn a living that places them in the middle class.

Living in the poor-quality housing common in low-income urban neighborhoods has numerous costs for families. Research has shown that stable and quality housing can help foster good parenting by providing families with a sense of control, choice, and well-being.[34] Conversely, housing in poor condition, with amenities in constant disrepair, reduces the quality of children's lives and hinders academic development by impeding their ability to learn or develop good study habits. Inadequate heat, lack of air conditioning, inoperable plumbing, or rodent infestation—common conditions in substandard housing—can be disruptive to any learner. Evidence suggests that neighborhood quality has profound effects on student outcomes.[35]

## IMPACTS ON TEACHERS AND CLASSROOMS

Teachers and classrooms in communities of concentrated poverty face unequal burdens compared to their counterparts in wealthier areas. One of the greatest discrepancies is access to instructional resources such as multimedia and other technologies. Schools in wealthier communities offer a range of educational resources that help teachers enhance traditional classroom practices. At the other extreme, many high-poverty school districts tend to have older books, out-of-date computers, and other old or failing technology. Higher pupil-to-teacher ratios, which typically result in poorer learning experiences, are often found in these schools. To make matters worse, teachers in high-priced housing markets are often in need of affordable housing for themselves.

Students living in poverty often require the largest amount of school-centered nutrition and healthcare intervention.[36] In the poorest school districts, funds for school nurses and counselors are the first cuts in school budgets, and some students attend even though they are sick, potentially risking the health of their peers and teachers. With little confidence that their students will be able to get support for homework, or even have a quiet place to study, teachers in urban schools often assign less homework than peers in wealthier school districts, leading to significant consequences for academic achievement.

Given all this, it is not surprising that urban school districts often have trouble attracting and retaining quality teachers, negatively impacting student outcomes. In

Charlotte, North Carolina, for example, one study found that almost one-third of teachers in high-poverty schools left the profession each year during the early 2000s.[37] Research demonstrates that high-poverty schools have more teachers without credentials and are the first to recruit from alternative teacher preparation and placement programs such as Teach For America. A 2004 U.S. Department of Education report found that schools with 75 percent low-income students had three times as many uncertified, out-of-field teachers in both English and science. In an environment where the challenges are great, the compensation small, and collegial support or collaborative opportunities are rare, constant teacher turnover and increasingly low teacher morale are a consistent problem, one that greatly hinders school stability and consistent school reform.[38]

## IMPACTS ON SCHOOLS AND SCHOOL DISTRICTS

For public schools district administrators, changing demographics present complex and intertwined challenges: student populations decline; school funding is reduced; and new demands are placed on basic school operations. Historically, local property taxes have been the major source of funding for public schools, so the relative wealth or poverty of the surrounding community has a direct impact on school funding.[39] State contributions to school district funding are determined by student enrollment and average daily attendance (ADA) calculations, so in communities losing students, state funding decreases and alternatively, where student population is growing, state funding increases.

Dealing with significant changes in budget and population directly affects the day-to-day operation of school districts across metropolitan areas. With fewer resources, high-poverty schools must cut school activities and services such as sports, art, music, healthcare, and security guards. In addition, the federal No Child Left Behind Act provides financial incentives for schools to focus more on test preparation than on elective classes such as art and music. The reduced school curriculum and limited extracurricular activities offered at urban schools are a central concern for many middle-class families seeking a rich and well-rounded education for their children.[40]

Population growth and neighborhood change put additional pressures on school districts in terms of providing adequate school facilities for students. Growth areas look to build schools while areas with student declines often look to close schools. In high-growth communities, housing developers are often charged impact fees for public infrastructure such as school facilities. Additionally, developers will often set aside land for a new school. However, this land often tends to be less than optimal in terms either of development potential or of proximity to adjacent neighborhoods. Districts with declining enrollments look to close schools, but risk losing scarce and expensive land should student populations rebound. In urban communities undergoing redevelopment, efforts to replace high-density public housing with lower-density mixed-income housing is reducing student population in the lowest-income communities. It is also contributing to gentrification of neighborhoods and further reducing density. In cities such as San Francisco, Washington, DC, New York, and Boston, land values are rapidly rising such that there is demand for public school land for real estate development.

### Housing Affordability, Mobility, and Student Achievement

In addition to the demographic shifts discussed above, another trend impacting schools is frequent student transfers due to the lack of affordable housing, even in the inner cities and first-ring suburbs, owing to rising costs, gentrification, and immigration. Steering on the basis of race or ethnicity worsens the affordability problem. According to NFHA, steering inflates the value of homes in certain majority-white school districts and limits demand for homes and schools in minority districts.[41] This artificial manipulation of the market depresses home values, and to compensate, these areas must raise taxes, providing a reason for agents to steer whites away.

Changes in the housing market put pressure on low-income families. A 2000 census study found that 51 percent of the 41.5 million people surveyed in the United States changed residences in 1999.[42] Thirty percent moved for positive housing reasons, such as moving from rental units to homeownership (11.5 percent) or to a new or better home (18.5 percent). However, nearly 10 percent, at least 2.3 million people, moved as a result of negative housing conditions, primarily the need for a better and safer neighborhood or cheaper housing. Overcrowded housing, in poor condition or with health hazards, puts enormous stress on families and can often lead to unplanned or unwanted moves. Moreover, when home prices and rents increase, families may be forced to move frequently. Too often, student mobility results from market forces that push families to poor or poorer neighborhoods and schools.

The issue of student mobility has received increasing attention in both educational and housing research. The *Journal of Negro Education* released a special edition in 2003 titled "Student Mobility: How Some Children Get Left Behind."[43] A growing literature investigates the impact of mobility on educational administration and student achievement. Researchers and practitioners alike agree that school instability is largely a function of residential instability.[44]

Finding an acceptable *and* affordable place to live is becoming difficult for many public school families. In 2000 the U.S. Department of Housing and Urban Development (HUD) reported that an all-time high of about 5.4 million households either live in severely inadequate housing or pay more than half their income on housing.[45] Recent reports by both the Center for Housing Policy and the Joint Center for Housing Studies at Harvard University also found that more than three-quarters of America's working families spend more than half their income on housing, compared to 20 percent in the 1960s.[46] The one-third of all U.S. households that rent their housing are especially affected. One analysis found that while the rent burden has increased only modestly in the past few decades, the most pronounced increases were borne by poor households.[47] Lack of affordable housing has increased residential mobility rates among low-income families, who are priced out of their neighborhoods.

Homeownership is also an important issue that relates to student mobility. Families owning homes tend to be more stable over time. Nearly 70 percent of Americans own their homes, but the rate of homeownership for working families with children is lower than in 1978, according to a study by the Center for Housing Policy.[48] The study indicates that the trend is being driven by a combination of factors: soaring housing costs that have overshot wage increases; higher healthcare bills; and a rise in the number of single parents. Hispanic and black working families with children have struggled the most; their homeownership rate has stagnated at about 45 percent, far below that of white families (71 percent) as of 2003.[49] The affordability of housing also affects the residential choices of new immigrants. Although this is beginning to change, new immigrant families tend to reside, at least initially, in lower-cost central city and older inner-ring suburban neighborhoods.[50] This trend places newly arriving school-age students—especially Latino and Asian students—in schools already troubled by declining resources.

### Impacts on Students and Families

In many urban centers, high housing costs often force parents to spend more time working to pay the rent or mortgage, with less time available to help their children with homework or be involved in their child's school. Study after study demonstrates the importance of parental involvement and how difficult this is to achieve in under-resourced, largely low-income schools.[51] Additionally, research has shown that stable and good-quality housing can help foster good parenting by providing families with a sense of control, choice, and well-being.[52]

As pressures from rising housing costs push vulnerable families from residence to residence, moving from school to school affects students' social and emotional life as well as their academic achievement.[53] Making new friends and learning new social expectations and norms are difficult tasks, demanding more time than frequent trans-fers allow. Student misbehavior and violence can also result from high mobility. A longitudinal study tracking 4,500 adolescents in California and Oregon from seventh grade demonstrated that violence increased by 20 percent among students who moved frequently in their elementary school years.[54] In the worst-case scenario, housing prices may force families with children to become homeless. As students in local schools, these children are at much greater risk of illness, injury, malnutrition, abuse, neglect, violence, separation from family, and delays in cognitive and language development.[55]

## Impacts on Teachers and Classrooms

When students are moving into and out of local schools, teachers are continuously getting to know new students as well as their learning needs and abilities. One of the most difficult aspects of student mobility is assigning transfer students to specific classes at their new schools. Inappropriate or incorrect ability grouping is particularly critical for mobile students; students with special needs or those who require individual education programs or English language accommodation can be misplaced.[56] The new teacher has limited information about mobile students, and discovering that students have been incorrectly placed can take weeks or even months. This crucial decision will influence not only how much the student will learn but also classroom placement for future years.[57]

High student mobility rates make it harder for *all* students to be prepared adequately for testing. A California study revealed that even nonmobile students had significantly lower average test scores in high schools that had high student mobility rates.[58] Those students who move frequently are particularly affected. Unless they attend for a certain percentage of days, mobile students simply "don't count": their scores are not considered in schools' reporting statistics. Because they are held accountable for test scores under the federal No Child Left Behind (NCLB) legislation, teachers may feel less incentive to focus their attention on transferring students whose scores do not matter. On the other hand, teachers may find themselves held responsible for the academic progress of students who were not in their class for the entire year but nevertheless met the score-reporting cutoff. Research indicates that high student mobility leads to teacher burnout and even resignation, creating more problems for schools.[59]

## Impacts on Schools and School Districts

School administrators are challenged to track the educational needs of students as they move into and out of the system. Transcripts rarely follow students in a timely fashion. Additionally, schools in low-income, high-mobility areas are often unable to rely on consistent participation from parents. Many of the transient families are poor or newly immigrated. Compared with parents in more privileged and better-resourced districts, lower-income parents tend to experience numerous barriers to effective school participation activities such as decision making, fund raising, or parent advocacy.[60] Language differences also increase the challenges of these relationships between parents and schools. The number and diversity of students from families speaking a language other than English rose rapidly in the 1990s; the number of children who speak a language other than English at home more than doubled from 5.1 to 10.6 million between 1980 and 2000.[61] Many of them are found in low-income urban schools.

## INNOVATIONS AT THE HOUSING–SCHOOLS NEXUS

Recognizing the linkage between the quality of housing and the quality of local schools, innovative leaders in both areas have developed a variety of strategies for improving educational outcomes and providing quality affordable housing. Some of these involve uncoupling urban schools from the poor neighborhoods through different assignment policies. This provides ways for students in the worst neighborhoods to get a quality education, as well as ways to even out the resources available to all schools, regardless of neighborhood. Other solutions link schools to residential and commercial development in ways that are designed to improve their resources and educational environment.

### Alternative School Assignment Policies

With school assignments traditionally based on school districts and neighborhood of residence, families living in poverty have had limited school options. To remedy this situation, a number of school assignment policies and practices have changed the traditional school and neighborhood relationship, providing opportunities for minority and low-income families. School districts have instituted policies to increase racial and economic integration in their schools. One of the least popular of these was "bussing," started in 1973. For the most part, it was court-ordered and designed to eliminate the institutional segregation that had defined public education. A more popular approach has been the use of magnet schools, introduced in the 1970s. A magnet school often features a specialized or unique curriculum or evaluation strategy to attract students of various social, racial, and economic backgrounds. In 2001, high numbers of magnet schools were found in Chicago, New York City, Puerto Rico, and Los Angeles.[62] Parents from the entire district, regardless of their residence within the district, may apply to send their children to a magnet school.

Another example of a school policy designed to foster better economic and racial integration is San Francisco's "Diversity Index." San Francisco Unified School District's

Diversity Index was adopted to guide school assignment, with the goal of achieving economic integration among students. The district uses a formula incorporating sixteen student measures to determine school assignment. Race is the last variable, and school assignments are often determined well before race comes into the equation. Students are assigned on the basis of a determination of optimal and acceptable diversity for a school. However, this policy has been very controversial in its implementation.

Charter schools offer another alternative. Developed in the mid-1990s, public charter schools are publicly funded, but controlled through charters to independent entities that operate a public school. Charter schools have school district boundaries, but are generally open by lottery or other broad-based access system to any student from the district.

A number of cities, including Washington, DC, Milwaukee, and Cleveland are using school vouchers. In theory, vouchers provide maximum access to choice among public schools or private schools, empowering families to choose the best educational option for their children. School choice proponents assert that free market forces on public education will improve all schools, public and private, because consumer demand will force schools to meet the standards of their customers. While choice has been hailed as a way to empower families and inject competition into the educational field, studies have shown mixed results.[63] One central critique is that school vouchers give additional advantage to already advantaged students, further fueling patterns of economic and racial segregation in schools.[64]

Research has yet to determine how these newer types of school assignment policies have affected housing patterns and prices and whether housing policies have taken new school assignment options for families into account. Rather than try to counter residential patterns through school assignment integration policies, another approach seeks to reinvigorate neighborhood schools to build stronger connections between families, schools, and communities. In this approach, neighborhood schools—ones that draw their students locally—become neighborhood centers of recreational, educational, and health services and support, with the goal of not only improving student achievement but also strengthening families and communities.

For example, community schools (sometimes called full-service schools) seek to bring educational, recreational, and health services together under one roof, particularly in disadvantaged neighborhoods, to better meet the wide variety of needs for children and their families.[65] The Coalition for Community Schools promotes this model as the vehicle for strengthening schools, families, and communities so that together they can improve student learning.[66] The result is a push away from desegregation policies that uncouple family residence and school assignment; instead, the link is reinvigorated, fostering neighborhood, family, and school cohesion. Some have argued that neighborhood schools are positively correlated with student achievement.[67] In particular, advocates believe that neighborhood schools will increase parental involvement, permit students to walk to and from school, and create local community social capital.

## Alternative Housing Policies

One way to increase integration within schools and to improve educational opportunities for low-income children is to give their families an opportunity to relocate to districts with higher-quality schools. A variety of housing policies have attempted to alleviate patterns of racial and economic segregation, with mixed results. The first effort—and one of the best-known—was the Gautreaux program, which relocated public housing families into different parts of the Chicago metropolitan area. Studies of the children involved show that, over a period of seven to ten years, those who moved to the suburbs had lower dropout rates (5 versus 20 percent) and higher rates of college attendance (54 versus 21 percent) than those who moved somewhere else within the city.[68] While the evidence is not decisive, the schools in suburban neighborhoods to which the students relocated had greater racial and economic integration.

In 1992 the U.S. Department of Housing and Urban Development launched the Moving to Opportunity for Fair Housing Demonstration Program (MTO), attempting to replicate the Gautreaux project's results. This effort sought to uncover what happens when very poor families have the opportunity to move out of subsidized housing in the poorest neighborhoods of Baltimore, Boston, Chicago, Los Angeles, and New York. The findings have been mixed. In Baltimore, one study found that elementary schoolchildren who moved from high-poverty to low-poverty neighborhoods had improved reading and math scores.[69] Other studies have not detected significant impacts on educational achievement.[70] One study found that many participating children actually remained at their original school rather than switching to a "better" school.[71] This may explain the insignificant improvement, and it points to a flaw in the policy. While gaining access to better schools by moving to a better neighborhood is one of the project's goals, policy mechanisms failed to encourage or assist families in transferring their students to these schools.

Another housing policy demonstrating a potentially positive impact is the federal HOPE VI urban revitalization program. The Urban Institute has shown very hopeful outcomes for low-income students enrolled in this program. The ongoing HOPE VI Panel Study showed that families who received Section 8 housing vouchers moved to neighborhoods with better schools, although residents who were simply reassigned to other public housing developments did not find better schools.[72] Key factors in better performance were having parents who have high school diplomas themselves, who are more engaged with their children's education, and who do not suffer from depression. In addition, the better-performing students were found to have higher levels of self-efficacy and social competence. While not conclusive, these findings indicate that, in addition to housing, social and health-related conditions correlate positively with a child's success in school.

An earlier study of Albuquerque, New Mexico, also revealed positive outcomes when low-income children in public housing are moved to high-income communities and schools. Metro Albuquerque has one dominant city government and one unified school system. As a result, public housing families live in a greater variety of neighborhoods, and a high percentage of the city's children attend the public schools (more than 92 percent at the time of this study in 1994). According to the study:

> Despite their family circumstances, children from public housing households living in middle-class neighborhoods and attending middle-class schools show measurable improvement in their academic performance over children of similar individual and family characteristics living in low-income neighborhoods and attending low-income schools.[73]

### Linking School Improvement to Housing Redevelopment

Neighborhood revitalization strategies are beginning to include schools in a more comprehensive approach to redevelopment. One survey showed that more than 200 community organizations are linking their work to school reform in a range of ways.[74] According to some researchers, "If urban school reform in the United States is to be successful, it must be linked to the revitalization of the communities around our schools."[75] Turnham and Khadduri conducted case studies of six revitalization programs, in Baltimore, Philadelphia, Washington, DC, Atlanta, St. Louis, and North Richmond, California.[76] Each case had a focus on different housing and educational strategies, ranging from public housing redevelopment and affordable housing improvements to greater homeownership opportunities. Some programs sought to attract middle-income families to a community by improving schools and offering better housing opportunities, whereas others sought to create more affordable housing and homeownership opportunities for local residents.

Developers working on impoverished sections of Baltimore, St. Louis, and Atlanta have formally coordinated school improvement, new housing development, and community services, with the particular goal of retaining old residents in the new diverse mixed-income communities.[77] In 1989 The Enterprise Foundation, now called Enterprise Community Partners, led by developer Jim Rouse, teamed up with the City of

Baltimore, churches, and local community organizations to launch the Neighborhood Transformation Initiative. This has brought education reform to center stage in the Sandtown–Winchester neighborhood. The goal was to "cement a relationship between community and school" as part of nearby housing renovation and construction in a seventy-two-block neighborhood about a mile and a half from downtown Baltimore. At the three elementary schools affected by the project, the percentage of students performing at a satisfactory level on the Grade 5 comprehensive state tests increased at a higher rate than in the city's public schools as a whole. At the same time, homeownership rates have risen, vacancy has declined, crime rates fell in all categories between 1997 and 2000, and real estate values increased during the 1990s.

Richard Baron, a well-known mixed-income housing developer, has had similar success in St. Louis and Atlanta. He recognizes school as being at "the center of virtually every residential real estate decision made in America."[78] In the 1990s he began working with the St. Louis Public Housing Authority and the U.S. Department of Housing and Urban Development (HUD) to renovate old public housing developments and the low-performing Jefferson Elementary School, raising an additional $3.5 million for the latter. Baron called for specific school reforms and a new principal, along with mixed-income development. As with the Baltimore example, these school reforms were meant to reinforce the new redevelopment and guide schools to play a central role in the process of revitalizing the neighborhood. A diverse set of residents and children are now socializing in the neighborhood and at school. Because the housing is attractive, well built, and formally linked to school reform, family mobility has been reduced, and children tend to stay at their school longer, reducing classroom disruptions.

Baron developed a similar project in Atlanta, known on Centennial Place. His partners were the federal HOPE VI redevelopment program, the Atlanta Housing Authority, the Atlanta Public School District, and the Integral Group, a local developer. Residents and the community helped to plan the transformation of a former public housing development into a mixed-income "community of choice." Their identified needs were (1) improved education, (2) day care, and (3) job opportunities.

In return for the developers' renovation of the public elementary school, the local school district agreed to make it a neighborhood school—that is, the school would draw its students primarily from nearby neighborhoods. By 2001, students at the Centennial Place Elementary School exceeded the standards in all categories tested by the State of Georgia. In the 2002–2003 school year, 93 percent of students met or exceeded math testing standards, and 98 percent of students met or exceeded standards in reading. The environment for learning had improved dramatically.

Against these positive findings, some research has found that redevelopment strategies can do harm to low-income households and to communities of color. In analyzing the Chicago Public Housing Transformation Program, which demolished many of the public housing developments in Chicago and relocated residents throughout the city, Pauline Lipman argues that the result has been gentrification of city neighborhoods. Along with local advocates, she argues that the gentrification was strategically—and purposefully—linked to one of the largest school reforms efforts in the United States: sixty low-achieving schools have been closed, and 100 new smaller schools were added, two-thirds of them run by charters or private contractors. Lipman argues that the combination of housing demolition, gentrification, and school reform is "concretely and symbolically linked to pushing out low-income people of color and destroying their communities."[79] Even if this outcome was not intentional, a negative potential exists. While mixed-income housing may initially include units that are affordable, as schools improve, housing costs are likely to increase. A key challenge is to ensure that housing remains affordable as the quality of education rises.

Two other housing policies show an increasing, although indirect, connection to education: (1) infill housing, which is residential development on small parcels of land surrounded by already developed areas; and (2) inclusionary zoning polices, which require specific percentages of affordable housing in new development. A recent study for the State of California found that school quality was one of the leading reasons families would be willing to relocate to an infill housing site—a strategy to attract families back to denser urban areas.[80] Regarding the latter innovation, former mayor and urban researcher David Rusk studies and advocates inclusionary zoning as a vehicle to bring more affordable housing to low-income families across regions. In effect, he positions inclusionary zoning as education policy.[81] An estimated 100 cities and counties have enacted inclusionary zoning laws that if adequately enforced would provide opportunities for more public school families to live in higher-income neighborhoods and attend higher-income schools.[82] However, inclusionary zoning often goes unenforced, and targeted goals remain unmet in most localities.

**Building New Schools**

Several efforts by neighborhood revitalization organizations have focused on creating new schools, both to attract new middle-income residents and to retain diverse families already in the community. In Baltimore the Patterson Park Community Development Corporation was formed in 1996 to address disinvestment in the community. Working in partnership with a local Catholic school and a local foundation, it provided school subsidies to families who bought homes through a special program designed to attract residents to the neighborhood.[83] The neighborhood went on to plan a neighborhood-based public charter school in hopes of creating an economically and racially diverse student body. Program designers used enrollment boundaries to draw students from local families because they hoped that local residents would contribute to the revitalization and integration of the neighborhood. The effort has been led by many of the 125 families who bought houses as part of the homeownership program.

There are community-based organizations (CBOs) that are creating charter schools as a way to expand their current services and provide "one-stop shopping" for the communities they serve. CBOs recognize that as neighborhood schools improve, fewer younger urban middle-income parents leave cities seeking areas with better schools.[84] They find, as other studies do, that with more middle-income families, classrooms become more diverse, and the economic base remains strong.[85] In many of these projects, local organizers conceive of charter schools before they have a building in place. This allows CBOs to purchase or lease vacant, dilapidated properties and renovate them, often into schools and community centers. In turn, the whole neighborhood is improved. Examples of CBO-driven charter schools are found at local and national levels.

A well-recognized example of improving a public school in conjunction with housing development is the community-managed public–private partnership between the District of Columbia James F. Oyster Bilingual Elementary School and a private developer.[86] The school was located on 1.67 acres of highly desirable land in Woodley Park, an upper-income residential area that nevertheless had a racially and economically mixed student body in the late 1980s. Understanding both the city's lack of financial resources and the value of the land that the school was on, Oyster School parents came up with the idea of selling part of the school's land to developers to pay for the necessary school improvements. These parents then started the 21st Century School Fund and in 1998 managed the process whereby the school district entered into an agreement with LCOR, a private property development firm, to build an apartment house on a portion of this land. In exchange for land and in lieu of property taxes, LCOR paid the debt service on a bond to design, construct, and furnish a new Oyster school. The agreement led to benefits for the whole city school system; the company also agreed to set aside $445,000 to fund other school modernization projects in the city.

Another example of innovation is found in San Diego. The city and school district teamed up on two redevelopment projects in the densely populated City Heights neighborhood. Nearly complete, the ten city block City Heights Urban Village has a pedestrian-friendly town square surrounded by retail, community, and educational facilities.[87] Already completed are a police substation, community gymnasium, elementary school, library, community service center, recreation center, continuing education center, and retail center. Still under construction are townhomes and an office center. Partners on this public-private project include the City of San Diego, San Diego Unified School District, CitiLink Investment Corporation, and Price Charities, among others.

Success breeds more innovation. The city and the school district are now working on another project in City Heights, the San Diego Model School Development. Again using an "urban village" concept, the smaller model school redevelopment site includes a new elementary school, new mixed-income family housing units, and community services. By forming a Joint Powers Authority (JPA) between local agencies, the goal is to work collaboratively to site a much-needed new school that takes up less space and provides a wide range of community amenities.[88]

### Smart Growth and Other New Initiatives

The Smart Growth movement, a major recent urban planning strategy, has also increasingly focused on the role of schools in urban growth and development. The smart growth agenda seeks to curb low-density development that leads to urban sprawl and to conserve resources and land in the process.[89] Affordable housing is a critical component, and advocates are interested in how changes in traditional school planning can foster sounder and healthier neighborhoods.[90] In particular, the Smart Growth-Smart Schools Initiative launched in 2004 by the Kellogg Foundation hopes to link an urban housing agenda to the movement for educational equity.[91]

Tied to smart growth issues is the notion of "schools as centers of community"—that is, that schools should be strategically located in neighborhoods so that they are easy to get to and act as central public spaces for events and community building, not just quality learning.[92] Planners, architects, and developers have been touting the role civic buildings, housing, and especially public schools can play in the life of a neighborhood, as both social and physical centerpieces. Many argue that the development (or redevelopment) of smaller schools on smaller sites can save time and money, put schools and homes closer together, and allow schools to better serve as centers of their communities.[93]

Additionally, there are new governance structures connecting housing and schools. In several states undergoing population growth, such as California and Ohio, governments are creating new administrative bodies. The Cities, Counties, Schools Partnership of California, for example, brings different actors together for dialogue across these policy divides.[94] The goal of these new structures is to align school planning with larger housing and metropolitan planning so that policy makers can share information, data, and projections and so that school districts and cities can better coordinate their development needs.

## CHALLENGES TO INTEGRATING HOUSING AND EDUCATION

Housing and education have always been organically connected, yet rarely has policy or practice in either field addressed the connection. Through specific project efforts, educators and housing polity makers are beginning to experiment with how to leverage these natural connections to the advantage of residential development and of public schools. However, the policy and research communities need to help develop a better understanding of the relationship between housing and schools for this to be a success. Following this, policy makers need to use the findings from practice and research to create a new policy framework for targeting the housing–school nexus effectively.

## Research Needs

Significant research voids exist at the housing–schools nexus. Specifically, we need to better understand the impact of mixed-income housing and other policies that seek to integrate communities on existing residents. For example, how does displacement affect student achievement? Research must explore the academic successes in mixed-income redevelopments to determine whether higher scores on standardized tests are due to improvements made by students who lived in these communities prior to redevelopment, or if they are attributable to an influx of higher-income students through gentrification. Finding this out is complicated by the fact that, as part of the federal NCLB policy, improvement is measured at the school level rather than the student level. Thus, the focus on improving failing schools may provide a subtle incentive for schools and cities to push out poorly performing students via school transfer or gentrification. Another impediment lies in the very nature of mixed-income housing—that is, that there is a need to sustain some level of affordable housing. As schools improve, market-rate developers may build housing that is expensive and out of reach for many of the families the school improvements were intended to help. Remembering that housing costs typically rise as school quality improves, how can housing remain affordable? There is little research to show that mixed-income housing programs actually lead to better and more economically integrated housing for all residents. Moreover, programs are unlikely to succeed if middle-income families avoid mixed-income communities because of deep racial biases.

On a related issue, while neighborhoods and schools become more diverse through mechanisms such as magnet schools or other reform efforts, internal problems may remain. For example, in Berkeley, California, one of the most celebrated models of racially integrated schools in the country, schools are overwhelmingly segregated inside their walls. While the overall student population is diverse, the more advanced college-prep classes are overwhelmingly filled with white and Asian students, while black and Latino students are tracked into less rigorous classes for those not expected to attend college.[95] This phenomenon, well known in the educational literature as tracking, remains a formidable hurdle for educational equity. Overall, research is needed to understand whether and how mixed-income housing leads to better and economically integrated housing for all residents, and how these actions ultimately impact schools. This work will form the basis for appropriate policy responses.

**Connecting Policy and Practice**

There is a structural disconnect between the education and housing sectors that presents a key barrier to successfully addressing the goals of advocates on both sides. School districts generally act autonomously from municipal authority, which makes it difficult to align plans, processes, and budgets for housing and school development.[96] Successful collaboration between the two sectors has often relied on the personal connections of individuals, rather than on formal established relationships between housing and education administrators. Although there have been a few successful efforts by actors such as New Schools, Better Neighborhoods, an organization that works to connect communities and schools in the Los Angeles area through housing and school facilities development, there are still considerable obstacles to aligning planning for building housing and schools. There is a general lack of understanding across disciplines and the absence of formal governance structures to sustain coordination across housing and education sectors.[97] Practitioners have voiced concern that the challenges to succeeding at collaboration often outweigh the possible rewards.[98]

More specifically, housing and education have different administrative practices, especially relating to funding, development regulations, and operational timelines. Though both the housing and education sectors are faced with inadequate funding, they may deal with this challenge differently. For example, developers may focus on the construction of housing that is designed to attract households without children so that they can avoid neighborhood opposition on the grounds that new construction will require increased taxes for education. Collaboration is further stymied by competing and noncomplementary regulations. Education is predominantly a public resource; whereas housing development occurs primarily in the private sector, driven by market forces.[99] This means that housing development can respond more quickly to demand, but school development is often slowed by more rigid funding structures. Furthermore, schools operate on a fixed and slow-moving academic schedule and are subject to project completion deadlines, while housing can be developed quickly and with more flexibility.

In the private sector time is money, while in the public sector plans must go through mandatory approval processes that often take significant time.

## CONCLUSION

Tremendous socioeconomic change has occurred in America's cities since the 1950s. During this time, both housing and public schools in older urban areas have experienced increasingly severe—and intertwined—problems. Yet rarely have policy responses been aimed at addressing the housing–schools nexus. As is shown in this chapter, the evidence has grown clearer: issues of housing and schools are far more interrelated and mutually dependent than previously acknowledged. Neighborhoods with poor housing too often have low performing schools while areas with good housing have higher performing schools. The first to notice, perhaps, were middle-income families, who now largely flood into the suburbs seeking not just a nice house at a reasonable price but also a fine education and promising future for their children—a goal that all families deserve to pursue. While innovative housing developers, cities, and community organizations are beginning to recognize the importance of high-quality schools to overall revitalization efforts, there are few formal mechanisms to institutionalize practices that address the housing–school nexus. Any effort to integrate education and housing policies and programs will face several challenges, most of them rooted in the way policy makers and practitioners historically think and act. Better understanding the housing–school nexus is an important first step.

## DISCUSSION QUESTIONS

1. Discuss some of the ways in which economic poverty affects quality of education at the community level.
2. What do the authors mean by the term "steering"? Why is this practice so devastating to urban school quality?
3. In your opinion, would an unfettered "free market" system of school choice increase or decrease the inequality in public schools, in the long run?

## NOTES

4. For example, Lloyd, Carol. 2005. The Home School Conundrum: Parents' Real Estate Decisions Often Based on Kids' Education Needs. *San Francisco Chronicle*, March 25; Ginsberg, Marsha. 2004. Educated Buyers; Test Scores, School Ratings Drive Decisions as Much as Floor Plans and City. *San Francisco Chronicle*, February 15, page G1.
5. Orfield, Myron. 2002. *American Metropolitics: The New Suburban Reality*. Washington, DC: Brookings Institution Press.

6. National Fair Housing Alliance. 2006. *Unequal Opportunity: Perpetuating Housing Segregation in America*, 2006 Fair Housing Trends Report. Washington, DC: National Fair Housing Alliance.

7. Stone, Clarence, Kathryn Doherty, Cheryl Jones, and Timothy Ross. 1999. Schools and Disadvantaged Neighborhoods. In *Urban Problems and Community Development*, edited by Ronald F. Ferguson and William T. Dickens. Washington, DC: Brookings Institution Press.

8. Coleman, James, Ernest Q. Campbell, Carol J. Hobson, James McPartland, Alexander M. Mood, Frederick D. Weinfeld, and Robert G. York. 1966. *Equality of Educational Opportunity*. Washington, DC: U.S. Government Printing Office; Rothstein, Richard. 2004. *Class and Schools: Using Social, Economic, and Educational Reform to Close the Black–White Achievement Gap*. Washington, DC: Economic Policy Institute.

9. Kingsley, G. Thomas and Kathryn L.S. Pettit. 2003. *Concentrated Poverty: A Change in Course*. Washington, DC: Urban Institute; Swanstrom, Todd, Colleen Casey, Robert Flack, and Peter Dreier. 2004. *Pulling Apart: Economic Segregation among Suburbs and Central Cities in Major Metropolitan Areas*. Washington, DC: The Living Cities Census Series, Brookings Institution.

10. Berube, Alan and William H. Frey. 2002. *A Decade of Mixed Blessings: Urban and Suburban Poverty in Census 2000*. Washington, DC: Brookings Institution.

11. U.S. Department of Health and Human Services. 2001. *Geographical Mobility, Population Characteristics: March 1999 to March 2000*. Washington, DC: U.S. Department of Health and Human Services, Office of the Assistant Secretary for Planning and Evaluation.

12. Orfield, Gary and Chungmei Lee. 2004. *Brown at 50: King's Dream or Plessy's Nightmare?* Cambridge, MA: Civil Rights Project, Harvard University.

13. Orfield, Gary and Chungmei Lee. 2005. *Why Segregation Matters: Poverty and Educational Inequality*. Cambridge, MA: Civil Rights Project, Harvard University.

14. Orfield, Myron. 2002. *American Metropolitics: The New Suburban Reality*. Washington, DC: Brookings Institution Press.

15. Crone, Theodore M. 1998. *Housing Prices and the Quality of Public Schools: What Are We Buying?* Federal Reserve Bank of Philadelphia.

16. Orfield, Myron. 2002. *American Metropolitics: The New Suburban Reality*. Washington, DC: Brookings Institution Press.

17. American Planning Association and American Institute of Certified Planners. 2000. *The Millennium Survey: A National Poll of American Voters' View on Land*

*Use*. Washington, DC: American Planning Association and American Institute of Certified Planners.

18. Baldassare, Mark. 2002. *Public Policy Institute of California Statewide Survey: Special Survey on Land Use*. San Francisco: Public Policy Institute of California.

19. Black, Sandra E. 1999. Do Better Schools Matter? Parental Valuation of Elementary Education. *Quarterly Journal of Economics* 114(2): 577–599.

20. Figlio, David. 2002. What's In a Grade? School Report Cards and House Prices. University of Florida, Department of Economics Working Paper.

21. Bogart, William T. and Brian A. Cromwell. 1997. How Much Is a Good School District Worth? *National Tax Journal* 50(2): 215–232.

22. National Fair Housing Alliance. 2006. *Unequal Opportunity: Perpetuating Housing Segregation in America*, Fair Housing Trends Report. Washington, DC: National Fair Housing Alliance. This measure does not include instances of discrimination against other protected classes, and discrimination in lending, insurance, planning, and zoning. Rental market discrimination is most common, with private fair housing groups reporting 12,651 complaints in 2005 against apartment owners and managers. In the same year, 747 complaints related to home sales were made. In an enforcement project involving 145 paired tests conducted in twelve major cities across the United States, the NFHA found evidence of steering on the basis of race or ethnicity in 87 percent of cases. Black and Latino testers were denied service or provided limited service by real estate agents in about 20 percent of instances, even though all black and Latino testers were better qualified for home purchase than their white counterparts. While white testers were shown an average of eight homes per test, black and Latino testers were shown an average of five homes per test. More often than their white counterparts, black and Latino testers were required to provide confirmation from a lender before being showed any homes.

23. Orfield, Myron. 2002. *American Metropolitics: The New Suburban Reality*. Washington, DC: Brookings Institution Press.

24. Orfield, Gary and Chungmei Lee. 2005. *Why Segregation Matters: Poverty and Educational Inequality*. Cambridge, MA: Civil Rights Project, Harvard University.

25. Rawlings, Lynette, Laura Harris, Margery Austin Turner, and Sandra Padilla. 2004. *Race and Residence: Prospects for Stable Neighborhood Integration*. Washington, DC: Urban Institute.

26. Orfield, Gary and Chungmei Lee. 2005. *Why Segregation Matters: Poverty and Educational Inequality*. Cambridge, MA: Civil Rights Project, Harvard University.

27. Rothstein, Richard. 2004. *Class and Schools: Using Social, Economic, and Educational Reform to Close the Black–White Achievement Gap.* Washington, DC: Economic Policy Institute.

28. Orfield, Myron. 2002. *American Metropolitics: The New Suburban Reality.* Washington, DC: Brookings Institution Press.

29. Van Hook, Jennifer and Michael Fix. 2000. A Profile of the Immigrant Student Population. In *Overlooked and Underserved: Immigrant Children in U.S. Secondary Schools,* edited by J.R. De Velasco, M. Fix, and T. Clewell. Washington, DC: The Urban Institute.

30. Briggs, Xavier de Sousa. 1998. Brown Kids in White Suburbs: Housing Mobility and the Many Faces of Social Capital. *Housing Policy Debate* 9(1): 177–221; Cattel, Vicky. 2001. Poor People, Poor Places, and Poor Health: The Mediating Role of Social Networks and Social Capital. *Social Science and Medicine* 52(10): 1501–1516.

31. Thernstrom, Abigail and Stephen Thernstrom. 2003. *No Excuses: Closing the Racial Gap in Learning.* New York: Simon & Schuster.

32. Foster-Bey, John A. 2004. Aiming for Integration? 50 Years after Brown. *National Review Online.* Available at http://www.nationalreview.com/comment/fosterbey200404150851 (accessed March 6, 2006).

33. Rothstein, Richard. 2004. *Class and Schools: Using Social, Economic, and Educational Reform to Close the Black–White Achievement Gap.* Washington, DC: Economic Policy Institute.

34. Orfield, Gary and Chungmei Lee. 2005. *Why Segregation Matters: Poverty and Educational Inequality.* Cambridge, MA: Civil Rights Project, Harvard University.

35. Ellen, Ingrid Gould and Margery Austin Turner. 1997. Does Neighborhood Matter? Assessing Recent Evidence. *Housing Policy Debate* 8(4): 833–866.

36. Rothstein, Richard. 2004. *Class and Schools: Using Social, Economic, and Educational Reform to Close the Black–White Achievement Gap.* Washington, DC: Economic Policy Institute.

37. Bartlett, Sheridan. 1998. Does Inadequate Housing Perpetuate Children's Poverty? *Childhood* 5: 405–428.

38. Ellen, Ingrid Gould and Margery Austin Turner. 1997. Does Neighborhood Matter? Assessing Recent Evidence. *Housing Policy Debate* 8(4): 833–866; Brooks-Gunn, Jeanne, Greg J. Duncan, and J. Lawrence Aber, eds. 1997. *Neighborhood Poverty: Contexts and Consequences for Children* (volume 1). New York: Russell Sage Foundation.

39. Rothstein, Richard. 2004. *Class and Schools: Using Social, Economic, and Educational Reform to Close the Black–White Achievement Gap.* Washington, DC: Economic Policy Institute.

40. Boger, John Charles. 2005. *The Socioeconomic Composition of the Public Schools: A Crucial Consideration in School Assignment Policy.* Chapel Hill, NC: Center for Civil Rights.

41. Holloway, L. 2000. Turnover of Teachers and Students Deepens the Troubles of Poor Schools *The New York Times*, May 28: A29.

42. While starting in the 1980s courts have ordered state governments to devise new ways to fund public schools more equitably, school finance systems today are still very decentralized and look dramatically different from state to state. Illinois and New Jersey, as well as many other states, depend somewhat on state funds but still rely most heavily on local property taxes. A few states, most notably California and Michigan, have state-controlled school finance systems. Hawaii is unique in that it has one statewide school district. Recent litigation across the country has challenged the notion of "adequacy" in school resources and conditions between districts.

43. Saulny, Susan. 2005. Middle Class, Signs of Anxiety on School Efforts. *New York Times*, December 27.

44. National Fair Housing Alliance. 2006. *Unequal Opportunity: Perpetuating Housing Segregation in America*, Fair Housing Trends Report. Washington, DC: National Fair Housing Alliance.

45. U.S. Department of Health and Human Services. 2001. *Geographical Mobility, Population Characteristics: March 1999 to March 2000.* Washington, DC: U.S. Department of Health and Human Services, Office of the Assistant Secretary for Planning and Evaluation.

46. *Journal of Negro Education.* 2003. Special Edition: "Student Mobility: How Some Children Get Left Behind." 72(1).

47. Rumberger, Russell W., K.A. Larson, R.K. Ream, and G.J. Palardy. 1999. *The Educational Consequences of Mobility for California Students and Schools.* Berkeley, CA: Policy Analysis for California Education; Crowley, Sheila. 2003. The Affordable Housing Crisis: Residential Mobility of Poor Families and School Mobility of Poor Children. *Journal of Negro Education* 72(1): 22–38.

48. U.S. Department of Housing and Urban Development. 2000. *The State of the Cities 2000: Megaforces Shaping the Future of America's Cities.* Washington, DC: HUD.

49. Lipman, Barbara J. 2005. The Housing Landscape for America's Working Families 2005. *New Century Housing* 5(1). Center for Housing Policy; Joint

Center for Housing Studies at Harvard University. 2004. *The State of the Nation's Housing 2004*. Boston: Joint Center for Housing Studies at Harvard University. Between 1960 and 1970 the median renter devoted 20 percent of income to rent. Most government housing assistance programs subsidize housing costs such that housing expenditures of recipients do not exceed 30 percent of household income.

50. Quigley, John M. and Steven Raphael. 2004. Is Housing Unaffordable? Why Isn't It More Affordable? *Journal of Economic Perspectives* 18(1): 191–214.

51. Lipman, Barbara J. 2005. The Housing Landscape for America's Working Families 2005. *New Century Housing* 5(1). Center for Housing Policy.

52. Lipman, Barbara J. 2006. *Locked Out: Keys to Homeownership Elude Many Working Families with Children*. Washington, DC: Center for Housing Policy.

53. Frey, William H. 2006. *Diversity Spreads Out: Metropolitan Shifts in Hispanic, Asian, and Black Populations since 2000*. Washington, DC: Brookings Institution.

54. Cotton, Kathleen and Karen Reed Wikelund. 1990. *Parent Involvement in Education*. School Improvement Research Series. Boston: Northwest Regional Laboratory.

55. Bartlett, Sheridan. 1998. Does Inadequate Housing Perpetuate Children's Poverty? *Childhood* 5: 405–428.

56. Scanlon, E. and K. Devine. 2001. Residential Mobility and Youth Well-Being: Research, Policy, and Practice Issues. *Journal of Sociology and Social Welfare* 28(1): 119–138.

57. Ellickson, P.L. and K.A. McGuigan. 2000. Early Predictors of Adolescent Violence. *American Journal of Public Health* 90(4): 566–572.

58. Molnar, J.M., W.R. Rath, and T.P. Klein. 1990. Constantly Compromised: The Impact of Homelessness on Children. *Journal of Social Issues* 46(4): 109–124; National Coalition for the Homeless. 2005. Education of Homeless Children and Youth: Factsheet No. 10. Washington, DC: National Coalition for the Homeless.

59. Schneider, Barbara, Christopher B. Swanson, and Catherine Riegle-Crumb. 1998. Opportunities for Learning: Course Sequences and Positional Advantages. *Social Psychology of Education* 2: 25–53.

60. Gamoran, Adam. 1986. Instructional and Institutional Effects of Ability Grouping. *Sociology of Education* 59(4): 185–198.

61. Rumberger, Russell W., K.A. Larson, R.K. Ream, and G.J. Palardy. 1999. *The Educational Consequences of Mobility for California Students and Schools*. Berkeley, CA: Policy Analysis for California Education.

62. Cohen, Deborah. 1994. Moving Images. Education Week on the Web. Available at http://www.edweek.org (accessed March 6, 2006).

63. Dauber, Susan L. and Joyce L. Epstein. 1993. Parents' attitudes and practices of involvement in inner-city elementary and middle schools. In *Families and Schools in a Pluralistic Society*, edited by N.F. Chavkin. Albany: State University of New York.

64. Fix, Michael and Jeffrey S. Passel. 2003. *U.S. Immigration: Trends and Implications for Schools*. Washington, DC: The Urban Institute.

65. U.S. Department of Education, National Center for Education Statistics, Common Core of Data, "Public Elementary/Secondary School Universe Survey," 2001–2002, Version 1a. Washington, DC: U.S. Department of Education.

66. Apple, Michael and Gerald Bracey. 2001. School Vouchers: An Education Policy Project Briefing Paper. Milwaukee: University of Wisconsin–Milwaukee School of Education, Center for Education Research, Analysis, and Innovation; Moe, Terry M. 2001. *Schools, Vouchers and the American Public*. Washington, DC: Brookings Institution Press.

67. Henig, Jeffrey R. 1994. *Rethinking School Choice: Limits of the Market Metaphor*. Princeton, NJ: Princeton University Press.

68. Dryfoos, Joy, Jane Quinn, and Carol Barkin. 2005. *Community Schools in Action: Lessons from a Decade of Practice*. Oxford: Oxford University Press; Blank, Martin, Atelia Melaville, and Bela P. Shah. 2003. *Making the Difference: Research and Practice in Community Schools*. Washington, DC: Coalition for Community Schools.

69. See http://www.communityschools.org.

70. Blank, Martin, Atelia Melaville, and Bela P. Shah. 2003. *Making the Difference: Research and Practice in Community Schools*. Washington, DC: Coalition for Community Schools.

71. Rubinowitz, Leonard and James Rosenbaum. 2000. *Crossing the Class and Color Lines: From Public Housing to White Suburbia*. Chicago: University of Chicago Press.

72. Ladd, Helen and Jens Ludwig. 2003. The Effects of MTO on Educational Outcomes in Baltimore: Early Evidence. In *Choosing a Better Life*, edited by John Goering and Judith Feins. Washington, DC: Urban Institute Press, pp. 117–152.

73. For example, Sanbonmatsu, Lisa, Jeffrey R. Kling, Greg J. Duncan, and Jeanne Brooks-Gunn. 2006. Neighborhoods and Academic Achievement: Results from

the Moving to Opportunity Experiment. *Journal of Human Resources* 41(4): 649–691.

74. Popkin, Susan J., Laura E. Harris, and Mary K. Cunningham. 2002. *Families in Transition: A Qualitative Analysis of the MTO Experience.* Washington, DC: U.S. Department of Housing and Urban Development.

75. Eisman, Michael, Elizabeth Cove, and Susan J. Popkin. 2005. Resilient Children in Distressed Neighborhood: Evidence from the HOPE VI Panel Study. Metropolitan Housing and Communities Center, Urban Institute. Brief 7.

76. Rusk, David. 1994. *The Academic Performance of Public Housing Children: Does Living in Middle-Class Neighborhoods and Attending Middle-Class Schools Make a Difference?* Washington, DC: Urban Institute.

77. Mediratta, Kavitha, Norm Fruchter, and Anne Lewis. 2002. *Organizing for School Reform: How Communities Are Finding Their Voices and Reclaiming Their Public Schools.* Institute for Educational and Social Policy, New York University.

78. Warren, Mark. 2005. Communities and Schools: A New View of Urban Education Reform. *Harvard Educational Review* 75(2): 133–173.

79. Turnham, Jennifer and Jill Khadduri. 2004. *Integrating School Reform and Neighborhood Revitalization: Opportunities and Challenges.* Cambridge, MA: Abt Associates.

80. Proscio, Tony. 2004. *Schools, Community and Development: Erasing the Boundaries.* Columbia, MD: The Enterprise Foundation.

81. Baron, Richard. 2003. The 2003 Rouse Lecture on the American City. Fannie Mae Foundation. Available at http://www.fanniemaefoundation.org/news/signature_events/rouse/rouse-index. shtml (accessed March 9, 2006).

82. Lipman, Pauline. 2004. *High Stakes Education: Inequality, Globalization, and Urban School Reform.* New York: Routledge.

83. Landis, John and Heather Hood. 2005. *California State Infill Housing Study Report.* Berkeley, CA: Institute of Urban and Regional Development, University of California.

84. Rusk, David. 2003. Housing Policy Is School Policy: Remarks to the 44th Annual Meeting of Baltimore Neighborhoods, Inc. May 6. Available at http://www.gamaliel.org/DavidRusk/Abell%202%20school%20final%20report.pdf (accessed March 9, 2006).

85. Burchell, Robert, C. Kent Conine, Richard Dubin, David Flanagan, Catherine C. Galley, Eric Larsen, David Rusk, Ann B. Schnare, Bernard Tetreault, and Richard Tustian. 2000. Inclusionary Zoning: A Viable Solution to the Affordable Housing Crisis? *New Century Housing* 1(2). The Center for Housing Policy.

86. Turnham, Jennifer and Jill Khadduri. 2004. *Integrating School Reform and Neighborhood Revitalization: Opportunities and Challenges.* Cambridge, MA: Abt Associates.

87. Halsband, Robin. 2003. Charter Schools Benefit Community Economic Development. *Journal of Housing and Community Development* November/December: 34–38.

88. Kahlenberg, Richard D. 2001. *All Together Now: Creating Middle-Class Schools through Public School Choice.* Washington, DC: Brookings Institution Press.

89. 21st Century School Fund. n.d. *Building Outside the Box.* Washington, DC: 21st Century School Fund.

90. City of San Diego Redevelopment Agency. Available at http://www.sandiego.gov/redevelopment-agency/majorproj.shtml (accessed March 9, 2006).

91. City of San Diego Redevelopment Agency. 2002. San Diego Model School Program in City Heights: Fact Sheet. The City of San Diego—its Housing Authority and Redevelopment Agency—and the school district entered into a joint powers of agreement that formed the San Diego Model School Development Agency.

92. Smart Growth Network. http://www.smartgrowth.org/about/overview.asp (accessed March 9, 2006).

93. Council of Educational Facility Planners International, Inc. and U.S. Environmental Protection Agency. 2004. *Schools for Successful Communities: An Element of Smart Growth.* Scottsdale, AZ: Council of Educational Facility Planners International; Smart Growth Network. 2001. *Affordable Housing and Smart Growth: Making the Connection.* Washington, DC: Smart Growth Network.

94. See http://www.smart-schools.org/.

95. U.S. Department of Education. 2000. *Schools as Centers of Community: A Citizen's Guide to Planning and Design.* Washington, DC: U.S. Department of Education.

96. Beaumont, Constance E. with Elizabeth G. Pianca. 2002. *Historic Neighborhoods in the Age of Sprawl: Why Johnny Can't Walk to School.* Washington, DC: National Trust for Historic Preservation.

97. See http://www.ccspartnership.org.

98. Noguera, Pedro. 2003. *City Schools and the American Dream: Reclaiming the Promise of Public Education.* New York: Teachers College Press.

99. Vincent, Jeffrey M. 2006. Public Schools as Public Infrastructure: Roles for Planning Researchers. *Journal of Planning Education and Research* 25: 433–437.

100. McKoy, Deborah L. and Jeffrey M. Vincent. 2005. The Center for Cities and Schools: Connecting Research and Policy Agendas. *Berkeley Planning Journal* 18: 57–77.

101. Vincent, Jeffrey M. 2006. Planning and Siting New Public Schools in the Context of Community Development: The California Experience. Unpublished dissertation. Department of City and Regional Planning, University of California, Berkeley.

102. Only an estimated 1 percent of the total housing stock in the nation is publicly owned.

# PART 2

---

## SPECIFIC WAYS THAT
## RACISM BECOMES MANIFEST

# CHAPTER 5

## Individual and Cultural Racism

### *Theoretical Framework*

# Hill, Thomas, and the Use of Racial Stereotype

## Neil Irvin Painter

J UST NOW I have had a teaching experience with Princeton graduate students, who were reading a lot and thinking hard, that reminds me of the formidability of seeing class and gender, as well as race, in matters African-American. The assignment challenged even thoughtful young people, who had an entire semester in which to work things out. But the Thomas-Hill hearings were entirely different, for few in the audience were graduate students dedicated to making sense of complicated issues. This time the scenario played itself out in the fast-paced medium of television before an audience unaccustomed to thinking about gender and race simultaneously. Because the protagonists of this American theatrical production were black, race stayed in the forefront nearly all the time. Even so, viewers realized, however fuzzily, that something else was going on. The unusual cast of characters made the viewers' task novel and hard: to weigh the significance of race in an intraracial drama. But the exercise proved too daunting, and stereotype, almost inevitably, became the medium of exchange. Even before the second part of the televised hearings began, Clarence Thomas had shown me that he would portray issues of gender as racial cliché.

As troubled as I was by what happened to the person and the persona of Anita Hill in the hearings, I had begun to have doubts about Clarence Thomas's manipulation of gender issues well before she entered the scene. My own difficulties with Thomas regarding women began when I learned that he had portrayed his sister, Emma Mae Martin, as a deadbeat on welfare. In a speech to Republicans (who practically invented the role of welfare queen), he had made Martin into a stock character in the Republican scenario of racial economics. His point was to contrast her laziness with his hard work and high achievement to prove, I suppose, that any black American with gumption and

Neil Irvin Painter; ed. Toni Morrison, "Hill, Thomas, and the Use of Racial Stereotype," from *Race-ing Justice, En-gendering Power: Essays on Anita Hill, Clarence Thomas, and the Construction of Social Reality*, pp 200–214. Copyright © 1992 by Knopf Publishing Group. Permission to reprint granted by Random House.

a willingness to work could succeed. Thus, a woman whom he had presumably known and loved for a lifetime emerged as a one-dimensional welfare cheat, one of the figures whom black women cite as an example of the pernicious power of negative stereotype. For Thomas, it seemed, all the information that needed to be known of his sister compared her to him: she was a failure on welfare and he was a high-ranking official. He left it to others—who were his critics—to describe his sister more completely.

Other people, like Lisa Jones in the *Village Voice,* had more to say about Emma Mae Martin. It turns out that she was only on welfare temporarily and that she was usually a two-job-holding, minimum-wage-earning mother of four. Unable to afford professional help, she had gone on welfare while she nursed the aunt who had suffered a stroke but who normally kept her children when Martin was at work. Feminists noted that Martin belonged to a mass of American women who were caregivers to the young, the old, and the infirm. She had followed a trajectory common in the experience of poor women, regardless of race; this pattern Clarence Thomas did not acknowledge.

That his life and the life of his sister had differed by virtue of their gender was not included in Clarence Thomas's rendition of contrasting destinies. He seemed not to have appreciated that he was the favored boy-child who was protected and sent to private schools and that she was the girl who stayed behind, married early, and cared for a relative who had fallen ill. If he realized how common his family's decisions had been, he gave no indication of seeing those choices as gendered. His equation balanced one thing only, and that was individual enterprise. Even though as a hospital worker his sister was a symbol of Jesse Jackson's masses of black folk who work every day, her life as a worker counted for naught in Thomas's story. His eagerness to shine on a conservative stage allowed him to obscure the actual circumstances of her life and her finances and to disregard her vulnerabilities as a poor, black woman. If he were ignorant of how very characteristic of poor women's her life's course had been, he would seem to have performed his job heading the Equal Employment Opportunity Commission in a perfunctory manner; if he were aware of how often families in need engage in such triage and distorted her situation to satisfy a Republican audience, he is guilty of outright cruelty.

Clarence Thomas's wielding of stereotype against his sister—a woman whose identity was already overburdened by stereotype—foreshadowed his strategy in the hearings that pitted him against another black woman, both in its heartlessness and its exploitation of racial imagery. Both times he distorted his relative position vis-à-vis a specific black woman, as though lacking a sense of social perspective.

Comparing his sister's failings to his own achievements, he spoke as though the two of them had played with the same advantages and handicaps, as though he had seized his chances while she had unaccountably kicked her own equal opportunities aside.

Later, as he confronted Anita Hill, his translation of the power relations of gender were similarly skewed. This time he ultimately portrayed himself as the person at the bottom facing terrible odds. His older adversaries were his favorite cardboard-cutout bogey-people: the (black, male) civil rights establishment and organized (white) feminists who persecuted him for being of independent mind. Squared off against his bogey-people, he saw himself as a symbol of integrity and as an underdog.

Thomas's version of American power dynamics reversed a decade's worth of his own rhetoric, in which he had castigated black civil rights advocates for whining about racist oppression. The haughty dismissal of claims that racism persisted had previously been his stock-in-trade. But once a black woman accused him of abusing his power as a man and as an employer, he quickly slipped into the most familiar role in the American iconography of race: that of the victim. Accused of misuse of power, he presented himself as a person with no power at all. It mattered not that the characterization was totally inappropriate, in terms of gender and of race. In a struggle between himself and a woman of his same race, Thomas executed a deft strategy. He erected a tableau of white-black racism that allowed him to occupy the position of "the race." By reintroducing concepts of white power, Thomas made himself into "the black person" in his story. Then, in the first move of a two-step strategy, he cast Anita Hill into the role of "black-woman-as-traitor-to-the-race."

The black-woman-as-traitor-to-the-race is at least as old as *David Walker's Appeal* of 1829, and the figure has served as a convenient explanation for racial conflict since that time. Although Thomas did not flesh out his accusation, which served his purposes only briefly, it should be remembered that in the tale of the subversion of the interests of the race, the black female traitor—as mother to whites or lover of whites—connives with the white man against the black man. Such themes reappear in *Black Skin, White Masks,* by Frantz Fanon; in *Black Rage,* by William Grier and Price Cobbs; and in *Madheart,* by LeRoi Jones, in which the figure of "the black woman," as "mammy" or as "Jezebel," is subject to loyalties to whites that conflict with her allegiance to the black man. Unable to extricate herself from whites, the black-woman-as-traitor misconstrues her racial interests and betrays black men's aspirations to freedom. Freedom, in this particular instance, meant a seat on the United States Supreme Court.

Although she is well known among African Americans, the black-woman-as-traitor-to-the-race is less familiar to white Americans and thus is not a useful trope in the television shorthand of race through which Clarence Thomas communicated. Having made Anita Hill into a villain, he proceeded—wittingly or not—to erase her and return to a simpler and more conventional cast. By the end of his story Anita Hill had lost the only role, that of villain, that his use of stereotype had allowed her. She finally disappeared, as he spun out a drama pitting the lone and persecuted figure of Clarence Thomas, the black man, against an army of powerful white assailants. Democratic senators became the lynch mob; Thomas became the innocent lynch victim. As symbol and as actual person, Anita Hill was no longer to be found.

Hill's strategy was different from Thomas's. But had she not stood on the ground of personal integrity and the truth of her own individual experiences, she might have sought to work within the framework of racial typecasting. To do so would have tested the limits of the genres of senatorial testimony and televised hearings, for she would have needed at least a semester to reveal, analyze, and destroy the commonplaces of American racism that Thomas manipulated so effectively. Her task could neither be undertaken, nor completed in sound bites and within a matter of days. Simply to comprehend Hill's identity as a highly educated, ambitious, black female Republican imposed a burden on American audiences, black and white, that they were unable—at least at that very moment—to shoulder. With breathtaking cynicism, Thomas evoked the pitiable image of the victimized black man, and his exploitation of the imagery of race succeeded. Such images, such stereotypes, of black women as well as of black men, bear closer inspection.

Black people of both sexes have represented the American id for a very long time, a phenomenon rooted in our cultural identities of race and class. The stereotypes are centuries old and have their origins in European typecasting of both the poor and the black, for sex is the main theme associated with poverty and with blackness. Even where race is not at issue, the presence of the poor introduces the subject of sex. William Shakespeare's characters provide a handy reminder across spectra of race, class, and ethnicity: the nurse in *Romeo and Juliet* speaks of sex purposefully and unintentionally, so that her every other utterance is characterized as bawdy; Caliban, in *The Tempest,* is a playfully uninhibited savage; and of course, there is Othello the Moor in a tortured saga of desire.

Sexuality, in the sense of the heightened desirability of working-class characters, figures centrally in the diaries of Arthur J. Munby and Hannah Cullwick, in *My Secret Life,* in D. H. Lawrence's *Lady Chatterley's Lover,* and, homo-erotically, in Hermann Hesse's *Demian.* In each case, members of the middle and upper classes seek sexual titillation or fulfillment with lovers of a lower class. Sigmund Freud, describing the complex family dynamics of bourgeois households, spoke of women in domestic service as people of low morals, because they were so likely to become entangled sexually with the men of the families that employed them. More recently, Susan Brown miller has noted that women who are particularly vulnerable to sexual violence by token of their ethnicity or race—Jews in Europe, Negroes in the United States—are viewed as especially provocative by potential assailants.

Over and over in European imaginations, the poor epitomize unfettered sexuality, and this convention has come to serve in the United States as well. American writing not only echoes the sexualization of the poor (Stephen Crane's *Maggie, A Girl of the Streets,* Wilbur Cash's *Mind of the South*), but, reflecting a history in which masses of workers were enslaved, also adds the ingredient of race. In American iconography the sexually promiscuous black girl—or more precisely, the yellow girl—represents the mirror image of the white woman on the pedestal. Together, white and black women stand for woman as madonna and as whore.

Today, as in the past, race and class are hopelessly intertwined in the United States. This is so even a generation after the end of legal segregation and the confusion of usages related to race and usages related to class. In eighteenth and nineteenth-century England, it was the lower classes who were expected to show deference toward the aristocracy by bowing their heads, doffing their hats, tolerating the use of their first names, entering by the service entrance, and, above all, revealing no sign of independent thought. In the era of American segregation these habits became the patterns of racial subordination that all black people, no matter what their class standing, were expected to observe. For most Americans race became and remains the idiom of expression of differences and characteristics of class. Just as slaves were the most exploited of workers, so blacks in the United States have become the sexiest of the American poor.

The imagery of sex in race has not and does not work in identical ways for black women and men, even though figures of educated black people, whether male or female, are not well enough established for quick recognition on TV, where the Thomas-Hill saga played and where so many American stereotypes are reinforced. Aside from Bill Cosby, there is no handy black character in our national imagination, male or female, who has strayed very far from the working class. And Cosby constitutes less a symbol than an individual phenomenon. If Clarence Thomas could not reach for a stereotypical black man who would be educated and respectable, Anita Hill (had she succumbed to the temptation) could not have done so either. To silence his questioners quickly, Clarence Thomas had to draw on older, better-known formulations of racial victimization, and he had to reach across lines of class and privilege to do so.

Thomas appropriated the figure of the lynch victim, despite glaring dissimilarities between himself and the thousands of poor unfortunates who, unprotected by white patrons in the White House or the United States Senate or by the law, perished at the hands of white southern mobs. As though education, status, and connections counted for nothing, Thomas grasped a chain of reference that begins with the stereotypical black-beast-rapist, as depicted in D. W. Griffith's *Birth of a Nation.* As Thomas knew well, however, those associations do not end with the rapist; they extend into meanings that subvert Griffith's brutalized invention.

The black-beast-rapist connects to the black man accused of rape, who, in turn, is only one link in a chain that also casts doubt on the validity of the charge of rape when leveled against black men. Ida B. Wells began to undermine the credibility of the accusation in the 1890s, and the NAACP and the Communist Party helped to discredit lynching even after trials, as in the case of the eight young black men summarily sentenced to hang in Scottsboro, Alabama, in 1931. Since that time the presumption (among non-Ku Klux Klansmen, at least) has been that the quintessential lynch victim was, like the Scottsboro boys, a casualty of the miscarriage of justice. To mention the figure of the southern black lynch victim is to cite a man unjustly accused, and this was the meaning that Clarence Thomas summoned. Had the sexualized figure of the black man not evolved past *Birth of a Nation,* he could not have served Thomas's purpose.

Anita Hill, on the other hand, had no comparable tradition of a stereotype that had been recognized, analyzed, and subverted to draw upon. The mammy image is in the process of being reworked, while the welfare queen and the oversexed-black-Jezebel are still unreconstructed. Considering that Hill is a beautiful young woman who was leveling a charge of sexual harassment, adapting herself to stereotype and then reworking the stereotype would not have been a simple matter. (No odder, perhaps, than assimilating the figure of a lynch victim to the person of a nominee for the United States Supreme Court.) Stereotypes of black women remain fairly securely in place, and the public discussion that would examine and dislodge them has only begun to occur around the mammy image. The oversexed-black-Jezebel is more likely than not still taken at face value.

The depiction of the oversexed-black-Jezebel is not so salient in American culture as that of the black-beast-rapist/lynch victim, but she has sufficient visibility to haunt black women to this day. This stereotypical black woman not only connotes sex, like the working-class white woman, but unlike the latter, is assumed to be the instigator of sex. Theodore Dreiser's Sister Carrie may have been seduced by a fast-talking city slicker she met on a train, but Rose Johnson, in Gertrude Stein's *As Fine as Melanctha,* positively revels in sexual promiscuity.

Overdetermined by class and by race, the black-woman-as-whore appears nearly as often as black women are to be found in representations of American culture. Mary Chesnut, in her Civil War diary, pities the virtuous plantation mistress surrounded by black prostitutes anxious to seduce white men and boys. The stereotype that averred there were no virginal black women over the age of fourteen was prevalent enough in the 1890s to mobilize black club-women nationally against it. The figure of the oversexed black-Jezebel has had amazing longevity. She is to be found in movies made in the 1980s and 1990s—*She's Gotta Have It, Jungle Fever, City of Hope*—in which black female characters are still likely to be shown unclothed, in bed, and in the midst of coitus.

Mammy, welfare cheat, Jezebel, period. These were the roles available to Anita Hill. Hill chose not to make herself into a symbol Americans could recognize, and as a result she seemed to disappear, a fate reserved for black women who are well educated and are thus doubly hard to see. Mammy and Jezebel and the welfare queen may be the most prominent roles for black women in American culture, but even these figures, as limited as is their range, inhabit the shadows of American imagination.

As commentators like Darlene Clark Hine and Patricia Hill Collins have noted, silence and invisibility are the hallmarks of black women in the imagery of American life. The most common formula for expressing minority status, in the nineteenth century as in the twentieth, is "women and blacks." As the emblematic woman is white and the emblematic black is male, black women generally are not as easy to comprehend symbolically. Barbara Smith, Gloria Hull, and Patricia Bell Scott noted in 1982 that while all the women seem to be white and all the blacks seem to be men, some of us are brave.

Because black women have been harder than men to fit into clichés of race, we often disappear. Few recall that after Bigger Thomas, in Richard Wright's *Native Son,* accidentally killed rich, white Mary Dalton, he committed the brutal, premeditated murder of his girlfriend, the innocent black Bessie. *Native Son* is generally summed up as the story of a racial crime in which a white woman dies and a black man emerges as the victim of society. Two generations later Eldridge Cleaver said in *Soul on Ice* that he raped black women for practice; he was honing his skills before attacking white women, who were for him real women. The poet Audre Lorde remembered and grieved for the twelve black women who were murdered in Boston in the spring of 1979, but their remembrance grows shadowy beside the figure of the Central Park jogger. Who recalls that Joan Little had been sexually assaulted by the man she killed?

Disregarded or forgotten or, when remembered, misconstrued, the symbolic history of black women has not functioned in the same way as the symbolic history of black men. If the reality of the Scottsboro boys and other black men accused of rape showed that the charge was liable to be false and thereby tempered the stereotype, the meaning of the history of black women as victims of rape has not yet penetrated the American mind. In the absence of an image equivalent to that of the Scottsboro boys, black women's reputed hypersexuality has not been reappraised. It is as though silence and invisibility had entirely frozen the image of black men at the black-beast-rapist stage. Lacking access to the means of mass communication, black women have not been able to use our history of abuse as a corrective to stereotypes of rampant sexuality.

Since the seventeenth-century beginnings of their forcible importation into what would become the United States, black women have been triply vulnerable to rape and other kinds of violence: as members of a stigmatized race, the subordinate sex, and people who work for others. The history of sexual violence against black women is rooted in slavery, but as bell hooks points out, it did not end there. Despite two centuries' worth of black women's testimony, as exemplified in Harriet Jacobs's *Incidents* in the Life of a Slave Girl, Alice Walker's The Color Purple, and the St. John's University rape case of 1991, our vulnerability to rape has not become a standard item in the list of crimes against the race. When the existence of rape is acknowledged, it is, as often as not, to name a crime of which the black man, rather than she who was raped, is the victim. Unable to protect "his" woman, the black man suffers the loss of his manhood when a female family member is assaulted. The belief persists that black women are always ready for sex and, as a consequence, cannot be raped. Introducing the specter of sex, Hill made herself vulnerable to Virginia Thomas's doubly stereotypical retort: Hill—as both the oversexed black Jezebel anxious for sex and as the rejected, vindictive woman who trumps up a charge of sexual harassment—really wanted to sleep with Clarence Thomas. The injury, then, is to him, not to her.

More, finally, is at stake here than winning a competition between black men and black women for the title of ultimate victim as reckoned in the terms of white racism, as tempting as the scenario of black-versus-white tends to be. Anita Hill found no shelter in stereotypes of race not merely because they are too potent and too negative to serve her ends. There was no way for Hill to emerge a hero of the race, because she would not deal in black and white. By indicting the conduct of a black man, Hill revealed the existence of intraracial conflict, which white Americans find incomprehensible and many black Americans guard as a closely held secret of the race. Keeping that secret in the interest of racial unity has silenced black women on the issue of sexual abuse, for our attackers have been black men as well as white, as The Black Women's Health Book poignantly reveals. Because discussions of the abuse of black women would not merely implicate whites, black women have been reluctant to press the point. Our silence, in turn, has tended to preserve intact the image of oversexed black Jezebel. Who knows how long Anita Hill would have held her tongue had not circumstances forced her to go public? As things turned out, in the short run at least, Clarence Thomas and his allies managed once again to "disappear" the black woman and to stage a drama of race. But the gender issue that Anita Hill raised, despite its potential for deep divisiveness, looks toward the future of racial politics in the United States (unless the David Dukes of the world force us back into a terrorized, defensive, androcentric unity). Ironically, black conservatism, which is not very hospitable to feminism, initially staked the claim for diversity within the race. Black feminists are enlarging this claim in the name of our history as black women.

Black women, who have traditionally been discounted within the race and degraded in American society, are becoming increasingly impatient with our devaluation. Breaking the silence and testifying about the abuse, black feminists are publishing our history and dissecting the stereotypes that have been used against us. So far, the discussion has not engaged large numbers of Americans, but I trust that Anita Hill will have helped us reach many more. If my experience with earnest and hardworking Princeton graduate students offers any guidance, the process, though ultimately liberating, will prove to be intellectually demanding. We will know we have succeeded in taking a first step when Americans greet the images of the mammy, the welfare queen, and the oversexed-black-Jezebel with the skepticism they turn toward the figure of the lynch victim accused of raping a white woman. Our work, however, cannot end there, for both the black-beast-rapist and the oversexed-black-Jezebel would still survive with enough vigor to dog both our tracks. The next step, which is just as necessary, will free African Americans from sexualized stereotypes that tyrannize us as black men and black women, for black men as well as black women feel their lives are circumscribed by just such stereotypes.

## DISCUSSION QUESTIONS

1.  What were the two contrasting ways that Thomas used to represent himself during the hearing?
2.  What were some of the stereotypes raised about black men and women during the trial? How did these stereotypes reflect historical depictions of African American men and women?
3.  What is the media's responsibility concerning stereotypes in journalism? Should the media censure sensitive content about racial minorities?

# Individual Racism

**Joseph Barndt**

*To be white in America is*
*not to have to think about it.*
—Robert Terry

Racism, then, creates two prisons, not just one. The first is the prison of oppressed people of color in America, the miserably uncomfortable, poverty-haunted ghetto. The inmates are African American and Hispanic people in the inner cities and rural areas of the United States, Native Americans confined on reservations, Asians in crowded "Chinatowns." Unless we have been totally deaf and blind during these past decades of social turmoil and racial conflict, we are at least aware of this prison's existence, though we may be unclear about the reality and its implications.

## THE COMFORTABLE PRISON

The other prison created by racism is for us, the white people of America. Although we are in a prison we don't believe it, for our prison is deceptively comfortable and disarmingly warm and friendly. But it is a prison, nonetheless. You and I are its inmates, and it exists wherever we live, learn, work, and play. The walls of this prison are the residential, cultural, and institutional boundaries of white America. Its bars may be less visible, but they evoke as much frustration, loneliness, fear, and anxiety as the bars of any penitentiary.

The inmates of this other prison have a desperate need to pretend that it does not exist. An intricate web of deception disguises its reality. The bars on the windows are hidden by expensive curtains. There is thick carpeting instead of institutional flooring. Flowers and vines hide the steel plate doors. In place of a meager cot, there is a luxurious bed. The disguise is complete; the lie is convincing. The inmates live in the firm belief that there is no prison; that they exist in total freedom. Whenever we become aware of the confining and dehumanizing walls that surround us, we are quickly assured that they are the outside walls of the other prison—the prison for people of color—not our own.

This comfortable prison is ruled by racism in its three interlocking forms: individual, institutional, and cultural. In this chapter, we will examine how the first of the three, individual racism, is systematically produced and perpetuated in white Americans. We will describe how individual racists are created, and how we can begin the task of dismantling and undoing our individual racism. We will also take special care to distinguish individual racism from racism in its institutional and cultural expressions, and at the same time to identify the linkages among the three. For, as we shall see, individual racism could not exist without the others.

## THE MAKING OF A RACIST

Racists are made, not born. As we said earlier, all of us are born with a natural propensity for prejudice, and are taught the biases and prejudices of our families and peers. But we are not born racist. Remember our definition of racism: prejudice plus power. An individual's personal racial prejudice are transformed, into racism by becoming linked to the power of societal systems. Without this linkage there could be no racism, and without the empowerment of systemic racism there could be no individual racists. Because of this linkage, however, an individual person whose prejudices might otherwise be limited to hurtful and ugly behavior in his or her private encounters becomes a violent and destructive instrument with far greater scope.

The linkage is automatic. As white individuals we unavoidably participate in a system that gives us power and privilege based on our racial identity. But our willing cooperation with this system is not automatic. Our active or passive acceptance of power and privilege requires a thorough process of socialization and conditioning. It begins early in our lives and continues throughout our childhood. By the time we are adults, our indoctrination is complete. The only escape is through a conscious decision to reject our right to this power and privilege and to participate in the struggle to dismantle the prison of racism.

How does this conditioning take place? How do we become so completely imprisoned that most of us are not aware of it, do not feel its restrictions and limitations? In the next few pages, we will examine four powerful forces that are brought to bear on every white individual, each of which contributes to this imprisonment.

## *Isolation*

The prison of white racism is maintained by keeping its inmates separate from and unaware of people of color and the world in which they live. Legal segregation created two ghettos, not one. Just as most people of color were isolated from us, so also were most of us isolated from them. Even if, from within our white communities, we became aware of African Americans, Native Americans, Hispanics, and Asians, they were somewhere out there, in another part of town or in another part of the country. We seldom experienced their reality. Everything we knew about them was secondhand information and filled with distortions.

Twenty-five years after the end of legal segregation, we are still a nation that lives racially apart. It is true that information about other racial groups now flows more readily. We know more about each other. We may have a friend or two of another race or culture. But, for the vast majority of us, that is as far as it goes. We may think there is more contact between whites and people of color than there was in the past. Don't we attend school together, work together, and play together? In fact, we do not actually do these things together; we do them in the same place and in each other's presence, but we still do them separately. In desegregated schools, workplaces, and recreation areas, a strict, but informal segregation still exists. True integration in such groups is relatively rare. And, as soon as school, work, or play is completed, whites and people of color still go home to their segregated communities knowing, for the most part, little or nothing of each others' lives.

One of the most familiar symbols of our isolation and separation is a suburban home. It is touted by the advertising world as an escape—the fulfillment of a person's dreams. But its distance from the city, at the end of a freeway, surrounded by six-foot fences, makes it seem in many ways more like a prison than an escape. The English author and theologian C. S. Lewis, in his book *The Great Divorce,* described a vision of hell as a place where people perpetually move away from one another because of their inability to get along with each other. They leave houses and entire blocks and neighborhoods empty and build new houses at the edge of hell, thereby creating an ever-expanding circle with houses at the edge, and with the abandoned center left behind them.[1] Lewis's description of hell could be a description of white flight from the city after World War II and the emergence of suburbs in the United States. The development of suburbs not only created a great gulf between suburban whites and people of color in the inner cities; it also led to a sense of great isolation for many suburbanites. Anyone who has spent several hours every day on the freeway or commuter train understands the need for tranquilizers and alcohol in order to survive and still insist with a smile, "It really isn't so bad."

## *Anesthesia*

*Anesthesia* is the word used here to describe a second powerful force that conditions us to accept our imprisonment. I first became aware of this phenomenon from an African American woman. She attended an interracial seminar, and became angry at white participants for being on a "head trip," that is, for staying on intellectual levels and not getting involved with their feelings. She said something like this.

> You people really don't give a damn! But it's not that you don't want to. You just don't know how to. You don't know how to feel! Your heads have been cut off from your guts, and you've lost touch with your own feelings. Sure, you can empathize with the feelings of others, with the pain of other people's oppression, but you can't feel the pain of your own oppression and brokenness. You have been anesthetized to the agony of the destruction inside yourselves. If you could see and feel the effects of racism on your own people, you would not be able to tolerate it. You would not be able to control your anger. There would be a white rage in your community that would make Black rage seem cool. But you white people have lost your ability to feel. The best you can do is understand with your minds, with no response from your emotions.

Anesthesiologists prescribe drugs to reduce or eliminate pain during surgery and convalescence. From aspirin to morphine, from slight loss of sensation to total unconsciousness, the medical profession can seal us off from our feelings. On a psychological level also, an anesthetizing process takes place when a person becomes trapped in painful human predicaments from which there seem to be no escape. Slum dwellers, for example, become less and less aware of their crowded conditions and of the debris and waste that surround them. Prison inmates anesthetize themselves into indifference to the claustrophobic effects of their confinement. Soldiers on patrol learn to prevent the fear of ambush from driving them insane. Unhappily married partners who no longer work at the marriage seal themselves off from each other's hostility. Anesthesia can be useful when a person is hopelessly and unalterably in pain. But it can also be evil by concealing reality; by encouraging the pretense that the pain is not real and, therefore, that there is no need to diagnose the cause. Throughout history, when tyrants have sought to enslave fellow human beings, a primary technique has been to anesthetize them to the effects of their bondage by removing their hope of ever returning to freedom.

People of color in America recognize that this process is used as a weapon against them. They see it in the false promises of the politicians. They see it in the escapist reassurances of pacifying religion disguised as Christianity. They see it in the oblivion of drugs available on every city street corner and in the deadening effects of alcohol on every Indian reservation. Whatever form the anesthesia takes, it results in the same repression of legitimate anger. Only when the rage builds up beyond even the anesthetic's power to prevent its expression, does one see the depth of the hurt and pain as it explodes in uncontrollable and irrational behavior. Numerous studies demonstrate a link between the internalized anger and repressed rage that results from racial injustice and the excessive violence and crime in communities of color. [2]

Anesthesia is also used against white people to deaden our feelings, in the comfortable prison. The most severe marks of our conditioned racism are not the bigotry and fear that have been brainwashed into us. Rather, they are the placid acceptance, of our ghettoized condition, and the permission implied by our silence and nonresistance to continued segregation from reality. The anesthetizing forces make it possible for us to go about our normal lives as though we were not being held in bondage; as though there were no alternatives to our present way of life. Robert Terry, an analyst and educator on racism and racial justice, puts it succinctly: "To be white in America," he says, "is not to have to think about it."[3]

## GERMANY: A PERSONAL WITNESS

In Germany, more than thirty years ago, I discovered how this socializing anesthesia, accompanied by layers of insulation, works to isolate us from reality. In 1960, I was a graduate student at a German university. There, my consciousness was first awakened to the reality of racism in America.

Before and during World War II, the National Socialists (or Nazis) had carried out the extermination of more than six million Jews. After the facts of this holocaust became known, the majority of Germans insisted that they didn't know it was happening. In response to these denials the entire world asked incredulously, "How can it be that you did not know?" I asked the same question of my German acquaintances and friends. With arrogance and self-righteousness, I challenged the assertion that they did not know about the persecution of the Jews that was happening before their very eyes.

Then, toward the end of my studies I participated in a seminar at the German Evangelical Academy on the subject, "Race Relations Around the World." There I was introduced to the reality of race relations in the United States, described in graphic historical and contemporary detail. It was the time of the civil rights movement when the push to desegregate schools and public accommodations in the South was causing major upheavals, such as the events at Little Rock, Arkansas. I was embarrassed to admit to my German colleagues that I knew virtually nothing about current racial realities in America. Most shocking, however, was an estimate by one of the speakers that the number of people of color who had been killed by white people in America since the time of Columbus was approximately six million, the same number as that of Jews who had been killed in the Holocaust! And I heard myself say the same words as the Germans: "I didn't know." And indeed, it had been hidden from me, and I was honestly not aware of it, at least on a conscious level. I had found the answer to why the Germans could say, "We didn't know it was happening."

### Privileges and Rewards

Even though we are using imagery of involuntary conditioning and imprisonment, each of us has. participated to a great degree in our own deception. This is nowhere more evident than in our willingness to accept the rewards and benefits, the payoffs of racism. As we grow older, we accept privileges, comforts, and often riches that come to us almost automatically as white middle and upper-class Americans. We join in the pretense that we earn these, privileges through our own efforts, initiative, and superior intelligence. We do not acknowledge that these gifts really fall into our laps; nor do we often admit that those who do not share the benefits are as deserving as we. We need to be honest with ourselves.

Often we remain under the control of our jailers because we wish to protect the benefits we have "worked so hard" to achieve. Bluntly put, it is our greed that keeps us attached to our chains, loyal to the warden of the prison.

What are these rewards and privileges? They are all around us, seemingly nameless and countless. But it is important that we begin naming and counting them. There are, of course, the rewards of better and more accessible education and jobs, and the benefits of higher salaries. And there are our better living conditions, our better health and health care, and many other large-scale rewards.

But there are also the smaller, day-to-day privileges that are so easily accepted and taken for granted. A list of these "White skin privileges," in comparison with people of color, might begin with the ease that we have in cashing a check, in walking without suspicion in a department store, or in having our contribution recognized in a discussion. The list could continue with the central place white people have in our history books, the image of white people compared with people of color in the media, or our power as white people in determining values and ethics in public life. Because of white skin privilege, we can also be confident that our racial identity will not be used against us in applying for a job, looking for a house, relating to public authorities, or using public accommodations. This list can go on and on. Readers need to develop their own lists and become conscious of their own rewards and benefits for white skin privilege.

At the same time, we must be absolutely clear that these privileges and rewards come to us automatically, whether we ask for them or not, whether we agree with having them or not. The very same institutions that are responsible for our socialization into racist beliefs and values also create and bestow the advantages of white skin privileges. Not only do they come to us automatically, but the socialization process make us oblivious to their existence. Even when we are directly confronted with the reality of racism's rewards, our first instinct is not to believe in their existence and especially to deny our possession of them.

The purpose of becoming aware of these privileges and rewards is not to make us feel bad, but to become more aware of that which we are struggling to change. As we shall see more clearly in the next chapter, the systems and institutions that bestow and control these privileges must be changed, and not simply our individual desire to receive them.

Our own awareness begins, however, not only with the realization of our imprisonment in racism, but also by realizing the purpose of these rewards, which is to keep us uncomplaining about our bonds. Only when we realize that our losses are far more than our benefits will we join fully in the effort to transform the institutions that both imprison and reward us. Robert Terry addresses this clearly:

> The better we are at pinpointing the losses of racism and highlighting the advantages of moving beyond those losses, the greater are our chances of dealing with the causes rather than the symptoms of racism.[4]

### Programming and Conditioning

In April 1968, shortly after the assassination of Dr. Martin Luther King Jr., Jane Elliot, a school teacher in Riceville, Iowa, led her all-white third grade class in a two-day experiment. She separated the blue-eyed children from the brown-eyed children. On the first day she taught them that blue-eyed children were-superior to brown-eyed children and instituted rules that gave the blue-eyed children more power and privileges than the brown-eyed children. The results were almost immediate and overwhelming. The blue-eyed students delighted in their new status, and adapted easily to a role of superiority and dominance. The brown-eyed students were docile in adapting to their new and inferior identity and subjugated role, accepting their new station in life with little resistance and behaving accordingly. Even their test scores took an immediate plunge. The next day, the roles were reversed. So also, and instantly, were the behavior patterns. This experiment has been repeated with both children and adults many times since

1968. Each time, it demonstrates how susceptible human beings are to indoctrination into superior and inferior roles. This is a true story that was recorded on film, and is widely used in antiracism education programs.[5]

This story illustrates how vulnerable human beings are to such conditioning. In a society that is isolated, unaware, and anesthetized into believing that the prison does not exist, making racists out of each of us is a relatively simple task. From earliest childhood each of us goes through a subtle (and sometimes, not so subtle) socializing process. Consciously and unconsciously, intellectually and emotionally, a racist mentality has been created in each of us. We are taught to respond to the stimulus of whiteness with pride and identity, a sense of ease and respect. To the stimulus of what is perceived by whites to be African American, Hispanic, Native American, and Asian we are taught to respond with fear and hate, suspicion, paternalistic concern, and pity. So deeply are these responses embedded in us that no matter how much we reject them, they still control our lives. The very core of our being is permeated with racist assumptions and values. Surrounding that core are many layers of insulation that muffle our feeling, our vision, and our memory, making racism appear to be subtle, elusive, and difficult to perceive. Most of this conditioning takes place before we are old enough to understand. If we knew what was happening, some of us might object and rebel. But how could we know at such an early age that growing up in an almost totally white environment is a forced and unnatural existence in a country that has a large population of people of color? How could we know that the values passed on to us are based on the fact of white control and the unspoken assumption of white superiority? How could we know that what we learn about the achievements of white people and the failures of people of color is twisted and untruthful? In our isolated and carefully protected white environment, we have no opportunity to doubt, let alone challenge the orientation to life that we were given. White power, white control, and white superiority are presented to us as natural, the way things are and the way things ought to be.

## DISCUSSION QUESTIONS

1. What are the four "forces" of White imprisonment?
2. Why are African Americans and Whites equally harmed by the forces of imprisonment?
3. What similarities exist between the Germans' treatment of Jews during World War II and European Americans' treatment of African Americans under Jim Crow segregation?

## NOTES

4. C. S. Lewis, *The Great Divorce* (New York: Macmillan, 1946), 18ff.

5. An important study of internalized anger is Price Cobbs and William Grier's *Black Rage* (New York: Basic Books, 1980). Also see Catherine Meeks, "Rage and Reconciliation: Two Sides of the Same Coin," *America's Original Sin: A Study Guide on White Racism,* 98ff.

6. Robert Terry, "The Negative Impact on White Values," *Impacts of Racism on White Americans,* edited by Benjamin P. Bowser and Raymond Hunt (Newbury Park, Calif.: Sage Publications, 1981), 120.

7. Ibid., 150.

8. "A Class Divided," a PBS video produced by Public Broadcasting Service, 1320 Braddock Place, Alexandria, VA 22314.

# Are Jews White?
## Or, The History of the Nose Job

Sander L. Gilman

[…]

THE PERSONAL COLUMNS in the *Washingtonian,* the local city magazine in Washington, D.C., are filled with announcements of individuals "in search of" mates ("in search of" is the rubric under which these advertisements are grouped). These advertisements are peppered with various codes so well known that they are never really explained: "DWM [Divorced White Male] just recently arrived from Boston seeks a non-smoking, financially secure 40+ who loves to laugh" … or "SJF [Jewish Single Female], Kathleen Turner type, with a zest for life in search of S/DJM … for a passionate relationship." Recently, I was struck by a notice which began "DW(J)F [Divorced White (Jewish) Female]—young, 41, Ph.D., professional, no kids … seeks S/D/WWM, exceptional mind, heart & soul …"[1] What fascinated me were the brackets: advertisements for "Jews" or for "African Americans" or for "Whites" made it clear that individuals were interested in choosing their sexual partners from certain designated groups within American society. But the brackets implied that here was a woman who was both "White" and "Jewish." Given the racial politics of post-civil rights America, where do the Jews fit in? It made me ask the question, which the woman who placed the personals advertisement clearly was addressing: are Jews white? and what does "white" mean in this context? Or, to present this question in a slightly less polemical manner, how has the question of racial identity shaped Jewish identity in the Diaspora? I am not addressing what the religious, ethnic, or cultural definition of the Jew is—either from within or without Judaism or the Jewish

Sander L. Gilman; eds. Les Black and John Solomos, "Are Jews White? Or, The History of the Nose Job," from *Theories of Race and Racism: A Reader,* pp 229–237. Copyright © 2000 by Routledge. Permission to reprint granted by Taylor & Francis.

community—but how the category of race present within Western, scientific, and popular culture, has shaped Jewish self-perception.

My question is not merely an "academic" one—rather I am interested in how the representation of the Jewish body is shaped and, in turn, shapes the sense of Jewish identity. My point of departure is the view of Mary Douglas:

> The human body is always treated as an image of society and … there can be no natural way of considering the body that does not involve at the same time a social dimension. Interest in its apertures depends on the preoccupation with social exits and entrances, escape routes and invasions. If there is no concern to preserve social boundaries, I would not expect to find concern with bodily boundaries.[2]

Where and how a society defines the body reflects how those in society define themselves. This is especially true in terms of the "scientific" or pseudo-scientific categories such as race which have had such an extraordinary importance in shaping how we all understand ourselves and each other. From the conclusion of the nineteenth century, the idea of "race" has been given a positive as well as a negative quality. We belong to a race and our biology defines us, is as true a statement for many groups, as is the opposite: you belong to a race and your biology limits you. Race is a constructed category of social organization as much as it is a reflection of some aspects of biological reality. Racial identity has been a powerful force in shaping how we, at the close of the twentieth century, understand ourselves—often in spite of ourselves. Beginning in the eighteenth century and continuing to the present, there has been an important cultural response to the idea of race, one which has stressed the uniqueness of the individual over the uniformity of the group. As Theodosius Dobzhansky noted in 1967: "Every person has a genotype and a life history different from any other person, be that person a member of his family, clan, race, or mankind. Beyond the universal rights of all human beings (which may be a typological notion!), a person ought to be evaluated on his own merits."[3] Dobzhansky and many scientists of the 1960s dismissed "race" as a category of scientific evaluation, arguing that whenever it had been included over the course of history, horrible abuses had resulted.[4] At the same time, within Western, specifically American culture of the 1960s, there was also a trans valuation of the concept of "race." "Black" was "beautiful," and "roots" were to be celebrated, not denied. The view was that seeing oneself as being a part of a "race" was a strengthening factor. We at the close of the twentieth century have, however, not suddenly become callous to the negative potential of the concept of "race." Given its abuse in the Shoah[5] as well as in neo-colonial policies throughout the world,[6] it is clear that a great deal of sensitivity must be used in employing the very idea of "race." In reversing the idea of "race," we have not eliminated its negative implications, we have only masked them. For it is also clear that the meanings associated with "race" impact on those included within these constructed categories. It forms them and shapes them. And this can be a seemingly positive or a clearly negative response. There is no question that there are "real," i.e., shared genetic distinctions within and between groups. But the rhetoric of what this shared distinction comes to mean for the general culture and for the "group" so defined becomes central to any understanding of the implications of race.

Where I would like to begin is with that advertisement in the *Washingtonian* and with the question which the bracketed (J) posed: are Jews white? To begin to answer that question we must trace the debate about the skin color of the Jews, for skin color remains one of the most salient markers for the construction of race in the West over time. The general consensus of the ethnological literature of the late nineteenth century was that the Jews were "black" or, at least, "swarthy." This view had a long history in European science. As early as 1691 François-Maximilien Misson, whose ideas influenced Bufon's *Natural History,* argued against the notion that Jews were black:

> 'Tis also a vulgar error that the Jews are all black; for this is only true of the Portuguese Jews, who marrying always among one another, beget Children like themselves, and consequently the Swarthiness of their Complexion is entail'd upon their whole Race, even in the Northern Regions. But the Jews who are originally of Germany, those, for example, I have seen at Prague, are not blacker than the rest of their Countrymen.[7]

But this was a minority position. For the eighteenth- and nineteenth-century scientist the "blackness" of the Jew was not only a mark of racial inferiority, but also an indicator of the diseased nature of the Jew, The "liberal" Bavarian writer Johan Pezzl, who traveled to Vienna in the 1780s, described the typical Viennese Jew of his time:

> There are about five hundred Jews in Vienna. Their sole and eternal occupation is to counterfeit, salvage, trade in coins, and cheat Christians, Turks, heathens, indeed themselves. … This is only the beggarly filth from Canaan which can only be exceeded in filth, … uncleanliness, stench, disgust, poverty, dishonesty, pushiness and other things by the trash of the twelve tribes from Galicia. Excluding the Indian fakirs, there is no category of supposed human beings which comes closer to the Orang-Utan than does a Polish Jew. … Covered from foot to head in filth, dirt and rags, covered in a type of black sack … their necks exposed, the color of a Black, their faces covered up to the eyes with a beard, which would have given the High Priest in the Temple chills, the hair turned and knotted as if they all suffered from the "plica polonica."[8]

The image of the Viennese Jew is that of the Eastern Jew, suffering from the diseases of the East, such as the *Judenkratze,* the fabled skin and hair disease also attributed to the Poles under the designation of the "plica polonica."[9] The Jews' disease is written on the skin. It is the appearance, the skin color, the external manifestation of the Jew which marks the Jew as different. There is no question for a non-Jewish visitor to Vienna upon first seeing the Jew that the Jew suffers from Jewishness. The internal, moral state of the Jew, the Jew's very psychology, is reflected in the diseased exterior of the Jew. As mentioned earlier, "plica polonica" is a real dermatologic syndrome. It results from living in filth and poverty. But it was also associated with the unhygienic nature of the Jew and, by the mid-nineteenth century, with the Jew's special relationship to the most frightening disease of the period, syphilis.[10] For the non-Jew seeing the Jew it mirrored popular assumptions about the Jew's inherent, essential nature. Pezzl's contemporary, Joseph Rohrer, stressed the "disgusting skin diseases" of the Jew as a sign of the group's general infirmity.[11] And the essential Jew for Pezzl is the Galician Jew, the Jew from the Eastern reaches of the Hapsburg Empire.[12] (This late eighteenth-century view of the meaning of the Jew's skin color was not only held by non-Jews, The Enlightenment Jewish physician Elcan Isaac Wolf saw this "black yellow" skin color as a pathognomonic sign of the diseased Jew.[13]) Following the humoral theory of the times, James Cowles Pritchard (1808) commented on the Jews' "choleric and melancholic temperaments, so that they have in general a shade of complexion somewhat darker than that of the English people …"[14] Nineteenth-century anthropology as, early as the work of Claudius Buchana commented on the "inferiority" of the "black" Jews of India.[15] By the mid-century, being black, being Jewish, being diseased, and being "ugly" came to be inexorably linked. All races, according to the ethnology of the day, were described in terms of aesthetics, as either "ugly" or "beautiful."[16] African blacks, especially the Hottentot, as I have shown elsewhere, became the epitome of the "ugly" race.[17] And being ugly, as I have also argued, was not merely a matter of aesthetics but was a clear sign of pathology, of disease. Being black was not beautiful. Indeed, the blackness of the African, like the blackness of the Jew, was believed to mark a pathological change in the skin, the result of congenital syphilis. (And, as we shall see, syphilis was given the responsibility for the form of the nose.) One bore the signs of one's diseased status on one's anatomy, and by extension, in one's psyche. And all of these signs pointed to the Jews being a member of the "ugly" races of mankind, rather than the "beautiful" races. In being denied any association with the beautiful and the erotic, the Jew's body was denigrated.[18]

Within the racial science of the nineteenth century, being "black" came to signify that the Jews had crossed racial boundaries. The boundaries of race were one of the most powerful social and political divisions evolved in the science of the period. That the Jews, rather than being considered the purest race, are because of their endogenous marriages, an impure race, and therefore, a potentially diseased one. That this impurity is written on their physiognomy. According to Houston Stewart Chamberlain, the Jews are a "mongrel" (rather than a healthy "mixed") race, who interbred with Africans during the period of the Alexandrian exile.[19] They are "a mongrel race which always retains this mongrel character." Jews had "hybridized" with blacks in Alexandrian exile. They are, in an ironic review of Chamberlain's work by Nathan Birnbaum, the Viennese-Jewish activist who coined the word "Zionist," a "bastard" race, the origin of which was caused by their incestuousness, their sexual selectivity.[20]

Jews bear the sign of the black, "the African character of the Jew, his muzzle-shaped mouth and face removing him from certain other races ... ," as Robert Knox noted at mid century.[21] The physiognomy of the Jew which is like that of the black " ... the contour is convex; the eyes long and fine, the outer angles running towards the temples; the brow and nose apt to form a single convex line; the nose comparatively narrow at the base, the eyes consequently approaching each other; lips very full, mouth projecting, chin small, and the whole physiognomy, when swarthy, as it often is, has an African look."[22] It is, therefore, not only the color of the skin which enables the scientist to see the Jew as black, but also the associated anatomical signs, such as the shape of the nose. The Jews were quite literally seen as black. Adam Gurowski, a Polish noble, "took every light-colored mulatto for a Jew" when he first arrived in the United States in the 1850s.[23]

[...] Jews look different, they have a different appearance, and this appearance has pathognomonic significance. Skin color marked the Jew as both different and diseased. For the Jewish scientist, such as Sigmund Freud, these "minor differences in people who are otherwise alike ... form the basis of feelings of strangeness and hostility between them."[24] This is what Freud clinically labeled as the "narcissism of minor differences." But are these differences "minor" either from the perspective of those labeling or those labeled? In reducing this sense of the basis of difference between "people who are otherwise alike," Freud was not only drawing on the Enlightenment claim of the universality of human rights, but also on the Christian underpinnings of these claims. For this "narcissism" fights "successfully against feelings of fellowship and overpower[s] the commandment that all men should love one another." It is the Christian claim to universal brotherly love that Freud was employing in arguing that the differences between himself, his body, and the body of the Aryan, are trivial. Freud comprehended the special place that the Jew played in the demonic universe of the Aryan psyche. But he marginalized this role as to the question of the Jew's function "as an agent of economic discharge ... in the world of the Aryan ideal" rather than as one of the central aspects in the science of his time.[25] What Freud was masking was that Jews are not merely the fantasy capitalists of the paranoid delusions of the anti-Semites, they also mirror within their own sense of selves the image of their own difference.

By the close of the nineteenth century, the "reality" of the physical difference of the Jew as a central marker of race had come more and more into question. Antithetical theories, such as those of Friedrich Ratzel, began to argue that skin color was a reflex of geography, and could and did shift when a people moved from one part of the globe to another. Building on earlier work by the President of Princeton University at the close of the eighteenth century, Samuel Stanhope Smith (1787), the Jews came to be seen as the adaptive people par excellence. "In Britain and Germany they are fair, brown in France and in Turkey, swarthy in Portugal and Spain, olive in Syria and Chaldea, tawny or copper-coloured in Arabia and Egypt."[26] William Lawrence commented in 1823 that "their colour is everywhere modified by the situation they occupy."[27] The questionability of skin color as the marker of Jewish difference joined with other qualities which made the Jew visible.

By the latter half of the nineteenth century, Western European Jews had become indistinguishable from other Western Europeans in matters of language, dress, occupation, location of their dwellings and the cut of their hair. Indeed, if Rudolf Virchow's extensive study of over 10,000 German schoolchildren published in 1886 was accurate, they were also indistinguishable in terms of skin, hair, and eye color from the greater masses of those who lived in Germany.[28] Virchow's statistics sought to show that wherever a greater percentage of the overall population had lighter skin or bluer eyes or blonder hair there was a greater percentage of Jews who also had lighter skin or bluer eyes or blonder hair. But although Virchow attempted to provide a rationale for the sense of Jewish acculturation, he still assumed that Jews were a separate and distinct racial category. George Mosse has commented, "the separateness of Jewish schoolchildren, approved by Virchow, says something about the course of Jewish emancipation in Germany. However rationalized, the survey must have made Jewish schoolchildren conscious of their minority status and their supposedly different origins."[29] Nonetheless, even though they were labeled as different, Jews came to parallel the scale of types found elsewhere in European society.

A parallel shift in the perception of the Jewish body can be found during the twentieth century in the United States. It is not merely that second- and third-generation descendants of Eastern European Jewish immigrants do not "look" like their grandparents; but they "look" American. The writer and director Philip Dunne commented on the process of physical acculturation of Jews in Southern California during the twentieth century:

> You could even see the physical change in the family in the second generation—not resembling the first generation at all. Of course, this is true all across the country, but it is particularly noticeable in people who come out of very poor families. ... One

dear friend and colleague of mine was a product of a Lower East Side slum. He was desperately poor. And he grew up a rickety, tiny man who had obviously suffered as a child. At school, he told me, the goyim would scream at him. Growing up in California, his two sons were tall, tanned, and blond. Both excelled academically and in athletics. One became a military officer, the other a physicist. They were California kids. Not only American but Californian.[30]

But the more Jews in Germany and Austria at the fin de siècle looked like their non-Jewish contemporaries, the more they sensed themselves as different and were so considered. As the Anglo-Jewish social scientist Joseph Jacobs noted, "it is some quality which stamps their features as distinctly Jewish. This is confirmed by the interesting fact that Jews who mix much with the outer world seem to lose their Jewish quality. This was the case with Karl Marx ..."[31] And yet, as we know, it was precisely those Jews who were the most assimilated, who were passing, who feared that their visibility as Jews could come to the fore. It was they who most feared being seen as bearing that disease, Jewishness, which Heinrich Heine said the Jews brought from Egypt.

In the 1920s, Jacob Wassermann chronicled the ambivalence of the German Jews towards their own bodies, their own difference. Wassermann articulates this difference within the terms of the biology of race. He writes that: "I have known many Jews who have languished with longing for the fair-haired and blue-eyed individual. They knelt before him, burned incense before him, believed his every word; every blink of his eye was heroic; and when he spoke of his native soil, when he beat his Aryan breast, they broke into a hysterical shriek of triumph."[32] Their response, Wassermann argues, is to feel disgust for their own body, which even when it is identical in *all* respects to the body of the Aryan remains different: "I was once greatly diverted by a young Viennese Jew, elegant, full of suppressed ambition, rather melancholy, something of an artist, and something of a charlatan. Providence itself had given him fair hair and blue eyes; but lo, he had no confidence in his fair hair and blue eyes: in his heart of hearts he felt that they were spurious."[33] The Jew's experience of his or her own body was so deeply impacted by anti-Semitic rhetoric that even when that body met the expectations for perfection in the community in which the Jew lived, the Jew experienced his or her body as flawed, diseased.[34] If only one could change those aspects of the body which marked one as Jewish!

But nothing, not acculturation, not baptism, could wipe away the taint of race. No matter how they changed, they still remained diseased Jews. And this was marked on their physiognomy. Moses Hess, the German–Jewish revolutionary and political theorist commented, in his *Rome and Jerusalem* (1862) that "even baptism will not redeem the German Jew from the nightmare of German Jew hatred. The Germans hate less the religion of the Jews than their race, less their peculiar beliefs than their peculiar noses. … Jewish noses cannot be reformed, nor black, curly, Jewish hair be turned through baptism or combing into smooth hair. The Jewish race is a primal one, which had reproduced itself in its integrity despite climactic influences. … The Jewish type is indestructible:"[35] The theme of the Jew's immutability was directly tied to arguments about the permanence of the negative features of the Jewish race.

On one count, Hess seemed to be wrong—the external appearance of the Jew did seem to be shifting. His skin seemed to be getting whiter, at least in his own estimation, though it could never get white enough. Jews, at least in Western Europe, no longer suffered from the disgusting skin diseases of poverty which had once marked their skin. But on another count, Hess was right. The Jew's nose could not be "reformed." Interrelated with the meaning of skin was the meaning of the Jew's physiognomy, especially the Jew's nose. And it was also associated with the Jew's nature. George Jabet, writing as Eden Warwick, in his *Notes on Noses* (1848) characterized the "Jewish, or Hawknose," as "very convex, and preserves its convexity like a bow, throughout the whole length from the eyes to the tip. It is thin and sharp." Shape also carried here a specific meaning: "It indicates considerable shrewdness in worldly matters; a deep insight into character, and facility of turning that insight to profitable account."[36] Physicians, drawing on such analogies, speculated that the difference of the Jew's language, the very mirror of his psyche, was the result of the form of his nose. Thus Bernhard Blechmann's rationale for the *Mauscheln* of the Jews, their inability to speak with other than a Jewish intonation, is that the "muscles, which are used for speaking and laughing are used inherently different from those of Christians and that this use can be traced … to the great difference in their nose and chin."[37] The nose becomes one of the central loci of difference in seeing the Jew. […]

## DISCUSSION QUESTIONS

1. How did Jews change their appearance over time to look more "White?"
2. What role did intermarriage play in the effort to alter their appearance?
3. What role did plastic surgery play in the effort to alter their appearance?

## NOTES AND REFERENCES

1. *Washingtonian* 26, 4 (January 1991), p. 196.
2. Mary Douglas, *Natural Symbols* (New York: Pantheon Books, 3970), p. 70.

3.  Theodosius Dobzhansky, "On Types, Genotypes, and the Genetic Diversity in Populations," in J.N. Spuhler, ed., *Genetic Diversity and Human Behavior* (Chicago: Aldine, 1967), p. 12.

4.  See for example, Peter A. Bochnik, *Die machtigen Diener: Die Medizin und die Entwicklung von Frauenfeindlichkeit und Antisemitismus in der europätschen Geschichte* (Reinbek bei Hamburg: Rowohlt, 1985).

5.  Robert Jay Lifton, *The Nazi Doctors: Medical Killing and the Psychology of Genocide* (New York; Basic Books, 1986).

6.  See Oliver Ransford, *"Bid the Sickness Cease": Disease in the History of Black Africa* (London: John Murray, 1983).

7.  Franoois-Maximilien Misson, *A New Voyage to Italy*, 2 vols. (London: R. Bonwicke, 1714), 2: 139.

8.  Johan Pezzl, *Skizze von Wien: Ein Kaltur- und Sittenbild aus der josepkinischen Zeit*, ed. Gustav Gugitz and Anton Scholssar (Graz: Leykam-Verlag, 1923), pp. 107–8.

9.  On the meaning of this disease in the medical literature of the period see the following dissertations on the topic: Michael Scheiba, *Dissertatio inauguralis medica, sistens quaedam plicae pathologica: Germ, Juden-Zopff, Polon. Kokun: qua … in Academia Albertina pro gradu doctori … subject defensurus Michael Scheiba …* (Regiomonti: Litteris Reusnerianis, 1739) and Hieronymus Ludolf, *Dissertatio inauguralis medica deplica, vom juden-Zopff …* (Erfordiae: Typis Groschianis, 1724)

10. Harry Friedenwald, *The Jews and Medicine: Essays. 2* vols. (Baltimore: The Johns Hopkins University Press, 1944), 2: 531.

11. Joseph Rohrer, … *Versuch über die jüdischen Bewohner der östereichischen Monarchic* (Vienna: n.p., 1804), p. 26. The debate about the special tendency of the Jews for skin disease, especially "plica polonica," goes on well into the twentieth century. See Richard Weinberg, "Zur Pathologie der Juden," *Zeitschrift fur Demographic und Statistik der Judea* 1 (1905): 10–11.

12. Wolfgang Häusler, *Das galizische Judentum in der Habsburgermonarchie im Lichte der zeitgenijssischen Puhlizistik und Reiseliteratur von 177–-1848* (Vienna: Verlag fur Geschichte und Politik, 1979). On the status of the debates about the pathology of the Jews in the East after 1919 see *Voprosy biologii i patologii evreev* (Leningrad: State Publishing House, 1926).

13. Elcan Isaac Wolf, *Von den Ktankheiten der Juden* (Mannheim: C.F. Schwan, 1777), p. 12.

14. James Cowies Pritchard, *Researches into the Physical History of Man* (Chicago: The University of Chicago Press, 1973), p. 186.

15. Claudius Buchanan, *Christian Researches in Asia, with Notices of the Translation of the Scriptures into the Oriental Languages* Boston: Samuel T. Armstrong, 1811), p. 169. On the background to these questions see George W. Stocking, Jr., *Victorian Anthropology* (New York: The Free Press, 1987).

16. Leon Poliakov, *The Aryan Myth: A History of Racist and Nationalist Ideas in Europe,* trans. Edmund Howard (New York: Basic Books, 1974), pp. 155–82.

17. Sander L. Gilman, *On Blackness without Blacks: Essays on the Image of the Black in Germany,* Yale Afro-American Studies (Boston: G. K. Hall, 1982).

18. See Cheryl Herr, "The Erotics of Irishness," *Critical Inquiry* 17 (1990): 1–34.

19. Houston Stewart Chamberlain, *Foundations of the Nineteenth Century,* trans. John Lees, 2 vols. (London: John Lane/The Bodley Head, 1913), 1: 389.

20. Nathan Birnbaum, "Uber Houston Stewart Chamberlain," in his *Ausgewählte Schriften zur jüdischen Frage* (Czernowitz: Verlag der Buchhandlung Dr. Birnbaum & Dr. Kohut, 1910), 2: 201.

21. Robert Knox, *The Races of Men: A Fragment* (Philadelphia: Lea and Blanchard, 1850), p. 134.

22. Knox, Races *of Men,* p. 133.

23. Adam G. De Gurowski, *America and Europe* (New York: D. Appleton, 1857), p. 177.

24. Sigmund Freud, *Standard Edition of the Complete Psychological Works of Sigmund Freud,* ed. and trans, J. Strachey, A. Freud, A. Strachey, and A. Tyson, 24 vols.(London: Hogarth, 19SS-74), 11: 199; 18: 101; 21: 114.

25. ibid. 21: 120.

26. Samuel Stanhope Smith, *An Essay on the Causes of the Variety of Complexion and figure in the Human Species* (Cambridge: MASS: The Belknap Press, 1965), p. 42.

27. William Lawrence, *Lectures on Physiology, Zoology, and the Natural History of Man* (London: James Smith, 1823), p. 468.

28. Rudolf Virchow, "Gesamtbericht über die Farbe der Haut, der Haare und der Augen der Schulkinder in Deutschland," *Archiv für Anthropologie* 16 (1886): 275–475.

29. George L. Mosse, *Toward the Final Solution: A History of European Racism* (New York: Howard Fertig, 197S), pp. 90–91.

30. Cited from an interview by Neal Gabler, *An Empire of Their Own: How the Jews Invented Hollywood* (New York: Crown, 1988), pp. 242–42.

31. "Types," *The Jewish Encyclopedia.* 12 vols (New York: Funk and Wagnalls, 1906), 12: 295.

32. Wassermann, *My life,* p. 156

33. Wassermann, *My Life,* p. 156.

34. On the cultural background for this concept see Jacob Katz, *Out of the Ghetto: The Social Background of Jewish Emancipation 1770–1870* (Cambridge, MASS: Harvard University Press, 1973) and Rainer Erb and Werner Bergmann, *Die Nachtseite der Judenemanzipation: Der Widerstand gegen die Integration der Juden in Deutschland 1780–1860* (Berlin: Metropol. 1989).

35. Moses Hess, *Rom und Jerusalem.* 2nd ed. (Leipzig: M. W. Kaufmann, 1899), Brief IV, Cited in the translation from Paul Lawrence Rose, *Revolutionary Antisemitism in Germany from Kant to Wagner* (Princeton: Princeton University Press, 1990),p. 323.

36. Eden Warwick, Notes *on Noses* (1848: London: Richard Bentley, 1864), p. 11. On the general question of the representation of the physiognomy of the Jew in mid-nineteenth-century culture see Mary Cowling, *The Artist as Anthropologist: The Representation of Type and Character in Victorian Art* (Cambridge: Cambridge University Press, 1989), pp. 118–19, 332–33.

37. Bernhard Blechmann, *Ein Beitrag zur Anthropologie der Juden* (Dorpat: Wilhelm Just, 1882), p. 11.

# CHAPTER 6

# Racism and Housing

# The Second Ghetto and the 'Infiltration Theory' in Urban Real Estate, 1940–1960

## Raymond A. Mohl

IN THE YEARS between 1940 and 1960, powerful demographic and structural shifts began to reshape neighborhood life in urban America. During these two decades, some five million African Americans migrated from the South to the urban North and West. Large numbers of Southern Blacks also moved from the rural to the urban South. At the same time, and especially after 1945, millions of White Americans began moving to the sprawling tract houses of the new postwar suburbs. In many cities, the suburban migration was also, in part, a racial response on the part of Whites seeking to escape what was perceived as a Black "invasion" of central-city residential neighborhoods. The period between 1940 and 1960, therefore, was one of dramatic racial and spatial reorganization of the American metropolis. African Americans who moved into the cities pushed out the residential boundaries of the inner-city ghettos, moving into the neighborhoods of Whites who had departed for the suburbs. Once the racial transitions began, more Whites moved out because of the Black in-migration. The creation of the "second ghetto," as historians have labeled this process of racial/spatial transition, emerges in retrospect as one of the most significant structural changes in the mid-twentieth-century American city.[1]

The process of residential transformation was not an easy one. Indeed, the frontiers of neighborhood change were marked by bitter protest, picketing, boycotts, demonstrations, intimidation, bombings, arson, and mob violence in many postwar cities. Neighborhood improvement associations actively participated in the defense of White communities faced with African American "infiltration." As one research report from 1947 noted, "the function of Negro exclusion" had become "the controlling motive" for

Raymond A. Mohl; eds. June Manning Thomas and Marsha Ritzdorf, "The Second Ghetto and the 'Infiltration Theory' in Urban Real Estate, 1940–1960," from *Urban Planning and the African American Community: In the Shadows*, pp 58–67, 71–74. Copyright © 1997 by Sage Publications. Permission to reprint granted by the publisher.

most neighborhood associations: "the maintenance of Caucasian-pure residence areas has come to be a dominant purpose." White communities mobilized to prevent the racial transition of urban neighborhoods.[2]

Propelling the process of second ghetto formation was the intensifying demand for new and better housing among Black Americans. The boundaries of the older, inner-city ghettos formerly had been maintained by racial zoning and restrictive covenants, as well as by the discriminatory policies of private lending firms. Federal housing agencies such as the Home Owners Loan Corporation (HOLC), the Federal Housing Administration (FHA), and the Veterans Administration (VA) supported lily-white housing practices, and public housing policies also adhered to the color line.[3] By midcentury, these discriminatory mechanisms could no longer contain the burgeoning Black populations of the American metropolis, now swelled by a decade of Southern Black migration. Court challenges supported by groups such as the National Association for the Advancement of Colored People (NAACP) resulted in the outlawing of restrictive covenants by the U.S. Supreme Court in 1948.[4] Many state and U.S. district courts in the South banned local racial zoning laws in the late 1940s.[5] Both the private sector and federal housing agencies began backing away from official policies of discrimination by the early 1950s, but not until the civil rights legislation of the mid-1960s was housing discrimination fully outlawed.[6] Nevertheless, throughout the 1940s and 1950s, although White neighborhood associations sought to maintain the color line in urban housing, African Americans who wanted better housing seized on opportunities presented by more liberal court decisions and by more open housing and lending policies. They were willing to challenge segregation and confront mob terror to achieve their objectives.[7]

There was one other mediating force facilitating, often manipulating, the racial/spatial transitions of the postwar American city. Indeed, central to the process of neighborhood change during these years was the real estate industry—the hidden hand that helped shape the postwar metropolis. Real estate professionals were fully cognizant, from an early period, of the demographic changes that were restructuring the city. Innumerable articles in the real estate trade journals not only demonstrated an awareness of racial change but provided prescriptive advice for real estate people confronted with racially changing neighborhoods. The responses were not monolithic by any means. Most in the real estate industry sought to hold off racial change and stabilize White neighborhoods; some others—blockbusters or builders of new Black housing, for instance—sought to profit from the demographic changes buffeting America; a very few hoped to facilitate residential integration and denied that racial change undermined property values.[8] With the growth of the second ghetto providing the background, this chapter will first discuss the Black migration and urban violence in the second-ghetto era and then outline the role and response of the real estate industry to urban change as reflected in the industry's professional and trade journals.

## BLACK MIGRATION AND SECOND GHETTO VIOLENCE

As noted, the demography of American cities and metropolitan areas began changing dramatically during the 1940s and after. The process of change began with new migratory patterns during World War II, as White and Black war production workers moved to new "war-industry centers," especially in the Northeast, Midwest, and Pacific Coast states. In the postwar years, urban America experienced a convergence of regional and metropolitan migration trends, as African Americans continued to move out of the South to new urban destinations and as urban Whites increasingly migrated to the suburban periphery of the large metropolitan areas.[9]

The U.S. metropolitan population more than doubled between 1940 and 1960, from 63 million to 133 million. Virtually all of the largest American metropolitan areas grew rapidly between 1940 and 1960; for instance, metropolitan Detroit increased in population by 64 percent, Philadelphia by 50 percent, Chicago by 38 percent, Los Angeles by 132 percent, and San Diego by 303 percent. However, almost all of that metropolitan growth was recorded in the suburbs. Many of the largest central cities (except those in the Sunbelt) had already stopped growing during these years, and some even began losing population. The trend was very clear—in mid-twentieth-century metropolitan America, population growth was a phenomenon that occurred mostly on the fringes and in the suburbs.[10]

Striking increases in the central-city Black population matched the White suburban surge. Virtually every big city in the United States recorded sharp gains in the Black population between 1940 and 1960. The big East Coast cities—New York and Philadelphia—and almost all of the industrial cities of the Midwestern heartland showed amazing Black population gains ranging from 100 percent in Philadelphia to 301 percent in Buffalo and 607 percent in Milwaukee. Even more startling was the West Coast experience; Los Angeles with a 425 percent increase was actually slow growth compared to the rate of increase in Seattle (592 percent), San Diego (721 percent), Oakland (882 percent), and San Francisco (1,425 percent). If the White population of the central cities was emptying out to the expanding suburban fringe, the cities themselves served as a massive human magnet attracting the African Americans migrating out of the South. Consequently, the proportion of Blacks in the central-city population was rising rapidly just about everywhere during these midcentury years. This experience of migration and metropolitan change established the basis for the later emergence of many majority Black central cities—the pattern most common at the end of the twentieth century.[11]

The conjunction of the African American migration to the city and the White migration to the metropolitan suburbs brought powerful social consequences. Despite large increases in Black population during the 1940s, the color line in housing continued to prevail. Severe housing congestion marked the confined Black residential areas in just about every big city and many smaller ones. Typically, as families doubled up in apartments, and as single-family residences were subdivided into multifamily units, overcrowded conditions worsened. These central-city housing pressures eventually contributed to the opening up of new areas for Black residence. The racial succession process varied in different cities, with some city governments providing new public housing for African Americans, others (especially in the South) zoning undeveloped spaces for new Black residence. Race advancement organizations such as the NAACP and the National Urban League pressured government agencies, and legal challenges produced some positive results. In most cities, some elements of the real estate industry facilitated the process of racial change through "blockbusting." But whatever the method, African Americans were eager for more and better housing, and they generally pushed the limits to achieve it. Thus, racial/spatial transitions took place in virtually every big city, as African American housing pioneers blazed new trails into White residential neighborhoods.

However, breaking the color line on housing was accompanied by great personal risk for African Americans. During the earlier "great migration" from the South to the urban North—the migration of 1915 to 1930—competition for housing and consequent racial conflicts touched off violent race riots in East St. Louis and Houston in 1917, in Philadelphia in 1918, in Chicago and Washington, D.C., in 1919, and in Tulsa in 1921. In Miami, Detroit, Baltimore, Kansas City, Memphis, and dozens of other cities, White mobs used intimidation, terror, and violence to maintain the color line in housing. The pattern of intimidation and violence surged once again in the midcentury decades, as the urban Black population began rising rapidly once again, as housing pressures intensified, and as new second ghettos sprouted all over urban America.[12]

The racial violence of the 1960s—the urban riots and ghetto insurrections of the Great Society era—is well known and much studied. Surprisingly little is known about the urban racial violence of the period between 1945 and 1960, when the victims were mostly Black people seeking better housing and the violent perpetrators were mostly White people trying to prevent African Americans from moving into their neighborhoods. Yet these racial incidents were ubiquitous at the time, even if they were not very well reported in the metropolitan press or by national news magazines. Indeed, as Herbert Shapiro has suggested, it appears that "all during this period news coverage of the racial violence was substantially suppressed." (The left-liberal press and the African American press did a much better job of reporting this surge of second ghetto housing violence.) Just barely hidden from general public awareness however, an era of "chronic urban guerrilla warfare" was emerging as the racial dynamics of neighborhood change produced violent responses from Whites who feared, resented, and often resisted Black "intrusion" into their neighborhoods.[13]

The White residents of midcentury Chicago could not have missed what was happening in working-class southside and westside neighborhoods. According to Arnold R. Hirsch, whose book *Making the Second Ghetto* (1983) provides a case study of the racial/spatial transitions in midcentury Chicago, more than 350 incidents of racial violence related to housing were reported to the Chicago Commission on Human Relations between 1945 and 1950; Chicago's racial troubles became even more intense in the 1950s. In Detroit, according to Thomas J. Sugrue, who studied the process of racial/spatial change in the auto city, "more than two hundred violent incidents occurred in racially transitional neighborhoods between 1945 and 1965, including the gathering of angry crowds, rock throwing, cross burning, arson, and other attacks on property." In Philadelphia, according to John F. Bauman, racial incidents were occurring with regularity by the 1950s: "Some 213 racial incidents during the first six months of 1955 alone reinforced an antiblack climate that cemented the boundaries of the city's North Philadelphia ghetto." In Miami, Florida, dozens of cross burnings, house burnings, bombings, and other forms of intimidation occurred between 1945 and 1951, as Blacks pushed out the boundaries of the confined inner-city ghetto. In the early 1950s, mob violence, arson, and bomb throwing occurred in Chicago, Atlanta, Dallas, Kansas City, East St. Louis, Birmingham, Louisville, Cleveland, Philadelphia, Indianapolis, Los Angeles, Tampa, and several California cities, to name just a few such cases.[14]

The violent responses to racial/spatial neighborhood transitions knew few bounds. They occurred in Northern and Southern cities, in the East and the West, in big cities and small cities, even in smaller suburban towns. Most of these incidents, which must have totaled many thousands nationwide, followed a similar pattern, usually touched off when a Black family bought or rented in a White district. During these midcentury years, as the Black migration intensified and as city neighborhoods began to experience racial succession, White people everywhere seemed easily riled up over the thought (or the reality) of African Americans moving into their neighborhoods. Carefully watching these events, and often heavily involved in them, local real estate people had a major interest both in the defense of White neighborhoods and in the making of the second ghetto.

## THE REAL ESTATE INDUSTRY AND THE "INFILTRATION THEORY"

The real estate industry had a major interest in the residential changes that accompanied the Black migration to the postwar American city. Many local real estate sales people and brokers confined their activities to specific urban neighborhoods or districts. Economic or social forces that affected such districts had consequences for their business and income. In many cities, real estate men served as officers and leaders of neighborhood improvement associations; in other cities they worked in concert with the associations in promoting restrictive covenants and maintaining White neighborhoods.[15] Similarly local banks, savings and loans, and mortgage firms had big investments in urban neighborhoods and kept a close watch on residential changes. Appraisal firms had to weigh the impact of racial transitions in revising and establishing property values. Builders and developers had to keep abreast of population trends and market forces to make intelligent business investment decisions. Apartment owners, landlords, and property management firms had to consider how residential transitions would affect their taxes, property values, and pricing structures.

The dominant belief in the nation's real estate industry held, as one appraisal expert put it in 1948, that "neighborhoods change, but never for the better." Real estate analysts uniformly ticked off a laundry list of explanations for the decline of residential neighborhoods. Ubiquitously present and high up on that list was the euphemistic notation: "infiltrations of unharmonious racial groups," real estate code for the movement of African Americans into new residential areas.[16] As far back as the 1920s, the National Association of Real Estate Boards (NAREB) drafted a code of ethics that made the sale of homes in White neighborhoods to African Americans a breach of professional standards. Most regional, state, and local real estate organizations replicated and adhered to the NAREB professional code. The National Association of Home Builders pursued similarly discriminatory practices, advocating home building for Blacks only in segregated neighborhoods. The NAREB deleted the racial provision of its ethics code in 1950, but the policy continued to be observed informally throughout the real estate industry. Most real estate people took it for granted that the movement of Blacks into White neighborhoods would undermine property values and destroy the community.[17]

These discriminatory perceptions were deeply embedded in the process of training and educating real estate professionals. The NAREB standards regarding race were written into virtually all of the real estate textbooks, appraisal manuals, and training materials at the time. As early as 1932, for instance, in his real estate text, *The Valuation of Real Estate*, Frederick M. Babcock of the University of Michigan devoted a full chapter to "The Influence of Social and Racial Factors on Value," Babcock advanced the concept that all residential neighborhoods gradually declined but that the downward trend in value could be speeded up by an "infiltration process" that "carries all residential communities not capable of other use downward in quality and value."[18]

In their book *Principles of Urban Real Estate* (1948), Arthur M. Weimer and Homer Hoyt also embraced the infiltration theory. Neighborhood stability, Weimer and Hoyt contended, could be maintained only "if the people living in an area are not threatened by the infiltration of people of another racial or national type." The migration of such groups into a neighborhood, they wrote, "frequently stimulates the out-migration of previous residents in the area." It is curious that those advancing the "infiltration" argument rarely mentioned Negroes or Blacks specifically, but given the real estate jargon of the time, everyone in the business knew what they meant.[19]

Even as official discrimination became less acceptable in the 1950s, real estate analysis of neighborhood change remained much the same. Henry E. Hoagland's 1955 text, *Real Estate Principles*, gave prominence to the infiltration theory. When "two or more incompatible groups" occupied any neighborhood, Hoagland wrote, "the tendency is for the group having the least regard for the maintenance of real estate standards to drive out the other group. ... The infiltration of additional representatives of the dominant group operates to put a blight on the neighborhood."[20] Even as late as 1984, one real estate appraisal text was still discussing the "introduction of contentious groups" as a factor threatening property values and promoting neighborhood decline.[21] Despite the changing euphemisms over thirty years (from "inharmonious" to "incompatible" to "contentious"), real estate people had a pretty good sense of how the cities were changing and what particular responses they should pursue.

The real estate industry did not stand alone in the effort to maintain segregated housing patterns. Equally significant, federal housing agencies beginning in the New Deal era—the Home Owners Loan Corporation (HOLC), the Federal Housing Administration (FHA), the Veterans Administration (VA), the U.S. Housing Authority, the Public Housing Administration, and the Housing and Home Finance Agency (HHFA), among others, all accepted the basic premise of the "infiltration" theory. HOLC, for instance, established an appraisal system (eventually used by other federal agencies and by local bankers and mortgage firms), that initiated the pernicious and discriminatory policy of "redlining."[22] The FHA's *Underwriting Manual*, first published in 1938 and reissued in 1947, opposed neighborhood "invasion by incompatible racial and social groups" and advocated residential segregation as a means of maintaining community stability (see Part 5.B, this volume).[23] The FHA, according to housing expert Charles Abrams, "set itself up as the protector of the all-white neighborhood" and "became the vanguard of white supremacy and racial purity—in the North as well as the South."[24] Federal public housing projects were segregated from the beginning almost everywhere, a policy that was maintained by local housing authorities that placed many public housing projects in segregated neighborhoods, or at least in the path of the expanding Black ghetto. Similarly, government urban renewal and highway projects often seemed to pursue a vigorous policy of Black removal while spending less effort on the relocation of families whose housing had been taken for redevelopment purposes.[25] As Arnold Hirsch has noted, "the most distinguishing feature of post-World War II ghetto expansion is that it was carried out with government sanction and support."[26]

Professional and trade journals in the various real estate and housing fields also adhered to the infiltration theory. These journals covering real estate, appraisal, banking, savings and loan, mortgage, property management, residential development, and building activities all kept real estate professionals aware of current trends and patterns. One such journal, the *Real Estate Analyst*, edited by Roy Wenzlick of St. Louis, was published regularly through the entire period between 1940 and 1960. Consistent readers of Wenzlick's journal got very good reports on the demographic, economic, and structural changes that were reshaping urban America during the midcentury decades. As early as 1942, Wenzlick reported on the decentralization of the urban population, with numerous follow-up reports on urban population shifts, including the Black migration to the central cities. Detailed population tables periodically provided the changing statistics for cities and standard metropolitan areas. Over many years, *The Real Estate Analyst* hammered home the basic message of the "infiltration" theory, noting in one 1949 article on St. Louis, for example, that for many White neighborhoods "it would be only a matter of time before ... Negro families encroached upon the districts in question." It was Wenzlick's expert advice that real estate appraisers should always carefully weigh the impact of "racial groups infiltrating a district." For Wenzlick, the problem was clear, and the solution clearer still—maintain the color line and hold back the encroaching second ghetto.[27]

The savings and loan industry had a big interest in neighborhood real estate, since most savings and loans were small institutions heavily tied to local housing markets. The major publication of the U.S. Savings and Loan League, *Savings and Loan Annals*, provided an annual snapshot of industry issues and concerns. Through the 1940s, the savings and loan people were mostly interested in the economic impact of the war on building materials, construction, and the new housing market. They were also extremely hostile to public housing and preferred programs, such as those later enacted in the Housing Act of 1949, that made it possible for private developers to assemble large parcels of inner-city land for private redevelopment. They rarely discussed Black housing and when they did so it was only in the context of the infiltration theory. Since most savings and loans generally practiced redlining and resisted the approval of mortgages in "second-grade districts," not many African Americans could get housing loans or even buy new houses.

## DISCUSSION QUESTIONS

1. What is a "second ghetto"? How did the real estate industry contribute to its existence?
2. How did racial violence lead to segregated communities between 1940 and 1960?
3. What were the commonly held beliefs by white real estate professionals about the outcome of racially mixed neighborhoods?

## NOTES

1. Second ghetto conceptualization was initiated in Arnold R. Hirsch, *Making the Second Ghetto: Race and Housing in Chicago, 1940-1960* (Cambridge: Cambridge University Press, 1983). On the demographic and economic shifts after World War II, see also Kenneth T. Jackson, *Crabgrass Frontier: The Suburbanization of the United States* (New York: Oxford University Press, 1985); Robert A. Beauregard, *Voices of Decline: The Postwar Fate of U.S. Cities* (Cambridge, MA: Blackwell Publishers, 1993); Raymond A. Mohl, "The Transformation of Urban America since the Second World War," in *Essays on Sunbelt Cities and Recent Urban America*, ed. Robert B. Fairbanks and Kathleen Underwood (College Station: Texas A&M University Press, 1990), 8–32.
2. Herman H. Long and Charles S. Johnson, *People vs. Property: Race Restrictive Covenants in Housing* (Nashville, TN: Fisk University Press, 1947), 40.
3. Charles Abrams, *Forbidden Neighbors: A Study of Prejudice in Housing* (New York: Harper, 1955), 205–43; Robert C. Weaver, *The Negro Ghetto* (New York: Harcourt, Brace, 1948), 211–303; Norman Williams Jr., "Discrimination and Segregation in Minority Housing," *American Journal of* Economics *and Sociology* 9 (October 1949), 85–101; Christopher Silver, "The Racial Origins of Zoning: Southern Cities from 1910-40," *Planning Perspectives* 6 (1991): 189–205.
4. Clement E. Vose, *Caucasians Only: The Supreme Court, the NAACP, and the Restrictive Covenant Cases* (Berkeley, CA: University of California Press, 1959).
5. Restrictive covenants were outlawed by the U.S. Supreme Court in *Shelley v. Kraemer*, 334 U.S. 1 (1948). The Florida Supreme Court outlawed racial zoning in Miami in *State of Florida v. Wright*, 25 So. 2d 860 (1946). A federal district court banned racial zoning in Birmingham in *City of Birmingham v. Monk*, 185 F. 2d 859 (5th Cir, 1950). See also Jack Greenberg, *Race Relations and American Law* (New York: Columbia University Press, 1959), 275–86.

6.  Arnold R. Hirsch, "With or Without Jim Crow: Black Residential Segregation in the United States," in *Urban Policy in Twentieth-Century America*, ed. Arnold R. Hirsch and Raymond A. Mohl (New Brunswick, NJ: Rutgers University Press, 1993), 90–91; Desmond King, *Separate and Unequal: Black Americans and the US Federal Government* (Oxford: Oxford University Press, 1995), 189–202.

7.  L. K. Northwood and Ernest A. T. Barth, *Urban Desegregation: Negro Pioneers and Their White Neighbors* (Seattle: University of Washington Press, 1965); John Fish, Gordon Nelson, Walter Stuhr, and Lawrence Witmer, *The Edge of the Ghetto: A Study of Church Involvement in Community Organization* (Chicago: Divinity School, University of Chicago, 1966).

8.  On this subject generally, see Davis McEntire, *Residence and Race* (Berkeley, CA: University of California Press, 1960), 175–250; and Rose Helper, *Racial Policies and Practices of Real Estate Brokers* (Minneapolis, MN: University of Minnesota Press, 1969).

9.  Catherine Bauer, "Cities in Flux," *American Scholar* 13 (Winter 1943–44): 70–84; Philip Funigiello, *The Challenge to Urban Liberalism: Federal-City Relations During World War II* (Knoxville, TN: University of Tennessee Press, 1978): 3–38; Reynolds Farley, "The Urbanization of Negroes in the United States," *Journal of Social History* 1 (Spring 1968): 241–58.

10. Kenneth Fox, *Metropolitan America: Urban Life and Urban Policy in the United States, 1940-1980* (Jackson, MS: University of Mississippi Press, 1986), 51; U.S. Census of Population, 1940, tables 35 and 36; U.S. Census of Population, 1960, tables 44 and 45.

11. U.S. Census of Population, 1940, tables 35 and 36; U.S. Census of Population, 1960, tables 44 and 45.

12. For the racial violence accompanying the earlier black migration, see Elliot M. Rudwick, *Race Riot at East St. Louis, July 2, 1917* (Carbondale, IL: Southern Illinois University, 1964); William M. Tuttle Jr., *Race Riot: Chicago in the Red Summer of 1919* (New York: Atheneum, 1970); David Allan Levine, *Internal Combustion: The Races in Detroit, 1915-1926* (Westport, CT: Greenwood Press, 1976); Herbert Shapiro, *White Violence and Black Response: From Reconstruction to Montgomery* (Amherst, MA: University of Massachusetts Press, 1988).

13. Shapiro, *White Violence and Black Response*, 377; Hirsch, *Making the Second Ghetto*, 40–67.

14. Hirsch, *Making the Second Ghetto*, 52; Arnold R. Hirsch, "Massive Resistance in the Urban North: Trumbull Park, Chicago, 1953-1966," *Journal of American History* 82 (September 1995): 522–50; Thomas J. Sugrue, "The Structures of

Urban Poverty: The Reorganization of Space and Work in Three Periods of American History," in *The "Underclass" Debate: Views from History*, ed. Michael B. Katz (Princeton: Princeton University Press, 1993), 111–12; John F. Bauman, *Public Housing, Race, and Renewal: Urban Planning in Philadelphia, 1920–1974* (Philadelphia: Temple University Press, 1987), 161; Raymond A. Mohl, "Making the Second Ghetto in Metropolitan Miami, 1940–1960," *Journal of Urban History* 21 (March 1995): 395–427.

15. Long and Johnson, *People vs. Property*, 67–69; Abrams, *Forbidden Neighbors*, 181–90.

16. George L. Schmutz, "Sidelights on Appraisal Methods," *Review of the Society of Residential Appraisers* 14 (June 1948): 18; George A. Phillips, "Racial Infiltration," ibid., 16 (February 1950): 7–9.

17. Long and Johnson, *People vs. Property*, 58; Hirsch, "With or Without Jim Crow," 75; McEntire, *Residence and Race*, 175–98; Abrams, *Forbidden Neighbors*, 150–68; National Association of Home Builders, *Home Builders Manual for Land Development* (Washington, DC: National Association of Home Builders, 1953), 17.

18. Frederick M. Babcock, *The Valuation of Real Estate* (New York: McGraw-Hill, 1932), 86–92.

19. Arthur M. Weimer and Homer Hoyt, *Principles of Urban Real Estate* (New York: Ronald Press, 1948), 123, 129.

20. Henry E. Hoagland, *Real Estate Principles*, 3rd. ed. (New York: McGraw-Hill, 1955), 64–65, 236.

21. Byrl N. Boyce and William N. Kinnard Jr., *Appraising Real Property* (Lexington, MA: D. C. Heath, 1984), 125.

22. On the HOLC appraisal system in practice, see Kenneth T. Jackson, "Race, Ethnicity, and Real Estate Appraisal: The Home Owners Loan Corporation and the Federal Housing Administration," *Journal of Urban History* 6 (August 1980): 419–52; Raymond A. Mohl, "Trouble in Paradise: Race and Housing in Miami During the New Deal Era," *Prologue: Journal of the National Archives* 19 (Spring 1987): 7–21.

23. Federal Housing Administration, *Underwriting Manual* (Washington, DC: U.S. Government Printing Office, 1938); Robert E. Forman, *Black Ghettos, White Ghettos, and Slums* (Englewood Cliffs, NJ: Prentice Hall, 1971), 69–72; Joe R. Feagin and Clairece Booher Feagin, *Discrimination American Style: Institutional Racism and Sexism* (Englewood Cliffs, NJ: Prentice Hall, 1978), 105–7.

24. Abrams, *Forbidden Neighbors*, 229–30.

25. McEntire, *Residence and Race*, 291–346; Long and Johnson, *People vs. Property*, 69–72; and for a case study of Black removal, Raymond A. Mohl, "Race and Space in the Modern City: Interstate 95 and the Black Community in Miami," in Hirsch and Mohl, *Urban Policy in Twentieth-Century America*, 100–158.

26. Hirsch, *Making the Second Ghetto*, 9.

27. Roy Wenzlick, "Land Appraising," *Real Estate Analyst* 18 (June 10, 1949): 233–36; Roy Wenzlick, "Migratory Population Changes by Race," ibid., 23 (June 30,1954): 260–61. On Wenzlick, see also Louise Cooper, "Real Estate's Prophet," *Freehold: The Magazine of Real Estate* 9 (May 1942): 39–44.

# A House Is Not a Home
## *White Racism and U.S. Housing Practices*

Joe R. Feagin

## THE FLIGHT FROM WHITE RACISM

WHITE RACISM IS the most fundamental if the least discussed of the causes of black-white tensions and conflict in U.S. cities. By *white racism* I mean the entrenched prejudices of white Americans, the subtle and blatant acts of discrimination by these whites, and the institutionalized system of oppression created by nearly 400 years of that prejudice and discrimination. White racism is antiblack prejudice added to the power of whites, acting on that prejudice, to change black lives—in workplaces, schools, and neighborhoods.

In April 1992 in Southern California the verdict of a suburban jury that included no black citizens exonerated four white Los Angeles police officers of police brutality. Several urban rebellions were triggered by this jury decision, and for a brief time the black urban rebellions brought issues of urban racial relations back into national media and policy discussions. Surveys of the black residents of central city areas where rebellions occur, in the 1960s as well as *the* 1980s and 1990s, have consistently found that those residents cite poor housing conditions, including racial discrimination in housing, as a major underlying cause of the uprisings (National Advisory Commission on Civil Disorders 1968; Feagin and Harm 1973).

In recent years the news media treatment of white racism has been poor. I recently searched for the term white racism in Mead Data Central's Lexis/ Nexis database of more than 160 magazines and newspapers. *Not one* of the many thousands of articles in the period February-May 1992 (before and after the Los Angeles rebellion) had a headline that included "white racism." This neglect of the centrality of white racism today extends from the mass media to social science research.

Of course, there have been some important shifts in mainstream social science thinking about racial issues since the 1960s. For example, as a result of the 1960s' civil rights movement and ghetto riots, many influential white social scientists, together with journalists and politicians, supported new civil rights laws and reconceptualized U.S. racial relations in relatively radical terms. The new intellectual discourse moved away from terms ' blaming black families and black culture to mostly new terms blaming whites. The latter included sharp terms, such as *white racism* and *institutional racism*. For example, the final report of the 1968 presidential Commission on Civil Disorders, drawing on research by social scientists, concluded that "our Nation is moving toward two societies, one black, one white—separate and unequal" and minced no words about white responsibility: "White society is deeply implicated in the ghetto. White institutions created it, white institutions maintain it, and white society condones it. … White racism is essentially responsible for the explosive mixture which has been accumulating in our cities." The report added that one of the major ingredients in white racism is "pervasive discrimination and segregation in employment, education, and housing, which have resulted in the continuing exclusion of great numbers of Negroes from the benefits of economic progress" (National Advisory Commission on Civil Disorders 1968, 1, 5).

In the 1970s there was discontent among influential whites in academia, the media, and government over affirmative action remedies and the growing power of blacks in traditionally white institutions. Since then there has been a significant shift in how most influential white scholars, journalists, politicians, and jurists view black-white issues. Recent media articles have concluded that the "two societies" verdict of the 1968 riot commission was much too harsh. For example, the authors of a March 1988 *Newsweek* article argued that "mercifully, America today is not the bitterly sundered dual society the riot commission grimly foresaw" (19). Terms such as institutional racism have mostly been eliminated from white media and government analyses, and from the most influential academic policy analyses, largely because they represent analytical concepts too uncharitable to white America.

### Studying White Racism in the Housing Sphere

Yet, tragically, the reality of racial discrimination in the United States is much different than this commonplace white portrait suggests. In my own work on the discrimination faced by middle-class blacks, I have found that one must leave the ivory tower and go out and talk to those most directly affected about their lived experience with everyday racism. Many recent studies of black American problems, adopting a neo-conservative approach, have *not* gone into the field to observe what is happening to black Americans in housing or other important institutional arenas.

To ascertain the current conditions of this black middle class, I undertook a study, using black interviewers, of 209 middle-class black respondents in sixteen cities across the country. The in-depth interviews consisted mostly of open-ended questions that elicited experiences with racial barriers on the street and in public accommodations, employment, housing, and education.[1] In this chapter I will explore the panoply of dimensions of racial discrimination in housing that is faced *by* black Americans, with illustrations from some of the interviews.

## THE BLACK AMERICAN DREAM OF HOUSE AND HOME

The right to a decent apartment or house is considered by most Americans, white and black, to be a central part of the American dream, one lived out in residential areas in every U.S. city. Middle-class black Americans clearly consider that part of the American dream to be very important; as one my respondents, an experienced teacher, expressed it: "I would like to have my dream home in the next year, and I'm serious." Similarly, in a recent survey of 1,500 Americans the polling firm Peter Halt and Associates found large percentages of Americans, black and white, viewing home ownership as a central part of the American dream, one worth sacrificing for. In an interview Peter Hart concluded: "Homeownership is really at the heart of middle-class values, of what America is about. … It is really all their dreams and all their hopes." John Buckley, a senior vice president of the agency Fannie Mae, commented on the survey s findings of strong black orientation to home ownership: "What was so significant about [these] findings for us was it made crystal-clear that the intensity of desire to own a home increases in inverse relationship to your ability to do it." He added that even those of moderate income in central cities do not need to be persuaded to desire home ownership (*American Political Network Hotline* 1992).

For most Americans, black and white, housing is more than a matter of a place to live. Housing represents not only pride of ownership of property but also a visible manifestation of accomplishments, one's standing in society, even one's character. Indeed, in the case of black Americans it is very important to understand just how important the home haven really is.

### *A Black Person's Home as a Place of Safety*

A black middle-class respondent working in a western state articulated this point: "Once we have a nice place to live, maybe we can think about becoming successful. Before we can move ahead, we have to have a place to go home to, You cannot be a doctor or a lawyer if you're worried about where you're going to be staying, and if you have a meal or a warm bed."

For most families, black and white, one's housing is usually one's *home,* one of the important anchors against the turbulence of daily life. Yet not all groups in this society are alike in the significance of places of refuge. For middle-class blacks pioneering in white institutions, home often represents the only reliable anchor available to them in a hostile white-dominated world.

Let me document how home is a central fortress for those black Americans I interviewed. Putting the subject succinctly, a corporate executive in the Northeast was clear about the only place he did not encounter racial discrimination:

> The only place it probably doesn't affect me, I guess, is in my home; specifically, actually, in the interior portions of my home.

The duality of the black daily experience was explained by a manager at an electronics firm:

> Well, I think you really kind of lead dual lives. You live a life that you can be black when you go home, and then a life you live white being at work.

In other words, one cannot be oneself in the white world.

But what of one's white friends? Supposedly the desegregation of the traditionally white worlds has opened up other places of refuge outside home. But very few whites can really relate to blacks in the intimate way that family and close black friends can, as an airline manager said:

> So I can't discuss it with white friends, and I do have white friends, but they're just, I mean, like I said, in the industry, the neighborhood, the situations that I'm in, there just aren't that many black people. So my husband and my family become the stabilizing force for bouncing off situations.

A college student at a predominantly white university explained that it is hard to make close friendships with whites outside the home:

> I said number one, that white people, an example is that, when you have a white person and a black person who are friends, and this comes from my own personal experience, the black person cannot be a true, whole person with that white person

without offending them, without embarrassing them, without putting them on the defensive because, I'm sorry, friendship to me is when you share your whole self. And if I have to leave my black self at home somewhere so the white person doesn't see it, that's not a friendship.

One respondent explained the problem of having to be superficial in white social networks:

So, you just keep on a level where everything's pretty much on the surface, and you don't have to delve into a lot of the personal characteristics, and you can get along easier I think. And most of the time black people have to be almost plastic in their own personal opinions just to go with the opinions of most white folks, just to get along, to do certain things, like going to movies, or just listening to bands. If you're with a large group of whites and there's a small number of blacks, you pretty much will get outvoted on where to go, so you pretty much pretend, or will put up with it just to go with the evening, when you'd rather possibly be someplace listening to a real good jazz, or whatever, black-oriented music place. So, I think most black people have hold to back their, the stuff that they really like, the stuff that would identify them and make them black, just so they can be accepted and get along and work with the white people, since they're going to have to be in a situation a majority of the time.

He then added sharply that home, the black family and friends network, is where you can be yourself as a black person:

I guess when they come home, is when they really become, that's when they're really black, and it's just a shame, because they have to hold that back when they're around white people because white people just probably won't be able to understand it, or really accept it or maybe they don't even want to accept it because it's something they don't want to do.

Another respondent discussed how he separates home from social interaction with coworkers:

I deal with it [racial discrimination] by basically being able to have my own home and my own circle of friends and communicating that with my several friends as to my experiences. When I have that in combination, I think that I'm able to have a normal lifestyle. When I say this, too, I don't really like to get involved with inviting my coworkers *to* my home or whatever. It's a funny thing that I feel this way.

Home is a place where blacks can retreat from racial discrimination and not have to deal with white America. This is a critical problem for middle-class black Americans, who must spend large amounts of time with white Americans as a consequence of their middle-class stature.

One respondent spoke of how quickly one may turn to the haven of one's home:

> And sometimes you can get enraged, and then you have to go home. You call and say, I'm going home no w, and you j ust leave, because you know if you don't leave, you're not going to be very professional in your behavior and you just leave.

Speaking in lucid language, yet another saw home as a healing place;

> My family helped me by giving me a strong *sense* of self-awareness. And my friends the friends that I have, we talk and we're able to process some things and be mutually supportive. But I think that's basically the way I am, I have a strong sense of community. One of the things that we have as black folk is that when the white world bites us, we know that we can come home and find some healing there. And when I say home, I mean community.

Home here has connotations of the larger black community. One's personal network broadens out to include many other networks, and ultimately the local black community.

An attorney described how home is used to discuss the solutions to specific white discrimination encountered during the day:

> With my husband, I guess, he's got a lot of little situations that may crop up mostly at work, and he would come home and tell me, and I would think about it and say, "You know, this is the way you should have handled it, because I've been in that situation before. And what they expect is typically the way you did. So why don't you do this at the next group meeting you have, or say this at the *next,* and see what their reaction is or something?" So we just work out a strategy to deal with them. The *next* time, it's totally not what they expected.

Another respondent discussed her husband and detailed the problems that she and the home must handle:

> He would bring home, and times, you know, you could say, "Did you have a nice day?" and he'd chew you up, you know what I'm saying? You can have dinner on the table and that's not what I want. And at first, my feelings would be hurt, you know,

'cause I'm trying to be a good wife I learned how to deal with that. I owe it to the times learning how to not bring it home, because I found myself jumping back on him, "Listen, I had a rough one, too. I left that stuff at work, and that's where you better leave yours, and you get that door again, you pick it back up and go ahead off.'" You know, home's where you can come and relax and, you know, don't have to worry about that outside world right now.

A school board member in an eastern city made it clear what letting down one's guard and "being real" at home entails:

My mother laughs now, because when all of us are home—I have five sisters and brothers—when we're all home—we're college educated, we speak distinctly, and we enunciate and enumerate our words appropriately—but when we're home, it's "get down." You know you don't care about how you say things, it's "dis" and "dat." And my mother laughs and says, "you wouldn't believe [it] if you came in here, they're all college graduates. Why do you speak that way?"

Middle-class black Americans live a dual life—one way with whites and *one* way in the home place. Even, or perhaps especially, well-educated and successful black Americans face a hostile white world that has allowed only one way integration. The traditional corporate and government workplace is white-normed and white-dominated; as a result, blacks must constantly be on guard and regularly find themselves, even subconsciously, on the defensive. The reason seems to be that societal integration has not meant radical institutional change, or personal change on the part of most whites. Whites in power have rarely restructured the warp and woof of their organizations to incorporate black subculture, values, or interests.

The importance of home puts the problem of blacks' getting decent housing in hospitable neighborhoods in the proper perspective. "Fair housing" must be more than a matter of getting a decent house. It must come to encompass the whole process of getting housing for *one's* family, including all contacts with whites involved in the housing selection and choice process and with whites in the neighborhood once one has the house or apartment. Only then can a house truly become a home.

### The Struggle for Decent Housing

U.S. cities have historically segregated black Americans from white Americans. Seen from a distance, the racial ecology of U.S. cities today is not much different from the segregation geography of the past, with most blacks living in mostly black areas and most whites living in almost all-white areas. Recent research using 1990 census data shows that blacks only became slightly less segregated during the 1980s. Black Americans are still the most segregated of all U.S. racial and ethnic groups, with nearly two-thirds today residing in residential blocks that are heavily black in composition (Vobejda 1992, AT). In addition, most white Americans still live in mostly white neighborhoods. Another analysis of 1990 census data found that black residents were highly segregated in most of the 47 large cities, such as Detroit, Chicago, and Miami, where they constituted at least one-fifth of the population (USA Today 1991).

The housing racism of the late twentieth century is somewhat different from the housing racism of earlier decades, in that a few black families now live, or have tried to reside, in many historically white areas in virtually every city in the United States. State and federal laws make official discrimination illegal. But this does not mean that there is no longer serious housing discrimination. There are still the informal patterns and mechanisms of housing discrimination.

## DISCUSSION QUESTIONS

1. What meaning do African Americans attach to their homes in relation to discrimination?
2. Why is it important to study middle-class African American attitudes and experiences with regard to housing and discrimination? How might these perspectives differ from low-income African Americans?
3. What shifts occurred in the thinking of social scientists about the subject of "White racism? " Why were these shifts important?

## NOTE

1. Using a snowball sample, I interviewed 209 black respondents in 1988–1990. About 65 percent of the respondents were residents of cities in the South and Southwest; about 6 percent were in West Coast or Midwest cities; and 29 percent were in Northeast or Middle Atlantic cities. Many have lived in several regions, and some comments refer to places other than where the individual resides now. Just over half are in the 36-to-50-years age bracket, with 32 percent in the 18-to~36 bracket and 16 percent in the 51-plus age bracket. Some are heads of their own businesses, and a few are students who probably will hold white-collar jobs. Most are corporate managers, doctors or other health care professionals, lawyers, electronic and computer professionals, teachers,

government officials, college administrators, journalists or others in mass media, or clerical or sales workers. Eight percent reported household incomes of $20,000 or less, while 22 percent reported incomes in the $21,000–35,000 range; 23 percent in the $36,000–55,000 range; and 47 percent in the $56,000 or more range. All but a handful, mostly students, had household incomes above the black median family income for 1989. The sample is well educated. All have at least a high school degree, and 96 percent have completed some college work. About 80 percent have a college degree. Most are thus in the upper reaches of the black middle class.

## REFERENCES

*American Political Network Hotline.* 1992. Interview: Hart and Buckley on home ownership survey. In Lexis Computer Database (June).

Bates, James. 1992. Obstacle course. *Los Angeles Times,* 6 September.

Bisceglia, Joseph G. 1973- Blockbusting: Judicial and legislative response to real estate dealers' excesses. *De Paul Law Review* 22 (Spring): 818–38.

Byrne, James. 1992. Lenders set plans to eliminate unintentional discrimination; more bad numbers expected. *American Banker-Bond Buyer,* 21 September.

Feagin, Joe R., and Clarece B. Feagin. 1986. *Discrimination American style.* 2d ed. Malabar, Fla.: Kriege.

Feagin, Joe R., and Harlan Hahn. 1973. *Ghetto revolts.* New York: Macmillan. Foundation for Change. 1974. *Fact sheets on institutional racism: White control and minority oppression.* New York: Foundation for Change.

Grezzo, Anthony D. 1972. *Mortgage credit risk analysis and servicing of delinquent mortgages.* Washington, D.C.: U.S. Department of Housing and Urban Development.

Helper, Rose. 1969. *Racial policies and practices of 'real estate brokers.* Minneapolis: University of Minnesota Press.

Jaynes, Gerald D., and Robin Williams, Jr. 1989. *A common destiny: Blacks and American society.* Washington, D.C.: National Academy Press.

Massey, Douglas S. 1992. Shrugging off racism. *Washington Post,* 17 May.

Massey, Douglas S., and Nancy A Denton. 1987. Trends in segregation of blacks, Hispanics and Asians, 1970–1980. *American Sociological Review* 52:802–25.

Myrdal, Gunnar. 1944. *An American dilemma.* New York: McGraw-Hill.

National Advisory Commission on Civil Disorders. 1968. *Report of the National Advisory Commission on Civil Disorders.* Washington, D.C.: U.S. Government Printing Office.

National Opinion Research Center. 1990. *General social survey.* Chicago: University of Chicago.

*Newsday.* 1990. The walls between us. 15 October.

*Newsweek.* 1988. Black and White America. 7 March.

Office of Thrift Supervision. 1989. *Report on loan discrimination. Washington,* D.C.: Office of the Treasury.

Pearce, Diana M. 1976. Black, white, and many shades of gray: Real estate brokers and their racial practices. Ph.D. diss., University of Michigan.

*USA Today.* 1991. World of difference. 11 November.

U.S. Census Bureau. 1985. *American housing survey.* Washington, D.C.: U.S. Government Printing Office.

U.S. Commission on Civil Rights. 1974. *Mortgage money: Who gets it,* Washington, D.C.: U.S. Government Printing Office.

U.S. Senate. 1990. Transcript of Confirmation Hearings for David Souter, 14 September.

Vobejda, Barbara. 1992. Neighborhood racial patterns little changed. *Washington Post,* 18 March.

Wilson, William J. 1987. *The truly disadvantaged: The inner city, the underclass, and public policy,* Chicago: University of Chicago Press.

——— (1978) *The declining significance of race,* Chicago: University of Chicago Press.

# CHAPTER 7

# Racism and Education

# Asian Americans and the Shifting Politics of Race
## *Asian Americans as Victim and Success Stories*

**Rowena Robles**

*Excerpter's note: In 1994 a group of students and their parents filed suit against the San Francisco Unified School District (SFUSD). They claimed its policy that required schools, such as Lowell High School, the premiere academic high school in the district, to enroll no more than a fixed percentage of students from a single racial group discriminated against Chinese American students based solely on their race.*

THE *Brian Ho, Patrick Wong & Hilary Chen v. SFUSD* lawsuit was waged by a group of Chinese Americans and effectively ended race-based school integration in the San Francisco Unifed School District. The Chinese American plaintiffs sued the San Francisco school district to contest the legal decision awarded to the National Association for the Advancement of Colored People (NAACP). It was the NAACP's original suit that resulted in the desegregation policy established in 1983, known as the San Francisco Unified School District's Consent Decree. The *Ho* lawsuit directly attacked one of the primary vestiges of the civil rights movement—the idea that all public school students are entitled to an equal education, from elementary to high school, regardless of race. More specifically, through desegregation, the Consent Decree has attempted to ensure that African Americans and other racial minorities are not relegated to "inherently unequal" public schools.

The *Brian Ho* lawsuit was evidence of political and public policy shifts away from an overt focus on race in education policy, as well as of how the Asian American supporters and plaintiffs of *Ho* have exploited this shift. Although *Ho* legally pointed to the dismantling of the Consent Decree, the main issue presented by the plaintiffs—that of race-based school assignments restricting the choice of Chinese American students[1]— was strengthened by a larger neoconservative project, namely the backlash against affirmative action and the rise of neoconservatism. *Ho* was not just a direct attack on the Consent Decree, it also "launche(d) a broad attack on race-based remedies."[2]

More generally, the *Ho* lawsuit demonstrated how far we have come as a nation from the civil rights movement that initiated African American struggles for social justice in the form of racial equality. Crenshaw states that,

> The image of a 'traditional civil rights discourse' refers to the constellation of ideas about racial power and social transformation that were constructed … by … the mass mobilization of social energy and popular imagination in the civil rights movements of the late fifties and sixties.[3]

This movement's victories and legal tenets, specifically "equal rights" and "equality of opportunity," were co-opted by a neoconservative movement to further its own agenda. This neoconservative agenda also incorporates a racial project in which the propagation of colorblindness, along with the idea of meritocracy, has worked to obscure the continuing significance of race in the debates around affirmative action, desegregation, and other race-conscious policies.

The Chinese students and parents behind the lawsuit contended that the goals and objectives of the Consent Decree never represented their particular group's interests, regardless of the fact that the desegregation mandate was designed to benefit all racial and ethnic groups. As the San Francisco Unified School District pointed out, "(the Decree) was not designed only to integrate African Americans with whites; the plan recognizes nine different racial and ethnic groups for desegregation purposes."[4] The *Ho* plaintiffs and supporters believed that they and other Chinese American public school students in San Francisco, were being discriminated against because of the stipulations of the 1983 Consent Decree.

The *Ho* plaintiffs embraced the Asian American Model Minority stereotype and articulated their cause through this racial myth. On the one hand, the dual construction of Asian Americans—as victims and as success stories—fit the agenda of the larger neoconservative political and social project. On the other, some Asian Americans also accepted this arguably positive racial construction. How did the plaintiffs' and supporters' framing of the case racially construct Chinese Americans, and how did they assert this racial construction? In a broader sense, how do the political sentiments of the Chinese American supporters of this case situate all other Asian Americans? The answers to these questions can be found in the way race, racial construction, and neoconservative politics meshed to produce the political and social climate in which the *Ho* lawsuit was filed.

A myriad of social and political factors come into play in a discussion of the *Ho* lawsuit. First, the Republican and neoconservative assault on affirmative action frames Asian Americans as a minority group that does not need racial considerations in admissions and is harmed by these policies. Second, the assertion of race by the *Ho* plaintiffs and supporters as the Model Minority fits squarely within the neoconservative propagation of colorblindness and meritocracy within education policy and politics. While these political catchphrases appear to be racially neutral, they still work to evoke race and construct African Americans and Latinos as undeserving beneficiaries of race-based policies, necessarily antithetical to the construction of Asian Americans as high-achieving victims of these policies. In this reading, I attempt to demonstrate how the Asian American supporters of the *Ho* lawsuit utilize a combination of racial stereotypes and neoconservative ideologies to further their cause within these highly politicized discursive contexts. While larger political and social forces racially construct minority groups such as African Americans and Latinos, the *Ho* plaintiffs and supporters demonstrate how Asian Americans possess the ability to transcend race—specifically negative racial stereotypes—and assert an arguably positive racial stereotype through the Model Minority Myth. In doing so, they effectively produce the simultaneous construction of victim and success story.

## SITUATING ASIAN AMERICANS WITHIN TRADITIONAL CIVIL RIGHTS GOALS AND THE NEW NEOCONSERVATIVE IDEOLOGY

The issues that underlie the lawsuit possess a larger history, involving both desegregation and affirmative action policies. The *Ho* plaintiffs, however, argued for colorblind policies that ensure meritocratic admissions and rearticulated recent history to situate the plaintiffs as both victims of past discrimination and victims of the policies addressing discrimination in the present. Ironically, their argument garnered widespread acceptance because they were Asian American and not white males crying reverse discrimination. The *Ho* lawsuit may not have been accepted judicially by the courts or socially by the public had not the tenor and meaning of equal rights and civil rights shifted in the larger political and social contexts. These shifts include the anti-affirmative action backlash as well as the growth and spread of neoconservative rhetoric, with the *Ho* lawsuit fitting squarely within and even complementing these political changes.

The success and widespread acceptance of the *Ho* lawsuit and the neoconservative and anti-affirmative action ideals it represents emerged within a context that is a turning point in the history of racial politics in the United States. Within this context, we can view the utilization of traditional civil rights demands for neoconservative ends. The *Ho* suit represents how the racist arguments of anti-affirmative action forces were changed to advocate an "end to discrimination" and a push for "equality of opportunity"—both rearticulated to demand an end to race-based policies such as affirmative action.

Although *Ho v. SFUSD* legally pointed to the dismantling of the Consent Decree and ending race-based desegregation, the main issue presented by the plaintiffs—that of race-based school assignment restricting the choice of Chinese American students[5]— was strengthened by the links between the backlash against affirmative action and the rise of neoconservatism. The politics of neoconservatism attempt to garner widespread support by simultaneously attacking anti-discriminatory policies such as affirmative action and advocating individual rights.[6] The cornerstone of this ideology rests on the "rearticulation of the meaning of racial equality as a matter of individual rather than group or collective concern."[7] In contrast, a basic tenet of the civil rights movement was group rights. Neoconservatives utilize the term, racial equality, yet envision racial equality to be the end of race-based policies. Instead, they put forth the belief that racial discrimination lies at the heart of these policies. The key in the political and legal strategy of the *Ho* plaintiffs was that by asserting a neoconservative stance, they were able to make the contradictory claims of being discriminated against while also taking an anti-affirmative action position.

The neoconservative stance propagated by the *Ho* plaintiffs and supporters both alludes to discriminatory treatment and encapsulates the larger backlash against affirmative action and other race-based policies. Their seamless merging of these contradictory ideals exemplifies the political strength of rearticulation. Michael Omi and Howard Winant define rearticulation by neoconservative forces as redefinitions of traditional civil rights ideals.

> The minority movements of the 1950s and 1960s ... definitively questioned (the) social assignment of identities and racial meanings. It was this questioning, this challenge, that the neoconservatives sought to confine and reorganize in their assault on affirmative action. They did this by limiting the meaning of racial discrimination to the curtailment of individual rights. ... The social logic of race was thus rendered opaque. ... [8]

This neoconservative assault on race-based policies has taken flight as the meanings of discrimination and equality have shifted to focus on the harm inflicted upon individuals as opposed to groups classified by race.

The neoconservative framing of race-based policies such as affirmative action, had been gaining momentum and garnering widespread support since the 1980s.[9] This political and social context created the space in which the *Ho* supporters were able to employ neoconservative language around racial equality and gain support. For example, the Chinese plaintiffs declared that "the justification for race-conscious assignment policies has ended."[10] The group believed that they were not being treated equitably or fairly and felt that this unfair treatment stemmed from the fact that they are Chinese. Lawrence Siskind, a San Francisco attorney and supporter of the lawsuit was quoted as stating, "A yellow skin can be a curse in San Francisco."[11]

In employing neoconservative definitions of racial discrimination, the *Ho* plaintiffs and supporters offered a convoluted version of equality that is widely accepted in the current political climate. The Chinese Americans involved in the *Ho* lawsuit claimed to "not (be) opposed to affirmative action."[12] The plaintiffs and supporters of the lawsuit, however, still put forth the racially coded language of neoconservative and anti-affirmative action forces and subliminally pointed to the undeserving beneficiaries of these policies—stereotypically framed as African Americans and Latinos. The *Ho* argument appeared to be one that included Chinese American students as a group, but it really focused on the individual rights of these students. Because they were actually arguing for the individual rights of Chinese American students, the contradictions in their argument lay in how they purported claims of discrimination against the group as a whole—an effective strategy for them politically but, in the end, detrimental to race-conscious policies.

The supporters of the *Ho* lawsuit simultaneously evoked racist and prejudicial treatment along with their rearticulated version of discrimination. This neoconservative version of racial equality confuses racist treatment with racial considerations in education policy. The supporters of *Ho* linked these racist experiences to the allegedly discriminatory aspects of the desegregation policy. The supporters and plaintiffs of the *Ho* suit directly appealed to the idea of being discriminated against—that they as minorities have experienced racial discrimination and now desire "equality." Lee Cheng, the vice-chair of the Chinese American Democratic Club's (CADC) Educational Reform Task Force, utilized his personal experiences to demonstrate this neoconservative rhetoric.

> "I grew up knowing a lot of racism," said Cheng, 23, (then) a UC Berkeley law student … "I was beaten up as a kid, referred to as a chink, a Chinaman. But in school I was taught that the laws will treat everyone the same, that discrimination was being eliminated. … Then my friends and I applied to public high school. We discovered that if you are Chinese, you have to do better than anyone else."[13]

Cheng equated desegregation, specifically Lowell High School's affirmative action policy, to that of discrimination. Several issues and concepts were combined here in order to affect a neoconservative tone that simultaneously evokes civil rights ideology—notably the elimination of what they perceive as racially discriminatory practices—and opposition to race-based policies.

For the supporters of the *Ho* lawsuit, racial discrimination was equated with the racial and ethnic caps imposed on all groups in order to achieve integrated schools. The CADC believed that these caps constituted discriminatory treatment. The *Ho* plaintiffs and supporters claimed that they have experienced racial discrimination firsthand, and equated the desegregation policy with racism. In comments made to a reporter, Daniel Girard, the attorney representing the (Ho) parents said, "Diversity doesn't justify racial discrimination in public assignments. ... Don't treat Chinese people differently and don't penalize them for being Chinese. Let's put an end to race-based assignments."[14] Girard alludes to racial discrimination in his statement while also denigrating race-based policies. In this statement, one can view how neoconservative "logic" situates the *Ho* plaintiffs as a racial minority group that is experiencing discrimination and that is being penalized in order to uphold desegregation policies. The underlying subtext is that Asian Americans are succeeding, yet are being penalized for this academic success.

Roland Quan, one of the leading members of the CADC, labeled the racial and ethnic ceilings imposed on all SFUSD schools as a form of discrimination.

> "We're just trying to end discrimination against Chinese Americans by lifting the caps," Quan said. "Last year, 94 students were rejected from Lowell because of their race. How can you tell a student you can't get in because you were born Chinese? If you tell them they couldn't get in because there weren't enough seats, that's something else."[15]

Quan reframed the debate on affirmative action admissions to Lowell by completely removing the larger context of the desegregation Consent Decree and its goals. He, instead, emphasized the rejection of Chinese American students, while omitting their over-representation at Lowell and other San Francisco magnet high schools. He pointed to their race as the sole reason for rejection.

Again, the goals of the Consent Decree and desegregation policies were rearticulated and presented by the CADC as attempts to disenfranchise Chinese-American students. While the original intent of both desegregation and affirmative action policies was to provide historically underprivileged groups access to educational equality, the CADC stance jeopardized these goals. The neoconservative rearticulation of these policies has been a concerted effort of those groups whom these policies do not include, such as white males and presently some Asian American groups, to ensure prime public education for their children without a concern for the greater social good. In addition to equating the desegregation policy to discriminatory treatment, the CADC also considered the policy "racist" and "unequal." Cheng referenced the civil rights movement in his stance against the consideration of race in pupil assignments and puts forth that the maintenance of race in student assignments is a racist throwback to George Wallace.

> Right about now … the disciples of preference appear ready to engage in a protracted campaign of trench warfare to maintain unequal, racist policies despite overwhelming public opposition to entitlements based on race. Vast amounts of resources and … creativity, have and are being spent in attempts to overturn or circumvent limitations on the use of racial preferences.[16]

Those who supported desegregation and affirmative action were now "disciples of preference"[17]—not civil rights activists, progressives, or liberals. They were essentially cast as upholding racism through their endorsement of racial considerations, which Cheng labels racial preferences, and victimizing Chinese American students in doing so.

The dual construction of Asian Americans as success stories as well as victims of discriminatory treatment through race-based preferences is complex and multi-layered. Beginning in the 1980s, portrayals of Asian Americans as the Model Minority filled newspapers and magazines. These range from labeling them as the "New Whiz Kids" to highlighting prestigious colleges and universities that were composed largely of Asian American students.[18] In the mid 1990s, these stereotypic constructions began to change along with an upsurge in the backlash against affirmative action. Asian Americans became viewed as victims of their own success. Whereas before they were lauded and praised for their achievements, now their success was arguably threatened by policies such as affirmative action, effectively creating their dual construction as both success stories and victims.

Along with the strategic political construction of Asian Americans as the Model Minority, neoconservative rearticulations of equality and discrimination have opened up a space in which traditional calls for civil rights and equal access are no longer politically powerful. While the supporters of the *Ho* lawsuit demanded that race-based policies be ended in the district, the SFUSD and NAACP fought back, arguing that racial diversity and representation was still necessary. Unfortunately, the court did not view their calls for equal access as legally and politically viable, proving that those who continue to support civil rights law and advocacy must find new ways to do battle with those who oppose race-based policies.[19]

By asserting this political stance and racial identity, the supporters of *Ho* "launch(ed) a broad attack on race-based remedies."[20] The *Ho* plaintiffs and supporters believed that they were furthering their legal case, yet they were also perpetuating harm on other groups who had benefited from the racial considerations in desegregation and affirmative action policies and who were eventually harmed by the outcome. The assertion of the Model Minority Myth[21] worked to situate African American and Latino students as the antithesis of this stereotype—the underachieving and undeserving beneficiaries of affirmative action policies.

## THE ASIAN AMERICAN MODEL MINORITY STEREOTYPE AS RACIAL CURRENCY IN A "COLORBLIND" SOCIETY

Interestingly and rather ironically, Asian Americans have been able to articulate race through the end of affirmative action policies and the ensuing incorporation of colorblindness, merit, and equality into educational policy debates. In contrast to African Americans and Latinos, who have been framed negatively as undeserving beneficiaries of these policies, Asian Americans have emerged with a positive stereotype. Further adding to the irony, the focus on the educational sector of society, the same site in which African Americans sought racial justice,[22] has enabled Asian Americans to assert themselves as the Model Minority.

This racial construct of the Model Minority Myth has gained its widespread currency because it functions within the American framework of meritocracy and equality. The *Ho* plaintiffs and supporters have been able to successfully play on a stereotype created by whites. This can be viewed in two ways. On the one hand, Asian Americans as a racial minority are able to exploit an arguably positive stereotype and be accepted into mainstream white society. In the acceptance of this stereotype, they also function as the good minority, in direct contrast to the other minorities who are framed by negative racial stereotyping. Asian Americans as the Model Minority get situated somewhere between black and white racial constructions.

The United States has historically and continues to operate within a simplistic paradigm of race. The black/white model of race relations informs historical as well as current battles around public policy, education, and politics.[23] Asian Americans, neither black nor white, are often constructed as "'near-white' or 'like Blacks.'"[24] This simplistic model of race and race relations and its fixity within the American mindset allows Asian Americans to transcend race to a certain extent. While the black/white racial paradigm remains fixed, Asian Americans, by virtue of the changeability and historical contexts of racial stereotypes, are situated and situate themselves at opposing ends of the model. Operating and shifting back and forth between the black and white ends of the U.S. racial paradigm, Asian Americans exist as both race-less and racially constructed at the same time. Okihiro presents a historical perspective on how Asian Americans have often traversed between black and white racial constructions in the

United States—being framed as black when they immigrated as railroad workers and migrant farm workers, and then as white when larger numbers of professionals from Asia composed a great number of immigrants to the United States[25].

This dynamic nature of the racial construction of Asian Americans works to support the assertions of the Asian Americans involved in the *Ho* lawsuit. Michael Omi and Dana Takagi assert that, "Unlike 'black' and 'white' as racial categories, there is a greater fluidity to 'Asian American' that can be manipulated in particular ways to suit particular positions."[26] They theorize that the media and politicians hold the power to frame and construct Asian Americans as the Model Minority or as more white than black or other. I would add to Omi and Takagi by suggesting that some Asian Americans accept and assert the racial identity of the Model Minority, situating themselves at the white end of the racial paradigm. The widespread acceptance of the black and white model of race could also be viewed as allowing Asian Americans the currency of leaving the black side of the model in favor of the white. This perceived ability of Asian Americans to transcend negative racial stereotypes might even be considered a privileged position.

For the *Ho* plaintiffs, such racial transcendence situated them in a powerful position as well. The power of racial transcendence for Asian Americans was enabled by the elimination of explicit talk about race in all public policy issues, especially in regards to education. Meritocracy, a concept initiated by neoconservatives in their assault on affirmative action, opened up a space in which the Asian American Model Minority gained more acceptance. Neoconservatives have advocated the use of merit to take the place of racial considerations in education policy. Meritocracy works well with the stereotype of the Model Minority—diligent, hard working, and quintessentially apolitical. What is then discussed explicitly within the space in which race was eliminated is the merit and achievement that these Asian American students possess; but what is evoked is race. The Model Minority Myth works both to deflect the need for affirmative action programs (in support of merit) while simultaneously invoking race (in the attempts to garner a political and social backlash against affirmative action and integration). In other words, if merit connotes Asian-ness, then lack of merit connotes black-ness or Latino-ness, which shifts the blame from structural inequalities to underachieving minority groups.

## THE DANGERS OF ASSERTING THE MODEL MINORITY MYTH

In the *Ho* lawsuit, the framing of Chinese Americans as victims of a desegregation policy lay entirely in the hands of a group of Chinese parents and their children. Thus, while the *Ho* lawsuit advocated an end to racial preferences and the institution of color-blindness in admissions policies, the supporters and plaintiffs also effectively employed a discursive strategy in which Asian Americans, specifically Chinese Americans, were cast as victims and African Americans and Latinos[27] were framed as undeserving beneficiaries of the desegregation policy.

While Asian Americans can be seen as political tools for the purposes and goals of conservative and neoconservative politicians and their respective agendas, in the *Ho* example, they can be seen as actively negotiating the racial, political, and social terrain of United States society. By situating themselves as the Model Minority and a "class of innocents"[28] being unfairly harmed by race-conscious policies, the *Ho* plaintiffs and supporters engage in constructing and asserting their race. On the one hand, they are the Model Minority, immigrants or children of immigrants who have achieved educational and professional success. On the other hand, they are also a minority group who believes that they have not personally discriminated against other racial minority groups and, therefore, should not bear the brunt of desegregation and affirmative action policies.

Asian Americans have been able to transcend notions of fault or blame for racial discrimination and prejudice because they themselves are racial minorities. This lack of "fault" on their part, coupled with the Model Minority stereotype, allows Asian Americans to frame themselves as innocents, making the *Ho* lawsuit that much stronger. Additionally, this lack of fault allowed the plaintiffs and supporters of *Ho* to distance themselves from the negative ramifications of their lawsuit, political stance, and racial assertions. The dangers that the *Ho* plaintiffs and supporters initiated with their assertion of the Model Minority Myth include obscuring the need for race-preferential policies and possibly engendering interracial conflicts with other racial minority groups.

This power and privilege of racial framing and constructionism, as well as the acceptance of a socially and politically constructed racial stereotype in the form of the Model Minority, functions to situate Asian Americans such that they may be held in positive esteem. These positive depictions can also work to their detriment when utilized to further neoconservative politics as well as interracial divisions. While the *Ho* plaintiffs and supporters assert the arguably positive aspects of the Model Minority Myth, these positive aspects can also be re-framed such that they are, in the end, damaging to Asian Americans.

In Takagi's study on the Asian Admissions Crisis at some of the United States' premier universities, admissions officers were quick to point out that Asians were "good, but not exceptional students."[29] The power of framing Asian Americans as good or bad, as deserving or not of admissions, resided with the admissions offices and university officials. Also in Nancy Abelmann and John Lie's analysis of the Black and Korean conflict in the aftermath of the 1992 Los Angeles Riots, many Korean American merchants claimed that the media too often took the easy way out and portrayed them as greedy yet successful immigrant entrepreneurs.[30] The power of framing Asian Americans lay in the hands of the mainstream media and university admissions offices; these forces merely extended and re-constructed the Model Minority Myth, negatively in these cases, to suit their political purposes.

While racial constructionism for all racial and ethnic groups has historically lain in the hands of larger political and social forces, 35 Asian Americans have recently been more actively participating in the articulation of their own race. Some Asian Americans, because of their economic and educational achievements, believe that they are now able to dictate their own racial constructions. This is evident in the *Ho* plaintiffs' and supporters' conflation of their racial positionality with that of being a Model Minority. Buying into the Model Minority Myth lends itself to the belief in the American Dream and individual success and away from group empowerment. Situating oneself and one's ethnic group within the hierarchical social formation is one thing. But what if these attempts at positively defining one's positionality negatively affect that of other minority groups, such as Blacks and Latinos?

Since the birth of the Model Minority Myth, Asian Americans have often been pitted against other minority groups. The Model Minority Myth publicizes the academic and professional success of Asian Americans, and attempts to prove that the American Dream is attainable—that minority groups can succeed in the United States. Before the Model Minority Myth, Asians often vacillated between being framed as part of a "yellow peril" invading the United States and the extreme opposite—as a successful minority student and professional, often times "outwhit[ing] the whites" and making great contributions to United States' society.[32] This key paradox embedded within the Model Minority Myth works to prove the inaccuracy of the Myth, but still does not detract from the power of invoking and asserting the Myth.

Many Asian American scholars demonstrate the inaccuracy of the Model Minority Myth with discussions and studies of the high poverty rate, extensive employment stratification, and relatively lower incomes of Asian Americans.[33] Although these scholars definitively dispel the Myth, they do not take power away from the widespread acceptance of the Model Minority stereotype by whites, African Americans, Latinos, and, as in the *Ho* case, Asian Americans. While Asian Americans are placed close to the top of this racial hierarchy, we must also pay attention to who is placed below them and why. Stereotypes regarding whiteness, blackness, and Asian-ness were exploited in order for the *Ho* lawsuit to gain viability within the current political and social contexts, which do not support any race-preferential policies, yet they also cast a negative light on African Americans and Latinos who are never characterized as the Model Minority.

Gary Okihiro recognizes that the Model Minority Myth is more than a mere construction but also a reality. "The construct, importantly, is not merely ideology but is a social practice that assigns to Asian Americans, and indeed to all minorities, places within the social formations."[34] Okihiro illustrates the dangers in accepting any stereotypes, regardless of the positive light they might shed on certain groups, stating that Asians are positioned within an insidious circle, in which the Model Minority can also be equated with the Yellow Peril. "Asian workers can be 'diligent' and 'slavish,' 'frugal' and 'cheap,' 'upwardly mobile' and 'aggressive. ...'"[35] Beyond the stereotypical framings of Asian Americans, their own decisions regarding their personal and political positionality have engaged neoconservative Asian Americans into a hegemonic compromise, in which they are attaining academic and professional success at the expense of African Americans and Latinos.

## CONCLUSIONS

In the case of the *Ho* lawsuit, the framing of Asians as victims of a desegregation policy lay entirely in the hands of a group of Chinese parents and their children. Thus, while the *Ho* lawsuit advocated an end to racial preferences and the institution of colorblindness in admissions policies, the supporters and plaintiffs also effectively utilized a discursive strategy in which Asians, specifically Chinese Americans, were cast as victims and African Americans and Latinos[36] were framed as undeservedly benefiting from a desegregation policy, which was framed by the plaintiffs as a racial preference policy. Omi and Takagi state that neoconservatives, what they term "the Right," frame Asian Americans as a minority group that has been wronged by racial preferences, "as the victims of affirmative action."[37] While the Right attempts to adhere to colorblindness and meritocracy in their quest to end all race-preferential policies, they also invoke race by utilizing Asian Americans. The complexity of this strategy comes across very simply—it is not just white men who are against affirmative action but some minority groups as well.

The discourse in the *Ho* lawsuit is emblematic of the larger national shifts away from support of affirmative action and any policy with racial or gender preferences. Stereotypes around whiteness, blackness, and Asian-ness are exploited in order for the *Ho* lawsuit to gain currency and viability within the current political and social contexts, which do not support any race-preferential policies. The *Ho* lawsuit has devised new arguments that are consonant with the current neoconservative political climate.

The danger lies not in the success of Asian-American individuals but how they are viewed and framed by other groups—most notably other minority groups, the media, and politicians. Anti-Asian sentiment, on the part of other minority groups, is brewing within the context of education. At UC Berkeley in the early 1990s, both African-American and Chicano/Latino students believed themselves to be stigmatized by their fellow Asian-American students. "(Some of them) saw Asian Americans as 'exclusionary,' 'isolationist,' and as wanting to distinguish themselves from the more pointedly stigmatized Chicano and Black students."[38]

Thus, while the *Ho* plaintiffs and supporters believe that they are discriminated against and attempt to fight for their rights, the larger issue really surrounds other minority groups and the negative stereotypes attached to them through and because of the Asian Model Minority stereotype. The *Ho* case and its surrounding political and social contexts also serve to frame another emerging conflict—that of Black/Brown vs. Yellow.

## DISCUSSION QUESTIONS

1. Discuss the harm done to other groups by asserting the Model Minority Myth as part of the *Ho* lawsuit arguments.
2. What are the unforeseen consequences of Asian Americans constructing themselves as the Model Minority?
3. What did the neoconservative movement gain from the *Ho* lawsuit and its arguments?

## NOTES

1. *Brian Ho, Patrick Wong, & Hilary Chen v. SFUSD*, p. 2.
2. Henry Der, *Preliminary Analysis of Brian Ho v. SFUSD,* Chinese for Affirmative Action, 9 September, 1994., 7.
3. Kimberle Crenshaw, Neil Gotanda, Gary Peller, and Kendall Thomas, "Introduction," in Kimberle Crenshaw, Neil Gotanda, Gary Peller, and Kendall Thomas, eds., *Critical Race Theory—The Key Writings that Formed the Movement,* (New York: The New Press, 1995), xiv.
4. San Francisco Unified School District, "Report on San Francisco School Desegregation plan to Judge William Orrick, United States District Court—Executive Summary," July 1992, 2.
5. *Brian Ho, Patrick Wong, & Hilary Chen v. SFUSD*, 2.
6. Michael Omi and Howard Winant, *Racial Formation in the United States—From the 1960s to the 1990s,* 2nd edition, (New York: Routledge, 1994), 130.
7. Omi and Winant, 130.
8. Omi and Winant, 131.
9. Edsall and Edsall chronicle the rise of neoconservative rhetoric through the politics of Ronald Reagan. The term "equality of opportunity" became a standard term that Reagan used to describe race-based policies. Edsall and

Edsall observe that, 'The power of conservative egalitarianism—based on an idealized concept of 'equal opportunity' and reinforced by free-market economic theory—is that it affirms basic American principles of equality while protecting, and in some cases reinforcing, the very unequal distribution of racial and economic benefits challenged by liberalism'. See Thomas Byrne Edsall with Mary D. Edsall, *Chain Reaction—The Impact of Race, Rights, and Taxes on American Politics,* (New York: W.W. Norton & Company, 1992), 147.

10. Gerard Lim, "Lawsuit Over Chinese American Enrollment: Class Warfare By the Bay," *AsianWeek,* 19 August, 1994.

11. Mamie Huey, "Chinese Americans Have Bone to Pick with Consent Decree," *Asian Week,* 27 January, 1995.

12. Elaine Woo, "Caught on the Wrong Side of the Line," *Los Angeles Times,* 13 July, 1995.

13. Woo, "Caught on the Wrong Side of the Line."

14. Nanette Asimov, "District's Long Struggle with Desegregation," *San Francisco Chronicle,* 19 June, 1995.

15. Alethea Yip, "Class-action Suit Sought on School Caps," *AsianWeek,* 6 October, 1995.

16. Lee Cheng, "Racialism Lives on in San Francisco Schools—SFUSD's New Assignment Plan Forces Race Mixing," *AsianWeek,* 7 October, 1999.

17. Cheng. "Racialism Lives On ..."

18. Keith Osajima notes, "The articulation of successful Asians in the popular press carried ramifications that extended well beyond the Chinatowns and Japantowns of America." See Keith Osajima. "Asian Americans as the Model Minority: An Analysis of the Popular Press Image in the 1960s and 1980s." In *Reflections on Shattered Windows—Promises and Prospects for Asian American Studies,* eds. Gary Okihiro, Shirley Hune, Arthur Hansen and John M. Liu, (Washington State University Press: Pullman, 1988),166.

19. Rowena Robles, "Articulating Race—Neoconservatve Renditions of Equality—An Analysis of the Brian Ho Lawsuit," AAPI Nexus, 2:1 (Winter/Spring 2004), 99.

20. Der, *Preliminary Analysis of Brian Ho,* 7.

21. Even though the plaintiffs and supporters of the *Ho* lawsuit are mostly Chinese Americans, the Model Minority Myth incorporates all Asian-American ethnic groups. Because they assert the Model Minority Myth, the assertion of race by the *Ho* plaintiffs and supporters may have worked inaccurately to include all Asian-American ethnic groups.

22. Through the *Brown* decision, the Supreme Court attempted to legislate racism as illegal and unconstitutional. The Supreme Court, along with the NAACP, believed that if schools could be desegregated, then so could the rest of society. David Kirp observes that, 'If the society as a whole cannot be integrated by law, it is thought, at least the schools can. Schools have also been regarded as a lever to more general social reform: integration in the schools just might catalyze wider change, brought about by a new and more tolerant generation.' The NAACP sought to end legalized desegregation in public education, believing that it would lead to more widespread change throughout American society. See David Kirp. *Just Schools—The Idea of Racial Equality in American Education,* (Berkeley: University of California Press, 1982), 22.

23. Omi and Takagi describe how the black/white paradigm of race relations frames how Americans view race and race relations. They state that, "(t)he hegemonic 'black/white' paradigm of race relations has fundamentally shaped how we think about, engage, and politically mobilize around racial issues." See Omi and Takagi, *Situating Asian Americans,* 155.

24. Gary Okihiro, *Margins and Mainstreams—Asians in American History,* (Seattle: University of Washington Press, 1994), 33.

25. See Okihiro, *Margins and Mainstreams,* 34.

26. Omi and Takagi, *Situating Asian Americans,* 156.

27. Takagi, *Retreat from Race,* 176.

28. Alan Freeman utilizes the "fault concept" in describing groups, "innocents," who do not support school integration because these groups believe that they have never personally discriminated against certain groups and, therefore, should not bear the brunt of any race-conscious policies such as bussing or Affirmative Action. See Alan Freeman, "Legitimizing racial discrimination through antidiscrimination law: a critical review of Supreme Court doctrine," in *Critical Race Theory: the Key Writings that Formed the Movement,* eds. Kimberle Crenshaw, Neil Gotanda, Gary Peller, and Kendall Thomas, (New York: New Press, 1995), 30.

29. Takagi, *Retreat from Race,* 79.

30. See Nancy Abelmann and John Lie, *Blue Dreams: Korean Americans and the Los Angeles Riots* (Cambridge: Harvard University Press, 1995).

31. See Omi and Winant, *Racial Formation,* 65–69.

32. See Okihiro for a historical perspective on how Asian Americans have often traversed between black and white racial constructions in the United States. Okihiro, *Margins and Mainstreams,* 34.

33. Suecheng Chan demonstrates that newly-arrived Asian immigrant groups are not as successful as their Chinese and Japanese American counterparts who have been in the U.S. for several generations. She specifically points to the high rate of poverty and welfare dependency among Vietnamese refugees in attempts to counter the Model Minority stereotype. See Suecheng Chan, *Asians Americans—An Interpretive History,* (Boston: Twayne Publishers, 1991), 170. Paul Ong demonstrates that "despite high level(s) of education, APAs have not been able to translate their credentials into commensurate earnings and occupational status." Through an analysis of the intersections of income and education levels, Ong shows that Asian Americans do not earn as much as their white counterparts even if they possess higher levels of education. See Paul Ong, "The Affirmative Action Divide," in *The State of Asian Pacific America—Transforming Race Relations,* ed. Paul Ong, (Los Angeles: LEAP Asian Pacific American Public Policy Institute and UCLA Asian American Studies Center, 2000), 329.
34. Okihiro, *Margins and Mainstreams,* 34.
35. Okihiro, *Margins and Mainstreams,* 170.
36. Takagi, *Retreat from Race,* 176.
37. Omi and Takagi, *Situating Asian Americans,* 157.
38. The Diversity Project, *Final Report,* November 1991, Institute of the Study for Social Change, Berkeley, November, 1991, 34.

# CHAPTER 8

# Racism and Employment

# The $40 Million Slave
## The Dilemma of Wealth Without Control

William C. Rhoden

*Niggas are players. Niggers are players, are players. Niggas play football, basketball and baseball while the white man is cutting off their balls.*

—THE LAST POETS, CIRCA 1969[1]

CURT FLOOD WAS THE FIRST PERSON I ever heard use a plantation metaphor in connection with professional athletes. I'm sure someone else had used the metaphor before him, but the first time the comparison really resonated in my soul was when Flood invoked the comparison in 1969. At the time he was probably the best centerfielder in baseball. He was a three-time all-star and a seven-time Gold Glove winner, with a career batting average of .293. Flood's brilliance went beyond numbers. He had the effortless, gliding speed that I first saw in Willie Mays. By 1969, Flood, in most minds, had replaced Mays as the greatest centerfielder in baseball. Flood, like Mays, wasn't just great—he was *cool* and great.

I had no idea just how cool Flood really was.

In the winter of 1969, he was traded from the St. Louis Cardinals, where he had played since 1958, to Philadelphia. Flood was stunned; a trade was the furthest thing from his mind. Flood had hit .285, knocked in 57 runs, and generally had another sound season. But Jim Tooney, the Cardinals' vice president, told Flood that he had been traded. Despite his time and stature in the game, Flood had not been given the courtesy of a call or a warning beforehand. Nothing. He was traded. That's how business was done. Athletes of his generation were powerless to determine their fate; they had limited options. Flood, who was making $92,500 at the time, exercised his option in the extreme: He refused to go to Philadelphia. In one of the most significant communications in sports labor history, Flood wrote to then baseball commissioner Bowie Kuhn that "after twelve years in the major leagues, I do not feel that I am a piece of property to be bought and sold irrespective of my wishes."

But that's exactly what he was; in fact, that's what all athletes were: so many pieces of property to be bought, sold, or discarded as their "owners" saw fit. This was—and still is—allowable in sports because athletes are supposed to be grateful for the opportunity. This mode of treatment was legitimized by the Reserve Clause in Major League Baseball.

The Reserve Clause allowed teams to hold on to players as long as they wanted but forbade the players from testing the market on their terms, an "iron fist" that Flood compared to sharecropping. "The reserve system was the same system used in the South where the plantation-owner owned all the houses that you live in,"[2] Flood said. "And you worked for him and you shopped in his store and you never got over the hump." In Flood's mind a divide between players and owners was ingrained in their roles: "They're the ranchers, and we're the cattle."

The owners were given license to do this by the federal government. The Reserve Clause prevented players from moving to another team unless they were traded or sold. Flood challenged the fairness of a system that kept players in perpetual servitude to their teams at the owners' pleasure.

Flood's dramatic action took place in the middle of my sophomore year in college. I was just beginning to become aware of the brutal business side of sports, of how athletes were economic creatures in a peculiar entertainment industry. The sports industry ran on the fuel of strong bodies—black or white, from small colleges or large—and an over-developed sense of gratitude. Athletes generally were just happy to be there, whether they were on scholarship or under contract. But by 1969 the tide had been shifting, giving way to a more aggressive sense of self-worth on the part of black athletes.

In 1967, Muhammad Ali was stripped of his heavyweight boxing championship for refusing to be drafted for religious reasons. In 1968, Kareem Abdul-Jabbar, then known as Lew Alcindor, refused to join the United States Olympic basketball team. And, of course, at the 1968 Mexico City Games, Tommie Smith and John Carlos staged their historic protest.

Flood filed his suit in 1970. During a meeting with the union's executive board in December 1969, Tom Haller, a white player, asked Flood if his action, then pending, was his response to baseball's history of racial discrimination. Flood said that he believed he had suffered harder times than white players; the change in black consciousness in recent years had made him "more sensitive to injustice in every area of my life." There was so much social turbulence in the United States that political and social neutrality wasn't really an option, particularly for black athletes who were aware of the recent controversy as well as the larger dramas of the civil rights movement.

What made Flood's fight resonate is that at one level his battle went beyond race. Flood said he was filing this suit against a "situation" that was "improper" for all ballplayers. Many white players never thought of themselves as being on a plantation or as being only so much chattel. But the legacy of black people in sports had sensitized Flood; that history had tuned him in to a different frequency than white players had access to. He used the insight born of that legacy to help all players, black and white, fight a corrupt system. The executive board of the Players Association liked what it heard and voted unanimously to support Flood.

But Flood had committed the cardinal sin: He'd challenged baseball bosses, and they went on to destroy him—as a player—with the help of other players and the sports media.

Marvin Miller, the attorney for the players' union, warned Flood from the start of his battle with Major League Baseball that if he went forward with the suit, his life in baseball was over; he would not be elected to the Hall of Fame, he would never manage or be given any significant management position in baseball. Undaunted, Flood pressed on. He decided to sit out the 1970 season, rather than report to Philadelphia and accept the $100,000 salary the Phillies offered. Sitting out was the ultimate sacrifice for a veteran player with limited seasons left to play and desperately needing to play to keep his skills sharpened.

But Flood was committed to the fight. What makes one man stand on principle and others sit quietly by and accept what is being handed out? Most of Flood's peers were terrified. Fast and courageous on the field, star players of the day—like star players today—were terrified of taking on their owners. Maury Wills, the daring base runner who set a base-stealing record in 1962, admitted, "Most of us were not courageous enough to take that stand and challenge the owners. I know I wasn't."[3]

But some were.

Flood's friend and teammate Bob Gibson came to Flood's trial. Jackie Robinson testified on Flood's behalf. In his autobiography, *The Way It Is*, Flood said that one of the most moving moments of the trial occurred when Robinson walked into the courthouse on the day he was scheduled to testify.

"As he and Rachel Robinson moved into the courtroom, you could hear a pin drop because he had a real presence about him."[4]

Robinson sat close to Flood. Flood later recalled, "Then he looked at me. I said, 'I really appreciate your taking the time and effort to do this.' And he said, 'Well, you can't be out there by yourself.' I remember these words very well: 'You can't be out there by yourself and I would be remiss if I didn't share these burdens with you.' "

Robinson understood history—he *was* history—and he understood the continuity of struggle, both the black struggle and the struggle for human freedom, which in Robinson's mind were intertwined. A year earlier, Robinson had supported John Carlos and Tommie Smith in their protest at the 1968 Summer Olympic Games in Mexico City.

Once, while explaining why he had reluctantly supported Nixon over John F. Kennedy, Robinson explained that he had not felt Kennedy was committed to the black cause and thus the cause of humanity.

He said, "I am most interested in a candidate who I think will be best for the Black American because I am convinced that the black struggle and its solution are fundamental to the struggle to make America what it is supposed to be."[5]

Robinson had long since stopped repaying baseball with "glad tidings," no matter what *The Sporting News* demanded.

While Curt Flood told the Major League Baseball executive board that his challenge was not coming out of the race-bag of the sixties, he also knew that he could not separate himself from the political and racial climate of the day.

"The sixties is an era that will never be forgotten. Being a child of those years between 1959 and 1969, America was coming apart at the seams and our boys were in Southeast Asia giving their lives, we were marching all over Berkeley. We lost Dr. King, we lost the Kennedys, we lost Medgar Evers, and true ugliness was happening to us as a people in the sixties. Little children were being shut out of education, and the mood of the sixties was dark and somber, and merely because you're a professional athlete does not defend you from that."[6]

Flood said that the currents of world affairs had a direct impact on him as an athlete and baseball player because "all of the things that we were fighting for all over the world, we weren't getting in my profession. And from the time someone made me stay in the colored section while the white kids stayed on the beach in the white high-rise hotel, I felt like 'a nigger,' whatever that means. Those years between 1960 and 1969 really were growing years for me."[7]

With the union executive board's support, Flood's case reached the Supreme Court two years later, in 1972.

He lost his case that year, in large part because no active players showed support.

Not only did Flood lose the case; he lost any chance he had to finish out his career with dignity. Joe Garagiola, a mediocre journeyman catcher, testified for baseball in the lawsuit. Years later Garagiola explained weakly, "I thought if the Reserve Clause went, baseball was going."

In 1973, when the owners agreed to federal arbitration of salary demands, the way was opened for the free agency that now makes players less the pieces of property they once were.

Flood was in Spain in 1975 when he learned that the Major League Baseball players had finally won free agency. Two white players, Dave McNally of Montreal and Andy Messersmith of Los Angeles, had brought a grievance against the owners, challenging the renewal clause in the basic player contract. The two pitchers won their case when the chairman of the arbitration panel ruled that they could bargain with other teams.

During a 1996 interview for a documentary I was writing for HBO, Flood said that he was happy for the victory, but that he felt the decisions had a tinge of racism. "It disappointed me that I didn't win," Flood said, "but I had to feel that somewhere in the equation, America was showing its racism again. They were just merely waiting for someone else to win that case."

As difficult as it was for even the most palatable African American to get a job in baseball after retirement, Flood's black mark made him untouchable. He was not welcomed back to the game. He played briefly for the Washington Senators in 1971, then, citing personal problems, left the Senators after thirteen games. He went to Majorca, Spain, for five years, where he painted and ran a café and struggled with alcoholism. He came back to the United States, went to Sweden, then came back home.

He returned to baseball briefly when he became a broadcaster for the Oakland A's in 1978. Later he operated a youth center in Los Angeles.

Flood died in January 1997, at the age of fifty-nine.

Thanks to Curt Flood, The Last Poets, and Fred Hampton, I emerged from 1969 much more aware, much less naïve. Flood put the sports industry in a whole new perspective—the new variation of the slave owner paradigm. He challenged the plantation mentality of big-time athletes, according to which the athlete was supposed to be grateful. Most athletes were and still are operating under that mentality: happy to be playing, not wanting to rock the boat.

## DISCUSSION QUESTIONS

1. What did Curt Flood achieve? How did it improve conditions for other athletes?
2. What were the parallels between working conditions for the enslaved and professional athletes?
3. What impact does discrimination have on relations between labor and management?

## NOTES

1. The Last Poets, "Scared of Revolution."
2. Curt Flood interview for HBO documentary *Journey of the African American Athlete* (1996).
3. Maury Wills interview for HBO documentary *Journey of the African American Athlete* (1996).
4. Curt Flood, *The Way It Is* (Trident Press, 1971).
5. Robinson, *I Never Had It Made.*
6. Curt Flood interview for HBO documentary *Journey of the African American Athlete* (1996).
7. Ibid.

# CHAPTER 9

# Racism and Criminal Justice

# The Race Card

**Renford Reese**

IN THE U.S. criminal justice system, race significantly affects the probability that a person will be convicted of a crime. Race also determines the severity of the punishment. Blacks receive on average six months more in jail time than whites for comparable crimes (National Urban League 2004, 1). There are racial disparities among black and Hispanic inmates versus white inmates in every slate in the union. Discrimination based on race violates the creed of the U.S. Constitution; more specifically, it violates the equal protection clause of the Fourteenth Amendment. This unattractive feature of American democracy represents a significant violation of human rights.

In his landmark book. *An American Dilemma: The Negro Problem and Modern Democracy*, Gunnar Myrdal poignantly discusses America's dilemma involving what to do with the black population. "There is a 'Negro problem' in the United States and most Americans are aware of it, although it assumes varying forms and intensity in different regions of the country and among diverse groups of the American people. Americans have to react to it, politically as citizens and, where there are Negroes present in the community, privately as neighbors" (1944, xlv). The question then was whether whites could peacefully and comfortably coexist with this population. In every period of American history, this has been the predominant theme. Perceptions and stereotypes of young black men as being lawless and dangerous have remained strong and consistent throughout the country's history.

In the 1950s, when segregation was legal, African Americans made up 30 percent of the nation's prison population. Today, they make up 49 percent of all prison inmates but only 12.6 percent of the general population. One out of every four black men aged

16–26 has some connection with the penal system; e.g., in prison, in jail, on parole, on probation. The federal government predicts that one of every four black men will be imprisoned during their lifetime (Reese 2001; Reese 2004). Waquant puts these startling statistics in perspective, when he says the incarceration of young black men in the U.S. "has escalated to heights experienced by no other group in history, even under the repressive authoritarian regimes and in Soviet-style societies" (Hallett 2003, 39).

What is the difference between the hyper-punitive, inequitable criminal justice policies of today with their emphasis on incarceration, and the black codes implemented in the South after the Civil War? The Jim Crow laws that existed in the South for more than fifty years? From a historical perspective, how has America changed its views of black men? The comments made by Martin Luther King Jr. more than four decades ago still resonate today.

Jailing the Negro was once as much of a threat as the loss of a job. To any Negro who displayed a spark of manhood, a southern law-enforcement officer could say: "Nigger watch your step, or I'll put you in jail." The Negro knew what going to jail meant. It meant not only confinement and isolation from his loved ones. It meant that at the jailhouse he could probably expect a severe beating. And it meant that his day in court, if he had it, would be a mockery of justice. (1964, 15)

Today, the U.S. is incarcerating an entire generation of black men. This trend is having a significant impact on black communities. Those incarcerated do not have jobs, pay taxes, or care for their children. Many cannot vote. "Felony disenfranchisement" restricts approximately four million Americans—mostly minorities—from voting. Because 45 states have laws restricting offenders from voting and 32 states deny those on parole the right to vote, at least one of every seven black men cannot vote, at least temporarily. Some 31 percent of the black men in Florida and Alabama are prohibited from voting because of felony convictions. On the national level, 13 percent of black men are disenfranchised because of felony convictions, compared to 2 percent of whites (Reese 2004; Cole 2000, 17A).

The opportunities for many young blacks to engage in full citizenship are restricted. In order for a democracy to thrive, all citizens must have the opportunity to engage in the various aspects of public life. As Kelman states, "Democracy recognizes the dignity and worth of each person ... by authorizing the lowliest as well as the mightiest to participate in governing, our government publicly affirms the value of every human" (1996, 7). The unequal treatment of young black men in the U.S. betrays the fundamental principles of democracy.

Lawmakers should reevaluate counterproductive criminal justice policies that lack vision, compassion, and practicality. Those who commit crimes should be punished. However, the punishment should always be proportional to the crime. The mean-spirited policy of "lock them up and throw away the key" might be expedient and useful to politicians, but it is not a long-term solution to the problem of crime in this country. More emphasis should be put on preventing crime by addressing its causes. More focus should be put on rehabilitating offenders so they can successfully reintegrate into society. Lawmakers should direct money into educational and recreational programs for youth, especially in areas acutely affected by crime. We must remember what Cesare Beccaria stated in 1764, because it rings true today: "It is better to prevent crimes than to punish them. That is the ultimate end of every good legislation" (Knepper 2003, 36).

### Race and Incarceration in the United States

Rates of incarceration in adult correctional and confinement facilities per 100,000 state residents, by race.

|  | *White* | *Black* | *Hispanic* | *Ratio Black/ White* | *Ratio Hispanic/ White* |
|---|---|---|---|---|---|
| Alabama | 373 | 1,797 | 914 | 4.8 | 2.4 |
| Alaska | 306 | 1,606 | 549 | 5.2 | 1.8 |
| Arizona | 607 | 3,818 | 1,263 | 6.3 | 2.1 |
| Arkansas | 468 | 2,185 | 1,708 | 4.7 | 3.7 |
| California | 487 | 3,141 | 820 | 6.4 | 1.7 |
| Colorado | 429 | 4,023 | 1,131 | 9.4 | 2.6 |
| Connecticut | 199 | 2,991 | 1,669 | 15.0 | 8.4 |
| Delaware | 361 | 2,500 | 330 | 6.9 | 0.9 |
| District of Columbia | 46 | 768 | 260 | 16.5 | 5.6 |
| Georgia | 544 | 2,153 | 620 | 4.0 | 1.1 |
| Hawaii | 173 | 577 | 587 | 3.3 | 3.4 |
| Idaho | 502 | 2,236 | 1,103 | 4.5 | 2.2 |
| Illinois | 216 | 2,273 | 426 | 10.5 | 2.0 |
| Indiana | 373 | 2,575 | 602 | 6.9 | 1.6 |
| Iowa | 300 | 3,775 | 923 | 12.6 | 3.1 |
| Kansas | 397 | 3,686 | 753 | 9.3 | 1.9 |
| Kentucky | 466 | 3,375 | 2,059 | 7.2 | 4.4 |
| Louisiana | 421 | 2,475 | 1,736 | 5.9 | 4.1 |
| Maine | 207 | 1,731 | 759 | 8.4 | 3.7 |
| Maryland | 282 | 1,749 | 230 | 6.2 | 0.8 |
| Massachusetts | 204 | 1,807 | 1,435 | 8.9 | 7.0 |
| Michigan | 357 | 2,256 | 951 | 6.3 | 2.7 |
| Minnesota | 197 | 2,811 | 1,031 | 14.3 | 5.2 |
| Mississippi | 353 | 1,762 | 3,131 | 5.0 | 8.9 |
| Missouri | 402 | 2,306 | 730 | 5.7 | 1.8 |
| Montana | 358 | 3,120 | 1,178 | 8.7 | 3.3 |

| Nebraska | 226 | 2,251 | 824 | 9.9 | 3.6 |
| Nevada | 630 | 3,206 | 676 | 5.5 | 1.1 |
| New Hampshire | 242 | 2,501 | 1,425 | 10.3 | 5.9 |
| New Jersey | 175 | 2,509 | 843 | 14.3 | 4.8 |
| New Mexico | 311 | 3,151 | 818 | 10.1 | 2.6 |
| New York | 182 | 1,951 | 1,002 | 10.7 | 5.5 |
| North Carolina | 266 | 1,640 | 440 | 6.2 | 1.7 |
| North Dakota | 170 | 1,277 | 976 | 7.5 | 5.8 |
| Ohio | 333 | 2,651 | 865 | 8.0 | 2.6 |
| Oklahoma | 682 | 4,077 | 1,223 | 6.0 | 1.8 |
| Oregon | 488 | 3,895 | 777 | 8.0 | 1.6 |
| Pennsylvania | 281 | 3,108 | 2,242 | 11.1 | 8.0 |
| Rhode Island | 199 | 2,735 | 817 | 13.8 | 4.1 |
| South Carolina | 391 | 1,979 | 871 | 5.1 | 2.2 |
| South Dakota | 440 | 6,510 | 1,486 | 14.8 | 3.4 |
| Tennessee | 402 | 2,021 | 790 | 5.0 | 2.0 |
| Texas | 694 | 3,734 | 1,152 | 5.4 | 1.7 |
| Utah | 342 | 3,356 | 998 | 9.5 | 2.9 |
| Vermont | 183 | 2,024 | 799 | 11.1. | 4.4 |
| Virginia | 444 | 2,842 | 508 | 6.4 | 1.1 |
| Washington | 393 | 2,757 | 717 | 7.0 | 1.8 |
| West Virginia | 375 | 6,400 | 2,834 | 17.1 | 7.6 |
| Wisconsin | 341 | 3,953 | 863 | 11.6 | 2.5 |
| Wyoming | 740 | 6,529 | 1,320 | 8.8 | 1.8 |
| *National* | **378** | **2,489** | **922** | **6.6** | **2.4** |

Figures calculated on basis of U.S. Census Bureau data from Census 2000 on state residents and incarcerated population.

Source: Human Rights Watch 2002

## DISCUSSION QUESTIONS

1.  What connection is made between race and conviction rates?
2.  How does Myrdal's "negro problem" relate to this contemporary phenomenon?
3.  What similarities exist between black codes, Jim Crow laws, and contemporary incarceration patterns?

# REFERENCES

Allen, James, Hilton Als, John Lewis, and Leon Litwack. 2000. *Without Sanctuary: Lynching Photography in America*. Santa Fe, NM: Twin Palms Publishing.

Baker, David V. 2003. The racist application of capital punishment to African Americans. In *Racial Issues in Criminal Justice, The Case of African Americans*, edited by Marvin D. Free Jr. Westport, CT: Praeger.

Blumberg, Rhoda Lois. 1984. *Civil Rights: The 1960s Freedom Struggle*. Boston: Twayne.

*Boston Herald*. 1991. Chronology of events. 21 October.

Cole, David. 2000. Denying felons vote hurts them. *USA Today*, 3 February.

Dorfman, Lori, and Vincent Schiraldi. 2001. *Off Balance: Youth, Race, and Crime in the News*. Justice Policy Institute (April).

Dye, Thomas R. 1995. *Understanding Public Policy*. Englewood Cliffs, NJ: Prentice Hall.

Feldman, Lisa, Vincent Schiraldi, and Jason Ziedenberg. 2001. *Too Little Too Late: President Clinton's Prison Legacy*. Justice Policy Institute. February.

Free, Marvin D., Jr. 2003. Race and presentencing decisions: the cost of being African American. In *Racial Issues in Criminal Justice, The Case of African Americans*, edited by Marvin D. Free Jr. Westport, CT: Praeger.

Glassner, Barry. 1999. *The Culture of Fear: Why Americans are Afraid of the Wrong Things*. New York: Basic Books.

Glassner, Barry. 2002. In *Bowling for Columbine*, a film by Michael Moore released in 2002.

Hallett, Michael A. 2003. Slavery's legacy? Private prisons and mass imprisonment. In *Racial Issues in Criminal Justice, The Case of African Americans*, edited by Marvin D. Free, Jr. Westport, CT: Praeger.

Human Rights Watch. 2002. Race and incarceration in the United States. *Press Backgrounder*, 22 February.

Kelley, Robin, and Earl Lewis. 1996. Introduction. In *From a Raw Deal to a New Deal: African Americans 1929–1945*, by Joe William Trotter Jr. New York: Oxford University Press.

Kelman, Steven. 1996. *American Democracy and the Public Good*. Fort Worth, TX: Harcourt Brace College Publishers.

King, Martin Luther, Jr. 1964. *Why We Can't Wait*. New York: Signet Classics.

Knepper, P. 2003. *Explaining Criminal Conduct: Theories and Systems in Criminology*. Durham, NC: Carolina Academic Press.

Myrdal, Gunnar. 1944. *An American Dilemma: The Negro Problem and Modern Democracy*. New York: Harper and Brothers.

NAACP Legal Defense and Educational Fund. 2003. *Death Row USA*. Washington, DC: NAACP.

National Urban League. 2004. *The State of Black America*. Washington, DC: National Urban League.

*New York Times*. 1994. Vice President rebukes Gingrich for citing murder case. 8 November.

Phillips, Frank. 1989. GOP's death penalty call brings rebuke from Flynn. *Boston Globe*, 25 October.

Reese, Renford 1999. The socio-political context of the integration of sport in the U.S. *Journal of African American Men* 4, no. 3 (Spring).

Reese, Renford. 2001. Criminal justice and social injustice: African American men in the U.S. *Journal of Ethics and Justice* 3, no. 2 (November).

Reese, Renford. 2004. *American Paradox: Young Black Men*. Durham, NC: Carolina Academic Press.

Royce, Edward. 1993. *The Origins of Southern Sharecropping*. Philadelphia: Temple University Press.

Schmidt, Steffen W., Mack C. Shelley, and Barbara Bardes. 1999. *American Government and Politics Today*. Belmont, CA: Wadsworth.

Terry, Don. 1994. False accusations anger black people. *Times-Picayune*, 6 November.

Thurman, Howard. 1979. *With Head and Heart: The Autobiography of Howard Thurman*. New York: Harcourt Brace Jovanovich.

Tompkins, Jonathan. 1995. *Human Resource Management in Government*. New York: Harper Collins College Publishers.

Trefousse, Hans L. 1971. *Reconstruction: America's First Effort At Racial Democracy*. New York: Litton Educational Publishing.

Waquant, L. 2001. Deadly symbiosis: When ghetto and prison meet and mesh. In *Mass Imprisonment: Social Causes and Consequences*, edited by D. Garland. Thousand Oaks, CA: Sage.

Wideman, John Edgar. 2003. The American dilemma revisited: Psychoanalysis, social policy, and the socio-cultural meaning of race. *Black Renaissance* (Spring) 2003:33.

www.filmsite.org. The "Birth of a Nation." Accessed at http://www.filmsite.org/birt.html.

www.insidepolitics.org. Independent ads: the National Security Political Action Committee, "Willie Horton." Accessed at http://www.insidepolitics.org/ps111/independentads.html.

# Capital Punishment as Legal Lynching?

Timothy V. Kaufman-Osborn

## SPECTACLE LYNCHINGS

IN THIS SECTION, I explore the post-Reconstruction articulation of the relationship between social and racial contracts, as that articulation was manifest in the conduct of lynchings. The first of the two parts in this section asks how what came to be known as "spectacle lynchings" participated in the generation of the class of subpersons (and, reciprocally, the class of persons as well). The second asks how the conduct of lynchings, spectacle and otherwise, often affirmed the racial contract by violating or, perhaps better, by paying no heed to the distinction drawn by the social contract between the law's official violence and its unofficial counterpart.

### Making Bodies Black

Prior to the Civil War, only rarely were the punishments imposed under what had come to be known as "Lynch's Law" specifically capital.[1] The most commonly inflicted extralegal penalties during the later decades of the eighteenth and the first half of the nineteenth century included whipping, tarring and feathering, beating, and sometimes expulsion from the community. This was true in the North (although, with increasing frequency, after 1850, vigilante groups adopted hanging as a method of punishment in the territories of the West); and it was equally true in the South, where, except for the crime of murder, slaves were often whipped but only occasionally executed, whether legally or extra legally, for the obvious reason that they were highly valued commodities.

Only during and after Reconstruction did the term "lynching" come to acquire its contemporary connotations, which characteristically include the punishment of death, the targeting of African-Americans, and, more specifically, African-American men, chiefly in the South, and absent due process of law.[2] Whether explained as a response to increased economic competition experienced by lower-class whites, or as retaliation for efforts at black political organization, or as punishment for the real or alleged crime of rape, or as a symptom of a premodern culture predicated on a chivalrous code of honor, or as a misdirected reprisal against Northern intervention, or as sacrificial atonement for the collective guilt incurred through loss of the Civil War, or as a means of reaffirming an endangered form of white masculine identity,[3] during the half century following the withdrawal of Federal troops in 1877, lynching became a lethal means of regenerating the racial contract once the racial polity could no longer be secured through the institution of chattel slavery. As such, it was part and parcel of a more comprehensive set of practices, including denial of access to education, race-specific codes of etiquette, systems of economic marginalization, especially debt peonage, and methods of political disenfranchisement, including denial of the right to vote and to serve on juries, that re-created the category of subpersons, but absent the legally codified construction of blacks as private property.

Although lynching, like slavery, helped to secure the racial polity, the differences between these two practices (like that between lynching and contemporary capital punishment) should not be elided. As I noted in the preceding section, so long as blacks remained slaves, so long as white supremacy remained the law of the land, membership in the racial and social contracts remained fully coextensive. That equation was disrupted, however, by Emancipation and, more particularly, by the Civil Rights Act of 1866, which conferred the rights of citizenship on freed male slaves, thereby removing them from the status of property and formally including them within the social contract.

Lynching responded to this rearticulation of the relationship between the racial and social contracts, and it did so by imposing on its victims a stark and all-consuming corporeal identity. That identity reduced lynching's targets, as well as the race they mimetically represented, to the status of mute black bodies, which, as such, were available for discursive construction in terms that reconsolidated the racial polity. By effectively equating the meaning of blackness with the predatory, the savage, the animalistic, the hypersexualized, lynchings demonstrated the patent ineligibility of those so marked to inhabit the category of citizen, while it simultaneously recertified the identity of those defined not by their degraded corporeality but by their white personhood and so their exclusive occupation of that same category.[4] As Mills puts the point, although not expressly in reference to lynching, "if the Racial Contract creates its signatories, those party to the Contract, by constructing them as 'white persons,' it also tries to make its victims, the objects of the Contract, *into* the 'nonwhite subpersons' it specifies."[5]

Just how post-Reconstruction lynchings marked the objects of the racial contract is perhaps best illustrated by what came to be known as "spectacle lynchings," which garnered far more publicity than did any other sort during the decades between 1880 and 1930.[6] Consider the following incident, one of many that might be cited:

> Accused of raping and killing Myrtle Vance, the three year old daughter of the local sheriff, seventeen year old Henry Smith was seized near Hope, Arkansas in February, 1893, and then returned by train to the scene of his alleged crime in Paris, Texas. After hundreds of spectators arrived from the countryside, along with those who had boarded special excursion trains in Dallas, Smith was driven from the depot, through the center of town, and then to an open prairie, strapped to a chair fixed atop an open cart drawn by four white horses and decorated to resemble a parade float. Upon arriving at a makeshift elevated platform, upon which the word "JUSTICE" had been painted in large white letters and to which the young man was secured, the sheriff was given the first opportunity to sear his flesh to the bone, using irons heated in a small furnace. After silencing Smith by burning his tongue and blinding him by putting out his eyes, the participants soaked the entire platform in oil and set it ablaze, as those with cameras, including the local press, snapped away. When the fire had cooled sufficiently, spectators began scouring the area for souvenirs, including buttons, teeth, and segments of the charred platform.[7]

As this account makes clear, spectacle lynchings are not well understood in strictly instrumental terms, i.e., as simple auxiliaries aimed at remedying the occasional failure of the official criminal justice system to accomplish expeditiously the ends of retribution and deterrence. Instead, they were, highly ritualized expressive performances aimed at communicating the terms of the racial contract to blacks and whites alike, and the medium of that message was the (sub)human body.

Unlike the very rare white targets of spectacle lynchings, whose bodies were almost never tortured or mutilated, black victims of this form of communal justice were routinely riddled with gunfire and as the example of Henry Smith indicates, often tortured and burned. The deployment of torture, aimed at inflicting unbearable pain, destroyed its victim's capacity to do other than cry out in anguish, and so transformed what might otherwise menace the regime of white supremacy into an inarticulate black body, denied its capacity for any sort of agency, political or otherwise: Smith's "tongue was silenced by fire," a local newspaper reported, "and henceforth he only moaned, or gave a cry that echoed over the prairie like the wail of a wild animal."[8] To burn and then display the corpse of a black man reduced to the status of a nonhuman creature, or to hang a sign on that corpse in order to warn others about the boundaries of acceptable race-specific conduct, or to photograph that corpse and then circulate its, image in the form of a postcard, as was often done,[9] is to compel that body to continue to signify long after its capacity to speak has been destroyed. To blacks, and especially black men, the lynched body communicated their vulnerability, their debasement, their exclusion from the community to which, by federal law, they now uneasily belonged. To whites, that same body reaffirmed the racial contract and, more particularly, the collective integrity of the master race at a time when its exclusive title to the rights and privileges afforded by the social contract was no longer altogether secure.

Relegation of black men to the status of subhuman things was additionally confirmed, as the example of Henry Smith once again suggests, by the common practice of dismembering the corpse of a lynching victim and then distributing its parts, whether finger, ear, or toe, as souvenirs. Such mutilation, which was reminiscent of the nonlethal punishments often meted out to slaves prior to the Civil War, also ensured that the lynched body serve as a sort of text, relaying to all the differential meanings essential to the reproduction of racial subordination. Indeed, in a sense, reduction of black bodies to their constituent parts, which were then bought, sold, and traded, restored formally free African-Americans to a status not unlike that of chattel slaves, i.e., to the status of commodities whose disposition was determined by white owners. That castration accompanied many spectacle lynchings, as was also done to many slaves accused of rape as late as the 1850s, should come as no surprise. Through this means, the white community literally emasculated (and so feminized) black men, thereby eliminating them as perceived threats to Southern white women, but also rendering them figuratively ineligible to enter into the company of formally equal male citizens.

### Law/Underlaw

Conventional definitions of lynching, virtually without exception, either presuppose or expressly draw a sharp line of demarcation between violence inflicted in the name of the law and that which stands outside or in violation of the law (the extralegal and the illegal, respectively). The *Oxford English Dictionary,* for example, defines lynching as "the practice of inflicting summary punishment upon an offender, by a self-constituted court armed with no legal authority." In much the same vein, in their *A Festival of Violence,* Stewart Tolnay and E. M. Beck, maintain that "[a]ll lynchings ... share one commonality: The mob acted illegally, choosing to circumvent the formal system of criminal justice in order to carry out the lethal punishment personally."[10] Similarly, Richard Maxwell Brown, in his oft-cited *Strain of Violence,* characterizes lynching as "the practice or custom by which persons are punished for real or alleged crimes without due process of law."[11] Finally, and as one would expect in a criminal code, much the same bifurcation was implicit in the antilynching statutes passed by various states during the late nineteenth and early twentieth centuries, beginning with Ohio in 1896: "That any collection of individuals, assembled for any unlawful purpose, intending to do damage or injury to any one or pretending to exercise correctional power over other persons by violence, and without authority of law, shall for the purpose of this act be regarded as a 'mob,' and any act of violence exercised by them upon the body of any person, shall constitute a 'lynching.' "[12] Lynching, according to each of these definitions, is construed as a paradigmatic instance of the extralegal or illegal, which, in turn, is typically taken to imply that the aim of reform is to secure state control over the exercise of such unauthorized violence and so bring this criminal practice to a halt.

Such definitions are of considerable utility to those who wish to tell a self-congratulatory tale about the ultimate victory of civilization over barbarism, of the duly constituted forces of law and order over lawless mobs acting absent all authority. However, they are a poor guide to a significant number of lynchings, and they are so precisely because they tacitly rely for their coherence on presuppositions drawn from the logic of the liberal social contract (which, in turn, renders them ill suited to an appreciation of the role of lynching in reproducing the racial contract). According to the terms of social contract theory, if it is to sustain its authority, the law of a liberal political order must distinguish unequivocally the harm it commands from that which it punishes. Thus, for example, the law must be able to differentiate the violence it inflicts when it carries out a death sentence from the violence for which that sentence is a punishment. The liberal state's capacity to create and sustain that distinction is, in turn, a function of its ability to demarcate the public from the private realms (just as the coherence of its abstract conception of citizenship presupposes that features of identity located in the private sphere, such as race, are formally irrelevant to determining one's participation in the social contract as well as membership in the political community it founds). One means of sustaining that demarcation is the state's adherence to norms of due process that are neither required nor expected of nonstate actors. It follows, accordingly, that the authority of the liberal state and, more particularly, the authority of its criminal law to punish are eroded when the distinction between lawful and unlawful violence, as well as that between public and private, are violated; and these distinctions are transgressed in an especially egregious way when the punishment of death, which is officially reserved to the state in a liberal political order on the ground that this penalty is the ultimate expression of its monopoly over the means of legitimate violence, is imposed by private agents who show no respect for the norms of due process. The integrity of liberal law therefore mandates, as the definitions cited above indicate, that official executions and unofficial lynchings be represented as categorically distinct events. Specifically, the former must be deemed a punishment performed by public officials, sworn to do their duty, after a dispassionate verdict has been reached following a fair trial before a jury of disinterested peers and supervised by an impartial judge, whereas the latter is prototypically construed as a lawless deed performed by an impassioned mob of private persons animated by a lust for vengeance and/or irrational race prejudice.

Yet, as the very phrase "lynch law" implies, and as Henry Smith's torture at the hands of the sheriff of Paris, Texas, suggests, the mutually exclusive opposition between the legal and the illegal fails to appreciate how unstable and often irrelevant was the liberal formulation of the distinction between the official and unofficial, public and private, in the conduct of lynching. Granted, the performance of spectacle lynchings did participate in elaborating a distinction between public and private, but the form assumed by that distinction was quite different from that mandated by the social contract. As a ritual that reaffirmed the racial contract, these lynchings were public not in the sense that they were authorized by a formal code of state law but, rather, in the sense that they ratified popular but unpromulgated norms regarding the superiority of the white race. Moreover, these lynchings were public not in the sense that they took place at sites officially designated by the state (e.g., a prison) but, rather, in the sense that they transpired at unbounded settings, typically outdoors, from which no one was excluded. Finally, spectacle lynchings were public not in the sense that they were accomplished by state agents acting in the name of a sovereign citizenry but, rather, in the sense that communal participation, often manifest in the traditional expectation that everyone present, without exception, fire shots at the victim's corpse, distinguished it from acts of private vengeance.

Spectacle lynchings, in short, are not well understood in terms of the oppositions conventionally drawn by social contract theory. A more promising route, one less prone to anachronism, is suggested not by the distinction between legal and illegal but between "law" and "underlaw." Jacquelyn Hall explains:

[L]ynchings often took the form not of frenzied killings but of deliberate, purposeful extensions of the administration of justice. Blacks were eliminated from juries, and courts meted out disproportionately harsh sentences to black defendants. In a system of what one scholar has termed "underlaw," police officials exploited areas of discretion in the legal process to translate local white custom into effective social control, regardless of the letter of the statute books. The broad discretionary power in the hands of local and county officials routinely verged on vigilantism. Whites acting as special deputies or posse members eagerly assisted in manhunts. If the lawful authorities failed to measure up to community demands, the initiative for law enforcement could easily pass into the hands of private citizens. The lynchings that followed were modeled after the public hangings that, until the second decade of the twentieth century, were carried out by local and county government officials.[13]

As the above passage indicates, many lynchings, especially of the spectacle sort, should be located not in the domain of the illegal or the extralegal but, rather, near the heart of a more comprehensive structure of racial control, one that vested informal police powers in members of the white race and that encouraged vigilantism as a necessary complement to its weak agencies of formally authorized political discipline.[14]

The permeability of the border between the legal and the extralegal, a key element of the post-Reconstruction racial polity, can be illustrated from both sides of liberalism's conceptual divide: "The distinction between legal lynchings and mob lynchings," writes George Wright, "was blurred by instances when the court assumed the role of the mob by holding a 'trial' even though the defendant stood no chance of being found innocent, as well as instances when the mob assumed the role of the court and gave the victim a 'trial' and allowed members of the lynch mob to render a verdict and select the method of execution."[15] To appreciate Wright's point from the perspective of the underlaw, consider the following example:

> In 1917, in Memphis, Tennessee, Ell Persons was accused of raping and murdering a sixteen year old white girl by the name of Antoinette Rappel. While shuttling Persons back and forth between Memphis and Nashville, local authorities were intercepted and overpowered by members of a lynching committee calling themselves the Shelby Avengers and presided over by a designated "master of ceremonies." After the next morning's newspaper announced that the Avengers intended to lynch Persons, several hundred persons gathered at the designated location, where the mother of Antoinette was given an opportunity to identify her alleged assailant and then to offer something akin to a victim impact statement, which included an expression of her desire that "the Negro" should "suffer as my little girl suffered, only ten times worse." Respecting her wishes, the Avengers collectively agreed to burn Persons, and to refrain from shooting him first, since that would abbreviate his agonies. On the day following Person's death and dismemberment, which included his decapitation, the *Commercial Appeal* reported that "throughout the entire proceedings there was perfect order. The crowd was dominated completely by the committee which had planned and executed the capture of the black slayer from the state authorities, and none offered violence not countenanced by the summary court." The *Appeal* concluded by praising the Avengers for their election of a treasurer who was assigned responsibility for securing compensation for those who had lost wages from their regular jobs while participating in the search for and execution of Persons.[16]

As the example intimates, it was not uncommon for lynching parties to mimic certain of the formal procedures that, according to the conventional definitions cited above, are said to distinguish lawful trials from extralegal lynchings.[17] In addition, a very large number of spectacle lynchings were conducted either with the active participation of police officers (along with other community elites), or with their obvious connivance.[18]

Moreover, as Brundage notes, it is not at all clear that these officers entertained the political convictions, crucial elements of the social contract, that might have invited them to deem their participation problematic: "[M]any local officials held a conception of law and order that neither stressed the abstract principles of justice nor drew precise distinctions between legal and extralegal justice. Instead, many saw mob violence as a means of carrying out the spirit of formal law, if not the letter."[19] In sum, many lynchings should be classified not as irrational deeds perpetrated by mobs of private persons, acting without legal authority but, rather, as ritualized enactments that drew their authority from the unwritten racial contract of the white community and that patterned their proceedings, to a greater or lesser extent, on the very judicial procedures they are characteristically said to flout.

In moving from the perspective of the underlaw to that of the law, again recognizing that these terms point not to a categorical distinction but to coconstitutive elements of a larger structure of racial domination, the historical record makes clear that many of the executions ordered by Southern courts, and performed by public officials during the post-Reconstruction decades were only barely distinguishable from the lynchings I have recounted thus far. Consider, for example, the following account of a 1929 execution in Brazos County, Texas, as related by the Southern Commission on the Study of Lynching in its 1931 publication, *Lynchings and What They Mean*:

> The sheriff arrested a Negro accused of raping a schoolteacher at Millican, just southwest of Bryan, and escaped with him. The mob followed. To prevent a lynching, a leading lawyer promised mob leaders that if they would leave the Negro in the custody of the law he would see to it that there would be an immediate conviction and death sentence. The case was called late one afternoon. The mob, jamming the courthouse, demanded that it be completed that night. Court officials, fearing that a recess would result in a lynching, went on with the case. The evidence and argument were finished by ten o'clock. The jury retired and in a few minutes returned a verdict of guilty. The lawyers appointed by the court for the defendant considered whether to appeal the case, calling into their deliberations other lawyers and leading citizens. They decided not to appeal, fearing that to do so would only result in a lynching that night. So it was that the Negro's case was not appealed and within a month he was executed. The mob dictated every move in this trial, and doubtless the Negro would

have been lynched had the court at any point failed to carry out promises made the mob by leading citizens.[20]

As Southern newspapers were often quick to point out, and as this example makes evident, the members of a community who engaged in a lynching were often the same persons who, should the accused be tried, would sit on the grand and petit juries that would convict and sentence him. Should the accused in fact be tried, as was the case here, the coercive presence of a band of potential lynchers, either within or just outside the courthouse, virtually guaranteed that adherence to the forms of due process generated the same verdict and punishment that its members would otherwise mete out in the streets. Should such proceedings take place before a jury from which all African-Americans had been excluded, either by law or by custom; should the interval between that trial's beginning and end prove exceedingly brief, as it was in the case of Allen Mathias, who, accused of rape in 1906, was tried, convicted, and executed in the space of one hour and two minutes;[21] should that trial deny to the accused the right to self-defense, as was George Dinning, also of Kentucky, when in 1897 he killed a member of an armed white mob seeking to seize his cattle and force him off his farm;[22] should that trial be presided over by a judge who acquiesced in these counterfeit proceedings, as was routinely the case, it is difficult to know what to call such incidents other than "legal lynchings," even though that phrase cannot help but appear oxymoronic from the standpoint of the social contract.

## CAPITAL PUNISHMENT AND THE CONTEMPORARY RACIAL CONTRACT

The last recorded spectacle lynching occurred in 1937 in the town of Duck Hill, Mississippi, where, after being arraigned for the murder of a white store owner, Roosevelt Townes and "Bootjack" McDaniels were seized by a party whose members removed them to a site near the scene of their alleged crime, tortured them with a chain as well as a blowtorch, and, finally, after each had "confessed," shot, mutilated and incinerated the two men.[23] Five years later, the Commission on Interracial Cooperation published a major report on the history of lynching in the post-Reconstruction era.[24] Analyzing the data presented in that document, Jessie Daniel Ames, executive director of the Association of Southern Women for the Prevention of Lynching, noted that, leaving aside occasional spikes, the number of lynchings had declined steadily from a peak in 1893, when, by the Commission's count, more than 150 blacks were killed. Indeed, in May of 1940, she concluded that, for the first time since the end of Reconstruction, a full year had elapsed without a single lynching.[25] To explain this accomplishment, among other factors, she pointed to an increase in the number of state radio police patrols, which, on her account, had the effect of introducing law enforcement officials into rural areas where, traditionally, most lynchings occurred. Ames's reading of lynching's history, in sum, is one that commends the victory of the social contract over its racial counterpart, however precarious, and which accounts for that victory, at least in part, by pointing to the state's more effective monopoly over the deployment of violence.

A less sanguine reading was offered by the National Association for the Advancement of Colored People, which was quick to respond to Ames's proclamation by arguing that what appeared to be a dramatic reduction in the number of lynchings was in fact simply an indication of their changing character.[26] As Ames and the NAACP both acknowledged, beginning in the mid-1930s, white bands seized fewer prisoners from officers and jails (or, when the accused remained unincarcerated, engaged in the customary manhunt). When they did so, almost never did their members resort to public torture, dismemberment, and/or burning of their victims; and only very rarely did they claim to be motivated by a code of chivalry, which demanded that they respond to injuries allegedly committed against white women. Curtailment of these features, maintained Walter White, executive secretary of the NAACP, indicated not that lynching had ceased but that the practice had simply "gone underground."[27] Setting aside its earlier definition, which required a mob acting in the name of community sentiment in order to qualify a killing as a lynching, the NAACP contended that lynchings were now more often conducted by small groups of white men who planned their deeds with considerable care, killed their victims in secret, attempted to hide the evidence of their crimes, and usually succeeded in escaping public identification and prosecution as a result of the clandestine participation or indifference of local law officers.

On this analysis, the end of spectacle lynchings did indeed signify a shift in the relationship between the social and racial contracts, as Ames's argument implied, but not one that could easily be folded into a narrative about the victory of the legal over the extralegal or illegal. As local and state elites sought to stabilize the sort of predictable legal order required by the imperatives of a slowly modernizing economy, as liberal reformers continued to afford lynchings national publicity and to press for passage of a federal bill that would impose heavy penalties on those who engaged in this practice, it grew more costly to reproduce the racial polity through an irregular and heavily ritualized brand of popular justice that relied on the undisciplined energies of untrained amateurs who, all too often, left the evidence of their handiwork swinging from tree limbs. That such rough justice proved eliminable may indicate not the growing authority of the social over the racial contract but, rather, as Jacquelyn Hall proposes, the latter's incorporation within the less overtly violent operations of rationalized institutions and routinized practices operating within the underlaw and law alike:

White supremacy, of course, did not rest on force alone. Routine institutional arrangements denied to the freedmen and women the opportunity to own land, the right to vote, access to education, and participation in the administration of the law. Lynching reached its height during the battles of Reconstruction and the Populist revolt; once a new system of disfranchisement, debt peonage, and segregation were firmly in place, mob violence gradually declined.[28]

In other words, more graphic forms of racial violence, such as spectacle lynching, became less imperative once white dominance was assured by less transparent but more calculable means (although cruder forms, such as privatized lynchings, remained available, should their more mundane kin fail). Perpetuation of the racial contract still required the coercive production of a class of subpersons, but no longer was it necessary to secure that end by visibly marking and publicly displaying the bodies of its members.

Taking Hall's contention as my cue, the question I wish to address in the remainder of this essay is not whether capital punishment is one of the political practices that now serves to reproduce the racial polity (which, for the purposes of this essay, I will assume to be the case).[29] Rather, I mean to ask how transformations in the conduct of capital punishment contribute to what Mills calls "the epistemology of ignorance," i.e., the sort of ignorance that renders its participation in reinforcing the terms of the racial contract less transparent and so less susceptible to challenge on the grounds of its dissonance with the norms of the social contract. To address this question, in the remainder of this section, I will consider two overlapping ways in which the practice of capital punishment has been rendered formally more consistent with the legitimating imperatives of liberalism. Each corresponds to one of the two features of spectacle lynching I emphasized in parts A and B of section II. The first concerns the gradual elimination of race-specific penalties, as well as methods of inflicting them, which, at least formally, moves the law closer to the liberal ideal of equality under the law; and the second concerns the construction of a less permeable wall between official and unofficial realms, which enhances the appearance of state neutrality and hence its authority in upholding the law. Each, I will suggest, is a vital means of hiding the play of the underlaw within the law itself.

## DISCUSSION QUESTIONS

1. What was spectacle lynching?
2. What are the parallels between spectacle lynching and capital punishment?
3. What are the consequences for African American offenders accused of harming whites?

## NOTES

1. For a useful account of the origins and history of the term "lynching," see James Cutler, *Lynch-Law* (Montclair, NJ: Patterson Smith, 1969).

2. The historical record explains and warrants these connotations. Specifically, in his *Lynching in the New South* (Urbana and Chicago: University of Illinois Press, 1993), W. Fitzhugh Brundage notes that, following the end of Reconstruction, the proportion of lynchings that occurred in the South rose each decade, increasing from 82 percent to 95 percent between 1880 and 1930. During these same decades, moreover, the proportion of lynching victims in the South who were black rose from 68 percent to 91 percent (pp. 8–9). The precise number of persons lynched following the withdrawal of Federal troops in 1877 will never be known with certainty, in part because many instances will remain forever unrecorded. That said, Brundage calculates that, between 1880 and 1930, 4,587 lynchings occurred in the United States, 3,943 in the South, and, of this number, 3,220 involved black victims.

3. For an overview of the principal accounts offered by scholars in order to explain lynchings in the post-Reconstruction South, see W. Fitzhugh Brundage's introduction to his *Under Sentence of Death* (Chapel Hill and London: University of North Carolina Press, 1997), pp. 1–20.

4. For an analysis of lynching in terms similar, but not identical, to those employed here, see Robyn Wiegman, "The Anatomy of Lynching," in *American Sexual Politics*, John Fout and Maura Tantillo, eds. (Chicago: University of Chicago Press, 1990).

5. Mills, *The Racial Contract*, p. 87.

6. See Brundage, *Lynching in the New South*, pp. 18–48, for a very helpful analysis of the principal types of post-Reconstruction lynchings. My particular concern is with those he labels "mass mobs," which, by his enumeration, accounted for 34 percent of all post-Reconstruction lynchings in Georgia and 40 percent of those in Virginia.

7. What I offer here is an abridged version of the more detailed accounts of the lynching of Henry Smith provided by Ida B. Wells, in her "A Red Record," in *Southern Horrors* (New York: Arno Press and the New York Times, 1969), pp. 25–32, as well as by Dray in his *At the Hands of Persons Unknown*, pp. 77–79.

8. Dray, *At the Hands of Persons Unknown*, p. 78.

9. Many of these photographs are reproduced in *Without Sanctuary: Lynching Photography in America* (Santa Fe, NM: Twin Palms Publishers, 2000).

10. Tolnay, Stewart, and E. M. Beck, *A Festival of Violence* (Urbana: University of Illinois Press, 1995), p. 56.

11. Richard Maxwell Brown, *Strain of Violence* (New York: Oxford University Press, 1977), p. 21. For another example of a definition that presupposes the coherence of the distinction between official and unofficial acts of violence, see Cutler, *Lynch-Law.* "Lynch-law has always been considered as operating wholly without, or in opposition to, established laws of government" (p. 15).

12. Quoted in Cutler, *Lynch-Low,* p. 235.

13. Jacquelyn Hall, *Revolt Against Chivalry* (New York: Columbia University Press, 1993), pp. 140–41. Hall appropriates the term "underlaw" from Peter Teachout, "Louisiana Underlaw," in *Southern Justice,* Leon Friedman, ed. (New York: Meridian, 1967).

14. Throughout the nineteenth century and well into the twentieth, the South was distinguished from the North by its weak institutions of legal and, more generally, state authority. In the North, explains Brundage, in his *Lynching in the New South,* "the accelerating pace of economic development and the growth of cities required the permanent and dependable exercise of state authority on behalf of capital and property. Consequently, courts and law enforcement agencies, including recently created urban police forces, assumed a greater role in preserving social order. In the South, planters were wary of the establishment of any powerful legal institutions that might challenge their autonomy … They preferred to rely on a code of honor and such traditional extralegal methods of punishment as whipping and ostracism to safeguard community morals and virtues" (p. 40.

15. George C. Wright, "By the Book: The Legal Executions of Kentucky Blacks," in Brundage, *Under Sentence of Death,* pp. 251–52.

16. I construct this account on the basis of the more extended version provided by Dray, *At the Hands of Persons Unknown,* pp. 231–34.

17. See George Wright, *Racial Violence in Kentucky* (Baton Rouge: Louisiana State University Press, 1990), pp. 93–95. For another example of a lynching party's respect for something akin to the norms of due process, see Leon Litwack, "Hellhounds" in *Without Sanctuary,* p. 18: In 1905, in Howard, Texas, after presenting a black man accused of rape to his alleged victim, so that she might confirm his identity before the community, the participants in his lynching elected to afford their victim two hours for prayers and family visitation prior to infliction of death. While waiting, they debated and then subjected to majority vote whether the sentence should be executed by means of hanging or by burning, with the latter eventually winning out on the grounds that the crime committed was unusually heinous. At the close of this "deliberately-planned

and calmly-executed spectacle," reported the editor of a local newspaper, the crowd dispersed.

18. See Arthur Raper, *The Tragedy of Lynching* (New York: Negro Universities Press, 1969), for accounts of numerous lynchings in which police officers either actively participated or passively condoned the conduct of others. For a good example of official approval given to lynchings, consider the following example, taken from *Without Sanctuary*, pp, 20–21. In 1911, those who killed and dismembered Willis Jackson in Honea Path, South Carolina, were led by Joshua W Ashleigh, who represented the district in the state legislature. When a group of South Carolinians demanded a state investigation, Governor Cole Blease refused, stating that, had he deemed it necessary, he would have resigned his office, come to Honea Path, and led the mob himself. The local newspaper in Spartanburg, praising the governor's refusal to initiate an investigation, cautioned against indicting Jackson's killers because that "would make heroes of the lynchers and eminently qualify them for public office."

19. Brundage, *Lynching in the New South*, p. 180.

20. Southern Commission on the Study of Lynching, *Lynchings and What They Mean* (Atlanta: The Commission, 1931), p. 52.

21. See Wright, "By the Book," pp. 256–57.

22. See ibid., pp. 258–59, In response to the public outrage occasioned by his conviction, Dinning was given a full pardon by the governor of Kentucky ten days after his arrival at the state prison.

23. See Dray, *At the Hands of Persons Unknown*, pp. 359–60, for a complete account of the lynching of Townes and McDaniels.

24. Jessie Daniel Ames, *The Changing Character of Lynching* (Atlanta: Commission on Interracial Cooperation, Inc., 1942).

25. See Hall, *Revolt Against Chivalry*, p. 256.

26. To be properly understood, Ames's pamphlet, as well as the response issued by the NAACP, should be read against the backdrop of a protracted argument among various antilynching groups about whether the end of specifically spectacle lynchings signified the end of lynching more generally. For a helpful account of this controversy, see Christopher Waldrep, "War of Words: The Controversy over the Definition of Lynching, 1899–1940," *Journal of Southern History* 66 (2000): 75–100.

27. Quoted in Waldrep, "War of Words," p. 96.

28. Jacquelyn Dowd Hall, " 'The Mind That Burns in Each Body': Women, Rape, and Racial Violence," in *Powers of Desire*, Ann Snitow, Christine Stansell, and Sharon Tompson, eds. (New York: Monthly Review Press, 1983), p. 331.

29. Were I to offer evidence to sustain this contention, I would start with the following: Although blacks now make up approximately 13 percent of the U.S. population, 35 percent of those executed since 1976 have been African-American, as are 43 percent of the inmates currently on death row (see Death Penalty Information Center, at http://www.deathpenaltyinfo.org/race.html). Moreover, capital punishment remains a largely southern practice, although there is some dispute as to whether this is because the homicide rate is higher in the South than in other regions or because southern juries are more prone than those in other regions to impose death sentences. In any event, as Stuart Banner notes in his *The Death Penalty: An American History* (Cambridge, MA: Harvard University Press, 2002), of the 598 executions conducted between 1977 and 1999, the overwhelming majority took place in Texas (199), Virginia (73), Florida (44), Missouri (41), Louisiana (25), South Carolina (24), Georgia (23), Arkansas (21), Alabama (19), Arizona (19), Oklahoma (19), and North Carolina (15) (p. 278). The geographical distribution of death sentences is not quite so unbalanced, but it is nonetheless true that of the 18 states that imposed more than 100 death sentences between 1973 and 1998, 13 are in the South. Furthermore, there are significant disparities in capital sentencing relative to race of the offender and the race of the victim. More specifically, as the U.S. General Accounting Office has indicated in the report "Death Penalty Sentencing: Research Indicates Pattern of Racial Disparities (1990)" reprinted in *The Death Penalty in America,* Hugo Bedau, ed. (New York: Oxford University Press, 1997), the percentage of death sentences imposed is highest in cases involving black defendants and white victims. This is so, explain William Bowers, Benjamin Steiner, and Maria Sandys in "Death Sentencing in Black and White: An Empirical Analysis of the Role of Jurors' Race and Jury Racial Composition," *University of Pennsylvania Journal of Constitutional Law* 3 (2001): 171–274, because, in black defendant/white victim cases, white male jurors are far less likely than are their black counterparts to experience doubts about the defendant's guilt, as well as far more likely to vote to impose a death sentence based on their perception of the defendant's future dangerousness. In terms of public opinion, the U.S. Department of Justice, in its Sourcebook of Criminal Justice Statistics 133, tbl. 2.60 (2000) available at http://www.albany.edu/sourcebook/1995/pdf/t260.pdf shows that support for the death penalty is far more pronounced among whites, and especially white males, than it is among blacks. And, from the work of Steven Barkan and Steven Cohn, "Racial Prejudice and Support for the Death Penalty by Whites," *Journal of Research on Crime and Delinquency* 31 (1994), we learn that white support for capital punishment is predicated in large part on racial prejudice and stereotyping.

# PART 3

---

## STRATEGIES OF
## ADDRESSING RACISM

# CHAPTER 10
## Strategies of Addressing Racism

# Racism and Feminism

## bell hooks

AMERICAN WOMEN OF all races are socialized to think of racism solely in the context of race hatred. Specifically in the case of black and white people, the term racism is usually seen as synonymous with discrimination or prejudice against black people by white people. For most women, the first knowledge of racism as institutionalized oppression is engendered either by direct personal experience or through information gleaned from conversations, books, television, or movies. Consequently, the American woman's understanding of racism as a political tool of colonialism and imperialism is severely limited. To experience the pain of race hatred or to witness that pain is not to understand its origin, evolution, or impact on world history. The inability of American women to understand racism in the context of American politics is not due to any inherent deficiency in woman's psyche. It merely reflects the extent of our victimization.

No history books used in public schools informed us about racial imperialism. Instead we were given romantic notions of the "new world," the "American dream," America as the great melting pot where all races come together as one. We were taught that Columbus discovered America; that "Indians" were scalphunters, killers of innocent women and children; that black people were enslaved because of the biblical curse of Ham, that God "himself" had decreed they would be hewers of wood, tillers of the field, and bringers of water. No one talked of Africa as the cradle of civilization, of the African and Asian people who came to America before Columbus. No one mentioned mass murders of Native Americans as genocide, or the rape of Native American and African women as terrorism. No one discussed slavery as a foundation for the growth of capitalism. No one described the forced breeding of white wives to increase the white population as sexist oppression.

I am a black woman. I attended all-black public schools. I grew up in the south where all around me was the fact of racial discrimination, hatred, and forced segregation. Yet my education as to the politics of race in American society was not that different from that of white female students I met in integrated high schools, in college, or in various women's groups. The majority of us understood racism as a social evil perpetuated by prejudiced white people that could be overcome through bonding between blacks and liberal whites, through militant protest, changing of laws or racial integration. Higher educational institutions did nothing to increase our limited understanding of racism as a political ideology. Instead professors systematically denied us truth, teaching us to accept racial polarity in the form of white supremacy and sexual polarity in the form of male dominance.

American women have been socialized, even brainwashed, to accept a version of American history that was created to uphold and maintain racial imperialism in the form of white supremacy and sexual imperialism in the form of patriarchy. One measure of the success of such indoctrination is that we perpetuate both consciously and unconsciously the very evils that oppress us. I am certain that the black female sixth grade teacher who taught us history, who taught us to identify with the American government, who loved those students who could best recite the pledge of allegiance to the American flag was not aware of the contradiction; that we should love this government that segregated us, that failed to send schools with all black students supplies that went to schools with only white pupils. Unknowingly she implanted in our psyches a seed of the racial imperialism that would keep us forever in bondage. For how does one overthrow, change, or even challenge a system that you have been taught to admire, to love, to believe in? Her innocence does not change the reality that she was teaching black children to embrace the very system that oppressed us, that she encouraged us to support it, to stand in awe of it, to die for it.

That American women, irrespective of their education, economic status, or racial identification, have undergone years of sexist and racist socialization that has taught us to blindly trust our knowledge of history and its effect on present reality, even though that knowledge has been formed and shaped by an oppressive system, is nowhere more evident than in the recent feminist movement. The group of college-educated white middle and upper class women who came together to organize a women's movement brought a new energy to the concept of women's rights in America. They were not merely advocating social equality with men. They demanded a transformation of society, a revolution, a change in the American social structure. Yet as they attempted to take feminism beyond the realm of radical rhetoric and into the realm of American life, they revealed that they had not changed, had not undone the sexist and racist brainwashing that had taught them to regard women unlike themselves as Others. Consequently, the Sisterhood they talked about has not become a reality, and the women's movement they envisioned would have a transformative effect on American culture his not emerged. Instead, the hierarchical pattern of race and sex relationships already established in American society merely took a different form under "feminism": the form of women being classed as an oppressed group under affirmative action programs further perpetuating the myth that the social status of all women in America is the same; the form of women's studies programs being established with all white faculty teaching literature almost exclusively by white women about white women and frequently from racist perspectives; the form of white women writing books that purport to be about the experience of American women when in fact they concentrate solely on the experience of white women; and finally the form of endless argument and debate as to whether or not racism was a feminist issue.

If the white women who organized the contemporary movement toward feminism were at all remotely aware of racial politics in American history, they would have known that overcoming barriers that separate women from one another would entail confronting the reality of racism, and not just racism as a general evil in society but the race hatred they might harbor in their own psyches. Despite the predominance of patriarchal rule in American society, America was colonized on a racially imperialistic base and not on a sexually imperialistic base. No degree of patriarchal bonding between white male colonizers and Native American men overshadowed white racial imperialism. Racism took precedence over sexual alliances in both the white world's interaction with Native Americans and African Americans, just as racism overshadowed any bonding between black women and white women on the basis of sex. Tunisian writer Albert Memmi emphasizes in The Colonizer and the Colonized the impact of racism as a tool of imperialism:

> Racism appears ... not as an incidental detail, but as a con-substantial part of colonialism. It is the highest expression of the colonial system and one of the most significant features of the colonialist. Not only does it establish a (fundamental discrimination between colonizer and colonized, a sine qua non of colonial life, but it also lays the foundation for the immutability of this life.

While those feminists who argue that sexual imperialism is more endemic to all societies than racial imperialism are probably correct, American society is one in which racial imperialism supersedes sexual imperialism.

In America, the social status of black and white women has never been the same. In 19th and early 20th century America, few if any similarities could be found between the life experiences of the two female groups. Although they were both subject to sexist victimization, as victims of racism black women were subjected to oppressions no white woman was forced to endure. In fact, white racial imperialism granted all white women, however victimized by sexist oppression they might be, the right to assume the role of oppressor in relationship to black women and black men. From the onset of the contemporary move toward feminist revolution, white female organizers attempted to minimize their position in the racial caste hierarchy of American society. In their efforts to disassociate themselves from white men (to deny connections based on shared racial caste), white women involved in the move toward feminism have charged that racism is endemic to white male patriarchy and have argued that they cannot be held responsible for racist oppression. Commenting on the issue of white female accountability in her essay "'Disloyal to Civilization': Feminism, Racism, and Gynephobia," radical feminist Adrienne Rich contends:

> If Black and White feminists are going to speak of female accountability, I believe the word racism must be seized, grasped in our bare hands, ripped out of the sterile or defensive consciousness in which it so often grows, and transplanted so that it can yield new insights for our lives and our movement. An analysis that places the guilt for active domination, physical and institutional violence, and the justifications embedded in myth and language, on white women not only compounds false consciousness; it allows us all to deny or neglect the charged connection among black and white women from the historical conditions of slavery on, and it impedes any real discussion of women's instrumentality in a system which oppresses all women and in which hatred of women is also embedded in myth, folklore, and language.

No reader of Rich's essay could doubt that she is concerned that women who are committed to feminism work to overcome barriers that separate black and white women. However, she fails to understand that from a black female perspective, if white women are denying the existence of black women, writing "feminist" scholarship as if black women are not a part of the collective group American women, or discriminating against black women, then it matters less that North America was colonized by white patriarchal men who institutionalized a racially imperialistic social order than that white women who purport to be feminists support and actively perpetuate anti-black racism.

To black women the issue is not whether white women are more or less racist than white men, but that they are racist. If women committed to feminist revolution, be they black or white, are to achieve any understanding of the "charged connections" between white women and black women, we must first be willing to examine woman's relationship to society, to race, and to American culture as it is and not as we would ideally have it be. That means confronting the reality of white female racism. Sexist discrimination has prevented white women from assuming the dominant role in the perpetuation of white racial imperialism, but it has not prevented white women from absorbing, supporting, and advocating racist ideology or acting individually as racist oppressors in various spheres of American life.

Every women's movement in America from its earliest origin to the present day has been built on a racist foundation—a fact which in no way invalidates feminism as a political ideology. The racial apartheid social structure that characterized 19th and early 20th century American life was mirrored in the women's rights movement. The first white women's rights advocates were never seeking social equality for all women; they were seeking social equality for white women. Because many 19th century white women's rights advocates were also active in the abolitionist movement, it is often assumed they were anti-racist. Historiographers and especially recent feminist writing have created a version of American history in which white women's rights advocates are presented as champions of oppressed black people. This fierce romanticism has informed most studies of the abolitionist movement. In contemporary times there is a general tendency to equate abolitionism with a repudiation of racism. In actuality, most white abolitionists, male and female, though vehement in their antislavery protest, were totally opposed to granting social equality to black people. Joel Kovel, in his study White Racism: A Psychohistory, emphasizes that the "actual aim of the reform movement, so nobly and bravely begun, was not the liberation of the black, but the fortification of the white, conscience and all."

It is a commonly accepted belief that white female reformist empathy with the oppressed black slave, coupled with her recognition that she was powerless to end slavery, led to the development of a feminist consciousness and feminist revolt. Contemporary historiographers and in particular white female scholars accept the theory that the white women's rights advocates' feelings of solidarity with black slaves were an indication that they were anti-racist and were supportive of social equality of blacks. It is this glorification of the role white women played that leads Adrienne Rich to assert:

> … It is important for white feminists to remember that—despite lack of constitutional citizenship, educational deprivation, economic bondage to men, laws and customs forbidding women to speak in public or to disobey fathers, husbands, and brothers—our white foresisters have, in Lillian Smith's words, repeatedly been "disloyal to civilization" and have "smelled death in the word 'segregation'," often defying patriarchy for the first time, not on their own behalf but for the sake of black men, women, and children. We have a strong anti-racist female tradition despite all efforts by the white patriarchy to polarize its creature-objects, creating dichotomies of privilege and caste, skin color, and age and condition of servitude.

There is little historical evidence to document Rich's assertion that white women as a collective group or white women's rights advocates are part of an anti-racist tradition. When white women reformers in the 1830s chose to work to free the slave, they were motivated by religious sentiment. They attacked slavery, not racism. The basis of their attack was moral reform. That they were not demanding social equality for black people is an indication that they remained committed to white racist supremacy despite their anti-slavery work. While they strongly advocated an end to slavery, they never advocated a change in the racial hierarchy that allowed their caste status to be higher than that of black women or men. In fact, they wanted that hierarchy to be maintained. Consequently, the white women's rights movement which had a lukewarm beginning in earlier reform activities emerged in full force in the wake of efforts to gain rights for black people precisely because white women wanted to see no change in the social status of blacks until they were assured that their demands for more rights were met.

At the beginning of the 20th century, white women suffragists were eager to advance their own cause at the expense of black people. In 1903 at the National American Woman's Suffrage Convention held in New Orleans, a southern suffragist urged the enfranchisement of white women on the grounds that it "would insure immediate and durable white supremacy." Historian Rosalyn Terborg-Penn discusses white female support of white supremacy in her essay "Discrimination Against Afro-American Women in the Woman's Movement 1830–1920":

> As early as the 1890s, Susan B. Anthony realized the potential to the woman suffrage cause in wooing southern white women. She chose expedience over loyalty and justice when she asked veteran feminist supporter Frederick Douglass not to attend the National American Woman Suffrage Association convention scheduled in Atlanta. …
>
> During the National American Woman Suffrage Association meeting of 1903 in New Orleans, the Times Democrat assailed the association because of its negative attitude on the question of black women and the suffrage for them. In a prepared statement signed by Susan B. Anthony, Carrie C. Catt, Anna Howard Shaw, Kate N. Gordon, Alice Stone Blackwell, Harriet Taylor Upton, Laura Clay, and Mary Coggeshall, the board of officers of the NAWSA endorsed the organization's states' rights position, which was tantamount to an endorsement of white supremacy in most states, particularly in the south.

Racism within the women's rights movement did not emerge simply as a response to the issue of suffrage; it was a dominant force in all reform groups with white female members. Terborg-Penn contends:

Discrimination against Afro-American women reformers was the rule rather than the exception within the woman's rights movement from the 1830s to 1920. Although white feminists Susan B. Anthony, Lucy Stone, and some others encouraged black women to join the struggle against sexism during the nineteenth century, antebellum reformers who were involved with women's abolitionist groups as well as women's rights organizations actively discriminated against black women.

In their efforts to prove that solidarity existed between 19th century black and white female reformers, contemporary women activists often cite the presence of Sojourner Truth at Women's Rights conventions to support their argument that white female suffragists were anti-racist. But on every occasion Sojourner Truth spoke, groups of white women protested. In The Betrayal of the Negro, Rayford Logan writes:

> When the General Federation of Women's Clubs was faced with the question of the color line at the turn of the century, Southern clubs threatened to secede. One of the first expressions of the adamant opposition to the admission of colored clubs was disclosed by the Chicago Tribune and the Examiner during the great festival of fraternization at the Atlanta Exposition, the Encampment of the GAR in Louisville, and the dedication of the Chickamauga battlefield. … The Georgia Women's Press Club felt so strongly on the subject that members were in favor of withdrawing from the Federation if colored women were admitted there. Miss Corinne Stocker, a member of the Managing Board of the Georgia Women's Press Club and one of the editors of the Atlanta Journal, stated on September 19: "In this matter the Southern women are not narrow-minded or bigoted, but they simply cannot recognize the colored women socially. … At the same time we feel that the South is the colored woman's best friend."

Southern white women's club members were most vehement in their opposition to black women joining their ranks, but northern white women also supported racial segregation. The issue of whether black women would be able to participate in the women's club movement on an equal footing with white women came to a head in Milwaukee at the General Federation of Women's Clubs conference when the question was raised as to whether black feminist Mary ChurchTerrell, then president of the National Association of Colored Women, would be allowed to offer greetings, and whether Josephine Ruffin, who represented the black organization the New Era Club, would be recognized. In both cases white women's racism carried the day. In an interview in the Chicago Tribune, the president of the federation, Mrs. Lowe, was asked to comment on the refusal to acknowledge black female participants like Josephine Ruffin, and she responded: "Mrs. Ruffin belongs among her own people. Among them she would be a leader and could do much good, but among us she can create nothing but trouble." Rayford Logan comments on the fact that white women like Mrs. Lowe had no objection to black women trying to improve their lot; they simply felt that racial apartheid should be maintained. Writing of Mrs. Lowe's attitude toward black women, Logan comments:

> Mrs. Lowe had assisted in establishing kindergartens for colored children in the South, and the colored women in charge of them were all her good friends. She associated with them in a business way, but, of course they would not think of sitting beside her at a convention. Negroes were "a race by themselves, and among themselves they can accomplish much, assisted by us and by the federation, which is ever ready to do all in its power to help them." If Mrs. Ruffin were the "cultured lady every one says she is, she should put her education and her talents to good uses as a colored woman among colored women."

Anti-black feelings among white female club members were much stronger than anti-black sentiment among white male club members. One white male wrote a letter to the Chicago Tribune in which he stated:

> Here we have the spectacle of educated, refined, and Christian women who have been protesting and laboring for years against the unjust discrimination practiced against them by men, now getting together and the first shot out of their reticules is fired at one of their own because she is black, no other reason or pretence of reason.

Prejudices white women activists felt toward black women were far more intense than their prejudices toward black men. As Rosalyn Penn states in her essay, black men were more accepted in white reform circles than black women. Negative attitudes toward black women were the result of prevailing racist sexist stereotypes that portrayed black women as morally impure. Many white women felt that their status as ladies would be undermined were they to associate with black women. No such moral stigma was attached to black men. Black male leaders like Frederick Douglass, James Forten, Henry Garnett and others were occasionally welcome in white social circles. White women activists who would not have considered dining in the company of black men welcomed individual black men to their family tables.

[…] Relationships between white and black women were charged by tensions and conflicts in the early part of the 20th century. The women's rights movement had not drawn black and white women close together. Instead, it exposed the fact that white women were not willing to relinquish their support of white supremacy to support the interests of all women. Racism in the women's rights movement and in the work arena was a constant reminder to black women of the distances that separated the two experiences, distances that white women did not want bridged. When the contemporary movement toward feminism began, white women organizers did not address the issue of conflict between black and white women. Their rhetoric of sisterhood and solidarity suggested that women in America were able to bond across both class and race boundaries—but no such coming together had actually occurred. The structure of the contemporary women's movement was no different from that of the earlier women's rights movement. Like their predecessors, the white women who initiated the women's movement launched their efforts in the wake of the 60s black liberation movement. As if history were repeating itself, they also began to make synonymous their social status and the social status of black people. And it was in the context of endless comparisons of the plight of "women" and "blacks" that they revealed their racism. In most cases, this racism was an unconscious, unacknowledged aspect of their thought, suppressed by their narcissism—a narcissism which so blinded them that they would not admit two obvious facts: one, that in a capitalist, racist, imperialist state there is no one social status women share as a collective group; and second, that the social status of white women in America has never been like that of black women or men.

When the women's movement began in the late 60s, it was evident that the white women who dominated the movement felt it was "their" movement, that is the medium through which a white woman would voice her grievances to society. Not only did white women act as if feminist ideology existed solely to serve their own interests because they were able to draw public attention to feminist concerns. They were unwilling to acknowledge that non-white women were part of the collective group women in American society. They urged black women to join "their" movement or in some cases the women's movement, but in dialogues and writings, their attitudes toward black women were both racist and sexist. Their racism did not assume the form of overt expressions of hatred; it was far more subtle. It took the form of simply ignoring the existence of black women or writing about them using common sexist and racist stereotypes. From Betty Friedan's The Feminine Mystique to Barbara Berg's The Remembered Gate and on to more recent publications like Capitalist Patriarchy and the Case for Socialist Feminism, edited by Zillah Eisenstein, most white female writers who considered themselves feminist revealed in their writing that they had been socialized to accept and perpetuate racist ideology.

In most of their writing, the white American woman's experience is made synonymous with the American woman's experience. While it is in no way racist for any author to write a book exclusively about white women, it is fundamentally racist for books to be published that focus solely on the American white woman's experience in which that experience is assumed to be the American woman's experience. For example, in the course of research for this book, I sought to find information about the life of free and slaveblack women in colonial America. I saw listed in a bibliography Julia Cherry Spruill's work *Women's Life and Work in the Southern Colonies*, which was first published in 1938 and then again in 1972. At the Sisterhood bookstore in Los Angeles I found the book and read a blurb on the back which had been written especially for the new edition:

> One of the classic works in American social history, *Women's Life and Work in the Southern Colonies* is the first comprehensive study of the daily life and status of women in southern colonial America. Julia Cherry Spruill researched colonial newspapers, court records, and manuscript material of every kind, drawing on archives and libraries from Boston to Savannah. The resulting book was, in the words of Arthur Schlesinger, Sr., "a model of research and exposition, an important contribution to American social history to which students will constantly turn."
>
> The topics include women's function in the settlement of the colonies; their homes, domestic occupation, and social life; the aims and methods of their education; their role in government and business affairs outside the home; and the manner in which they were regarded by the law and by society in general. Out of a wealth of documentation, and often from the words of colonial people themselves, a vivid and surprising picture—one that had never been seen before—emerges of the many different aspects of these women's lives.

I expected to find in Spruill's work information about various groups of women in American society. I found instead that it was another work solely about white women and that both the title and blurb were misleading. A more accurate title would have been *White Women's Life and Work in the Southern Colonies*. Certainly, if I or any author sent a manuscript to an American publisher that focused exclusively on the life and work of black women in the south, also called Women's Life and Work in the Southern Colonies the title would be automatically deemed misleading and unacceptable. The force that allows white feminist authors to make no reference to racial identity in their books about "women" that are in actuality about white women is the same one that would compel any author writing exclusively on black women to refer explicitly to their racial identity. That force is racism. In a racially imperialist nation such as ours, it is the dominant race that reserves for itself the luxury of dismissing racial identity while the oppressed race is made daily aware of their racial identity. It is the dominant race that can make it seem that their experience is representative.

In America, white racist ideology has always allowed white women to assume that the word woman is synonymous with white woman, for women of other races are always perceived as Others, as de-humanized beings who do not fall under the heading woman. White feminists who claimed to be politically astute showed themselves to be unconscious of the way their use of language suggested they did not recognize the existence of black women. They impressed upon the American public their sense that the word "woman" meant white woman by drawing endless analogies between "women" and "blacks." Examples of such analogies abound in almost every feminist work. In a collection of essays published in 1975 titled Women: A Feminist Perspective, an essay by Helen Hacker is included called "Women as a Minority Group" which is a good example of the way white women have used comparisons between "women" and "blacks" to exclude black women and to deflect attention away from their own racial caste status. Hacker writes:

> The relation between women and Negroes is historical, as well as analogical. In the seventeenth century the legal status of Negro servants was borrowed from that of women and children, who were under the patria potestas, and until the Civil War there was considerable cooperation between the Abolitionists and woman suffrage movement.

Clearly Hacker is referring solely to white women. An even more glaring example of the white feminist comparison between "blacks" and "women" occurs in Catherine Stimpson's essay "'Thy Neighbor's Wife, Thy Neighbor's Servants': Women's Liberation and Black Civil Rights." She writes:

> The development of an industrial economy, as Myrdal points out, has not brought about the integration of women and blacks into the adult male culture. Women have not found a satisfactory way to bear children and to work. Blacks have not destroyed the hard doctrine of their unassimilability. What the economy gives both women and blacks are menial labor, low pay, and few promotions. White male workers hate both groups, for their competition threatens wages and their possible job equality, let alone superiority, threatens nothing less than the very nature of things. The tasks of women and blacks are usually grueling, repetitive, slogging, and dirty ...

Throughout Stimpson's essay she makes woman synonymous with white women and black synonymous with black men.

[...] Whenever black women tried to express to white women their ideas about white female racism or their sense that the women who were at the forefront of the movement were not oppressed women they were told that "oppression cannot be measured." White female emphasis on "common oppression" in their appeals to black women to join the movement further alienated many black women. Because so many of the white women in the movement were employers of non-white and white domestics, their rhetoric of common oppression was experienced by black women as an assault, an expression of the bourgeois woman's insensitivity and lack of concern for the lower class woman's position in society.

Underlying the assertion of common oppression was a patronizing attitude toward black women. White women were assuming that all they had to do was express a desire for sisterhood, or a desire to have black women join their groups, and black women would be overjoyed. They saw themselves as acting in a generous, open, non-racist manner and were shocked that black women responded to their overtures with anger and outrage. They could not see that their generosity was directed at themselves, that it was self-centered and motivated by their own opportunistic desires.

Despite the reality that white upper and middle class women in America suffer from sexist discrimination and sexist abuse, they are not as a group as oppressed as poor white, or black, or yellow women. Their unwillingness to distinguish between various degrees of discrimination or oppression caused black women to see them as enemies. As many upper and middle class white feminists who suffer least from sexist oppression were attempting to focus all attention on themselves, it follows that they would not accept an analysis of woman's lot in America which argued that not all women are equally oppressed because some women are able to use their class, race and educational privilege to effectively resist sexist oppression.

Initially, class privilege was not discussed by white women in the women's movement. They wanted to project an image of themselves as victims and that could not be done by drawing attention to their class. In fact, the contemporary women's movement was extremely class bound. As a group, white participants did not denounce capitalism. They chose to define liberation using the terms of white capitalist patriarchy, equating liberation with gaining economic status and money power. Like all good capitalists, they proclaimed work as the key to liberation. This emphasis on work was yet another indication of the extent to which the white female liberationists' perception of reality was totally narcissistic, classist, and racist. Implicit in the assertion that work was the key to women's liberation was a refusal to acknowledge the reality that, for masses of American working class women, working for pay neither liberated them from sexist oppression nor allowed them to gain any measure of economic independence. In Liberating Feminism, Benjamin Barber's critique of the women's movement, he comments on the white middle and upper class women's liberationist focus on work:

Work clearly means something very different to women in search of an escape from leisure than it has to most of the human race for most of history. For a few lucky men, for far fewer women, work has occasionally been a source of meaning and creativity. But for most of the rest it remains even now forced drudgery in front of the ploughs, machines, words or numbers—pushing products, pushing switches, pushing papers to eke out the wherewithal of material existence.

… To be able to work and to have work are two different matters. I suspect, however, that few liberationist women are to be found working as menials and unskilled laborers simply in order to occupy their time and identify with the power structure. For status and power are not conferred by work per se, but by certain kinds of work generally reserved to the middle and upper classes. … As Studs Terkel shows in Working, most workers find jobs dull, oppressive, frustrating and alienating—very much what women find housewifery.

When white women's liberationists emphasized work as a path to liberation, they did not concentrate their attention on those women who are most exploited in the American labor force. Had they emphasized the plight of working class women, attention would have shifted away from the college-educated suburban housewife who wanted entrance into the middle and upper class work force. Had attention been focused on women who were already working and who were exploited as cheap surplus labor in American society, it would have de-romanticized the middle class white woman's quest for "meaningful" employment. While it does not in any way diminish the importance of women resisting sexist oppression by entering the labor force, work has not been a liberating force for masses of American women. And for some time now, sexism has not prevented them from being in the work force. White middle and upper class women like those described in Betty Friedan's The Feminine Mystique were housewives not because sexism would have prevented them from being in the paid labor force, but because they had willingly embraced the notion that it was better to be a housewife than to be a worker. The racism and classism of white women's liberationists was most apparent whenever they discussed work as the liberating force for women. In such discussions it was always the middle class "housewife" who was depicted as the victim of sexist oppression and not the poor black and non-black women who are most exploited by American economics.

[…] Feminism as a political ideology advocating social equality for all women was and is acceptable to many black women. They rejected the women's movement when it became apparent that middle and upper class college-educated white women who were its majority participants were determined to shape the movement so that it would serve their own opportunistic ends. While the established definition of feminism is the theory of the political, economic, and social equality of the sexes, white women liberationists used the power granted them by virtue of their being members of the dominant race in American society to interpret feminism in such a way that it was no longer relevant to all women. And it seemed incredible to black women that they were being asked to support a movement whose majority participants were eager to maintain race and class hierarchies between women.

Black women who participated in women's groups, lectures, and meetings initially trusted the sincerity of white female participants. Like 19th century black women's rights advocates, they assumed that any women's movement would address issues relevant to all women and that racism would be automatically cited as a force that had divided women, that would have to be reckoned with for true Sisterhood to emerge, and also that no radical revolutionary women's movement could take place until women as a group were joined in political solidarity. Although contemporary black women were mindful of the prevalence of white female racism, they believed it could be confronted and changed.

As they participated in the women's movement they found, in their dialogues with white women in women's groups, in women's studies classes, at conferences, that their trust was betrayed. They found that white women had appropriated feminism to advance their own cause, i.e., their desire to enter the mainstream of American capitalism. They were told that white women were in the majority and that they had the power to decide which issues would be considered "feminist" issues. White women liberationists decided that the way to confront racism was to speak out in consciousness-raising groups about their racist upbringings, to encourage black women to join their cause, to make sure they hired one non-white woman in "their" women's studies program, or to invite one nonwhite woman to speak on a discussion panel at "their" conference.

When black women involved with women's liberation attempted to discuss racism, many white women responded by angrily stating: "We won't be guilt-tripped." For them the dialogue ceased. Others seemed to relish admitting that they were racist but felt that admitting verbally to being racist was tantamount to changing their racist values. For the most part, white women refused to listen when black women explained that what they expected was not verbal admissions of guilt but conscious gestures and acts that would show that white women liberationists were anti-racist and attempting to overcome their racism. The issue of racism within the women's movement would never have been raised had white women shown in their writings and speeches that they were in fact "liberated" from racism.

As concerned black and white individuals tried to stress the importance to the women's movement of confronting and changing racist attitudes because such sentiments threatened to undermine the movement, they met with resistance from those white women who saw feminism solely as a vehicle to enhance their own individual, opportunistic ends. Conservative, reactionary white women, who increasingly represented a large majority of the participants, were outspoken in their pronouncements that the issue of racism should not be considered worthy of attention. They did not want the issue of racism raised because they did not want to deflect attention away from their projection of the white woman as "good," i.e., non-racist victim, and the white man as "bad," i.e., racist oppressor. For them to have acknowledged woman's active complicity in the perpetuation of imperialism, colonialism, racism, or sexism would have made the issue of women's liberation far more complex. To those who saw feminism solely as a way to demand entrance into the white male power structure, it simplified matters to make all men oppressors and all women victims.

[...] The emergence of black feminist groups led to a greater polarization of black and white women's liberationists. Instead of bonding on the basis of shared understanding of woman's varied collective and individual plight in society, they acted as if the distance separating their experiences from one another could not be bridged by knowledge or understanding. Rather than black women attacking the white female attempt to present them as an Other, an unknown, unfathomable element, they acted as if they were an Other. Many black women found an affirmation and support of their concern with feminism in all-black groups that they had not experienced in women's groups dominated by white women; this has been one of the positive features of black women's groups. However, all women should experience in racially mixed groups affirmation and support. Racism is the barrier that prevents positive communication and it is not eliminated or challenged by separation. White women supported the formation of separate groups because it confirmed their preconceived racist–sexist notion that no connection existed between their experiences and those of black women. Separate groups meant they would not be asked to concern themselves with race or racism. While black women condemned the anti-black racism of white women, the mounting animosity between the two groups gave rise to overt expression of their anti-white racism. Many black women who had never participated in the women's movement saw the formation of separate black groups as confirmation of their belief that no alliance could ever take place between black and white women. To express their anger and rage at white women, they evoked the negative stereotypical image of the white woman as a passive, parasitic, privileged being living off the labor of others as a way to mock and ridicule the white women liberationists.

[...] Animosity between black and white women's liberationists was not due solely to disagreement over racism within the women's movement; it was the end result of years of jealousy, envy, competition, and anger between the two groups. Conflict between black and white women did not begin with the 20th century women's movement. It began during slavery. The social status of white women in America has to a large extent been determined by white people's relationship to black people. It was the enslavement of African people in colonized America that marked the beginning of a change in the social status of white women. Prior to slavery, patriarchal law decreed white women were lowly inferior beings, the subordinate group in society. The subjugation of black people allowed them to vacate their despised position and assume the role of a superior.

Consequently, it can be easily argued that even though white men institutionalized slavery, white women were its most immediate beneficiaries. Slavery in no way altered the hierarchical social status of the white male but it created a new status for the white female. The only way that her new status could be maintained was through the constant assertion of her superiority over the black woman and man. All too often colonial white women, particularly those who were slavemistresses, chose to differentiate their status from the slave's by treating the slave in a brutal and cruel manner. It was in her relationship to the black female slave that the white woman could best assert her power. Individual black slave women were quick to learn that sex-role differentiation did not mean that the white mistress was not to be regarded as an authority figure. Because they had been socialized via patriarchy to respect male authority and resent female authority, black women were reluctant to acknowledge the "power" of the white mistress. When the enslaved black woman expressed contempt and disregard for white female authority, the white mistress often resorted to brutal punishment to assert her authority. But even brutal punishment could not change the fact that black women were not inclined to regard the white female with the awe and respect they showed to the white male.

By flaunting their sexual lust for the bodies of black women and their preference for them as sexual partners, white men successfully pitted white women and enslaved black women against one another. In most instances, the white mistress did not envy the black female slave her role as sexual object; she feared only that her newly acquired social status might be threatened by white male sexual interaction with black women. His sexual involvement with black women (even if that involvement was rape) in effect reminded the white female of her subordinate position in relationship to him. For he could exercise his power as racial imperialist and sexual imperialist to rape or seduce black women, while white women were not free to rape or seduce black men without fear of punishment. Though the white female might condemn the actions of a white male who chose to interact sexually with black female slaves, she was unable to dictate to him proper behavior. Nor could she retaliate by engaging in sexual relationships with enslaved or free black men. Not surprisingly, she directed her anger and rage at the enslaved black women. In those cases where emotional ties developed between white men and black female slaves, white mistresses would go to great lengths to punish the female. Severe beatings were the method most white women used to punish black female slaves. Often in a jealous rage a mistress might use disfigurement to punish a lusted-after black female slave. The mistress might cut off her breast, blind an eye, or cut off another body part. Such treatment naturally caused hostility between white women and enslaved black women. To the enslaved black woman, the white mistress living in relative comfort was the representative symbol of white womanhood. She was both envied and despised—envied for her material comfort, despised because she felt little concern or compassion for the slave woman's lot. Since the white woman's privileged social status could only exist if a group of women were present to assume the lowly position she had abdicated, it follows that black and white women would be at odds with one another. If the white woman struggled to change the lot of the black slave woman, her own social position on the race-sex hierarchy would be altered.

Manumission did not bring an end to conflicts between black and white women; it heightened them. To maintain the apartheid structure slavery had institutionalized, white colonizers, male and female, created a variety of myths and stereotypes to differentiate the status of black women from that of white women. White racists and even some black people who had absorbed the colonizer's mentality depicted the white woman as a symbol of perfect womanhood and encouraged black women to strive to attain such perfection by using the white female as her model. The jealousy and envy of white women that had erupted in the black woman's consciousness during slavery was deliberately encouraged by the dominant white culture. Advertisements, newspaper articles, books, etc. were constant reminders to black women of the difference between their social status and that of white women, and they bitterly resented it. Nowhere was this dichotomy as clearly demonstrated as in the materially privileged white household where the black female domestic worked as an employee of the white family. In these relationships, black women workers were exploited to enhance the social standing of white families. In the white community, employing domestic help was a sign of material privilege and the person who directly benefited from a servant's work was the white woman, since without the servant she would have performed domestic chores. Not surprisingly, the black female domestic tended to see the white female as her "boss," her oppressor, not the white male whose earnings usually paid her wage.

[…] Resolution of the conflict between black and white women cannot begin until all women acknowledge that a feminist movement which is both racist and classist is a mere sham, a cover-up for women's continued bondage to materialist patriarchal principles, and passive acceptance of the status quo. The sisterhood that is necessary for the making of feminist revolution can be achieved only when all women disengage themselves from the hostility, jealousy, and competition with one another that has kept us vulnerable, weak, and unable to envision new realities. That sisterhood cannot be forged by the mere saying of words. It is the outcome of continued growth and change. It is a goal to be reached, a process of becoming. The process begins with action, with the individual woman's refusal to accept any set of myths, stereotypes, and false assumptions that deny the shared commonness of her human experience; that deny her capacity to experience the Unity of all life; that deny her capacity to bridge gaps created by racism, sexism, or classism; that deny her ability to change. The process begins with the individual woman's acceptance that American women, without exception, are socialized to be racist, classist, and sexist, in varying degrees, and that labeling ourselves feminists does not change the fact that we must consciously work to rid ourselves of the legacy of negative socialization.

If women want a feminist revolution—ours is a world that is crying out for feminist revolution—then we must assume responsibility for drawing women together in political solidarity. That means we must assume responsibility for eliminating all the forces that divide women. Racism is one such force. Women, all women, are accountable for racism continuing to divide us. Our willingness to assume responsibility for the elimination of racism need not be engendered by feelings of guilt, moral responsibility, victimization, or rage. It can spring from a heartfelt desire for sisterhood and the personal, intellectual realization that racism among women undermines the potential radicalism of feminism. It can spring from our knowledge that racism is an obstacle in our path that must be removed. More obstacles are created if we simply engage in endless debate as to who put it there.

## DISCUSSION QUESTIONS

1. On what grounds does bell hooks contend that racism has not been adequately acknowledged and addressed by feminists?
2. According to the author, why did many Black women react negatively to invitations by white upper and middle class feminists to join the women's movement of the 1960s and 1970s?
3. What is the problem with defining women's liberation in terms of gaining greater economic status and money power?

## REFERENCES

Barber, Benjamin, *Liberating Feminism*. New York: Delta, 1976.

Berg, Barbara, *The Remembered Gate: Origins of American Feminism*. NewYork: Oxford University Press, 1979.

Douglass, Frederick, *Narrative of the Life of Frederick Douglass.* Edited by Benjamin Quarles. Cambridge, Mass.: Belknap Press, 1969.

Eisenstein, Zillah, ed., *Capitalist Patriarchy and the Case for Socialist Feminism.* New York: Monthly Review Press, 1979.

Logan, Rayford, *The Betrayal of the Negro.* New York: Collier, 1954.

Spruill, Julia, *Women's Life and Work in the Southern Colonies.* New York: W.W. Norton, [1938] 1972. Chapter 26

# CHAPTER 11

## Confronting Racism on a Macro Level

# The Mississippi Civil Rights Movement and Its Legacy

## Kenneth T. Andrews

DO SOCIAL MOVEMENTS matter? When people come together to challenge inequalities and face powerful authorities and opponents, what hope can they have of bringing about significant changes? This question has puzzled movement participants and observers throughout history. There are numerous examples to inspire confidence in the power of social movements, and there are equally plentiful cases to support a pessimistic assessment that movements are more likely to fail, invite repression, become co-opted, or produce polarization and violence than to achieve success.

The civil rights movement has raised the same questions for its participants and subsequent observers. John Lewis, one of the early SNCC leaders from Nashville, argues that "so many things are undeniably better. ... But there is a mistaken assumption among many that these signs of progress mean that the battle is over, that the struggle for civil rights is finished, that the problems of segregation were solved in the '60s and now all we have to deal with are economic issues" (1998, 490). Mary King is critical of a flippant view, writing:

> Those who sardonically claim "not much has changed for American blacks" must not know how bad it was. Such a comment reveals ... that the speaker was not on the front lines in the southern civil rights movement and never experienced the brutality that was directed against blacks and their supporters at that time. (1987, 544)

Others have painted a less optimistic assessment, pointing to the limited gains, continuing inequality and injustices, and the costs that were suffered through the fierce struggles of the movement. Annie Devine, a legendary activist from Canton, Mississippi, wonders whether "all we may have done through the civil rights movement is open Pandora's box" (quoted in Dent 1997, 347).

L. C. Dorsey, a civil rights leader from Bolivar County, observes that "to the optimist, things are beautiful and even the small changes take on grand dimensions. For the pessimist, the changes may seem miniscule when viewed from eyes that expect the rubble from the fallen walls of racism already to be cleared away" (1977, 41). From the perspective of the activist, change can be measured relative to the goals that were sought or against the conditions that prevailed before the movement began. In this study, I use the tools of historical and social scientific analysis to shed new light on the legacy of the civil rights movement.

Many scholars of social movements assume that movements are, at least under certain conditions, effective agents of social change, especially for poor and powerless groups. This belief in the efficacy of protest and collective action underlies much of the scholarship by historians and social scientists on social movements. This is especially true for scholars of the civil rights movement. In fact, many studies of the origins and development of the movement have been justified by pointing to its success in challenging and transforming the southern system of racial domination. For example, Aldon Morris, in *The Origins of the Civil Rights Movement*, argues that the movement had "a profound impact on American society" (1984, 266). Similarly, Dennis Chong points to the movement as "the quintessential example of public-spirited collective action in our time" that "spark[ed] radical changes in American society" (1991, 1). Although these and many other scholars make strong assertions about the success of the civil rights movement, they do not examine this basic question. Surprisingly, we know more about the origins and early development of the civil rights movement than about the role the movement played in transforming the institutions and social relations of the South.

Adding to the confusion are disagreements about how movements influence social change. Some scholars locate the power of movements in disruptions and threats that force concessions from powerful opponents and authorities. In contrast, other scholars see movements as engaged in a form of persuasive communication designed to bring about change by appealing to the "hearts and minds" of bystanders. In this view, effective protest can win influential allies and secure much-needed resources. Finally, another line of argument claims that movements are efficacious when they adopt the organizational forms, institutionalized tactics, and rhetorical frameworks of interest groups and abandon the "politics of protest." Professionalization and moderation are the necessary steps to winning new advantages as groups make the transition from outsiders to insiders. These alternatives were well represented within the civil rights movement as leaders debated the strengths and weaknesses of strategies built around the basic mechanisms of disruption, persuasion, and negotiation as tools of social change.

In this study, I address these long-standing questions about the impacts of social movements through a multilayered study of the Mississippi civil rights movement. Mississippi stood most firm in its resistance to the civil rights movement and federal efforts to enforce racial equality. Tom Dent, a native of New Orleans who worked in the Mississippi movement for many years, tells us that "if racial change and justice meant anything anywhere, change in Mississippi, to the degree it existed, would be … the surest barometer of progress in the American South" (1997, 338). By examining this historically important case, I clarify our broader understanding of the ways in which movements transform social and political institutions as well as the constraints and obstacles that movements face when they try to do so. Through this analysis, I shed light on the movement building that took place in Mississippi and the resilience of the movement in the face of massive repression. I trace the movement's development beginning in the early 1960s, and I analyze its impact and setbacks during the 1970s and 1980s. This time period includes the expansion of voting rights and gains in black political power, the desegregation of public schools and the emergence of "white flight" academies, and the rise and fall of federally funded antipoverty programs. I chart the movement's engagement in each of these arenas as well as the tactical interaction between local civil rights movements and white power holders.

Research on the civil rights movement has focused primarily on the period up to the passage of the Voting Rights Act in 1965, often regarded as the final chapter of the southern phase of the black movement. However, many important struggles took place after 1965 as local movements tried to shape electoral politics, increase access to and improve the quality of public schools, and secure public resources like Head Start and community action programs.

Furthermore, historians of the civil rights movement have focused most heavily on the national leaders, the major civil rights organizations, and a handful of key protest campaigns. These are, of course, appropriate topics for research. However, this disproportionate focus on the national level of the movement obscures the depth and breadth of the civil rights struggle. Moreover, this focus locates the potential impacts of the movement in major court decisions and legislative reforms without asking whether or to what extent these legal changes were realized in the institutions throughout the South. The major legal reforms of the civil rights era only beg the question of whether the implementation of new laws and policies made the functioning of politics, schools, and social policies more equitable in the post–civil rights South.

Movements rarely, if ever, achieve all of their goals, but they can and do generate enduring consequences. Sidney Tarrow notes that "protest cycles do not simply end and leave nothing but lassitude or repression in their wake; they have indirect and long-term effects that emerge when the initial excitement is over and disillusionment passes" (1994, 172). Tarrow's observation is widely regarded as accurate by scholars of social movements and contentious politics. This study broadens and refines our understanding of movement impacts. Underlying this study is an argument that explains how movements have long-term and short-term impacts. I claim that focusing at the local level provides the best opportunity and the most important barometer for examining the consequences of social movements. In addition, I show that there is continuity between the heyday of movement activity and the period of movement decline.

Clayborne Carson, one of the leading historians of the civil rights movement, wrote an incisive essay about the historical scholarship on the movement, making three major criticisms that have influenced my argument. Carson observes that "because the emergent goals of American social movements have usually not been fulfilled, scholars have found it difficult to determine their political significance" (1986, 19). From this complexity and causal ambiguity, some scholars assume that movements are important and others assume that they are inconsequential. Some scholars assume that professional interest groups and routine political processes are the key actors because they are more likely to persist once mass mobilization wanes.[1] Second, there is the assumption "that the black struggle can best be understood as a protest movement, orchestrated by national leaders in order to achieve national civil rights legislation" (Carson 1986, 23). This assumption leads to an inaccurate view of the tactics, organizations, leaders, goals, and impacts of the movement. Throughout the civil rights movement, campaigns and tactics targeted change at the local level. In a small handful of campaigns such as in Birmingham and Selma, there was a complex effort to use local mobilization to leverage federal action. These highly visible cases represent a small fraction of the broader civil rights struggle. The assumption of a national movement effecting national legislation leads to a third error—"the prevailing scholarly conception … that [the movement] ended in 1965" with the passage of the Voting Rights Act (Carson 1986, 27). Rather, Carson argues that there is substantial continuity alongside transformation in the broader struggle by blacks after the Voting Rights Act.

Clayborne Carson's insights are a key starting point for this study of the continuity and transformation of the Mississippi civil rights movement from the early 1960s through the early 1980s. This focus allows us to better understand the consequences of social movements. In short, to understand the history of the black freedom struggle, we must examine in detail the ongoing conflicts after the major legislative victories of the civil rights movement. The question here is a rather direct and obvious one, and it grows out of a straightforward concern on the part of social movement participants and observers to understand the consequences of social movements. While the question is generally acknowledged to be important, research and theory remain sparse.[2] Many barriers stand in the way of insightful research on the impacts of movements—both methodological and conceptual. In the next section, I describe the research that has allowed me to address these challenges and develop my analysis of the impact of the civil rights movement.

## OVERVIEW OF THE STUDY

The argument developed through this study demonstrates the importance of movement dynamics for explanations of political change. In addition to the actions of elites, courts, legislatures, and countermovements, social movements can and sometimes do play a key role in the process of social change. I show how the Mississippi movement built indigenous organizations and facilitated the growth of new leadership. I call this combination of leaders, indigenous resources, and local organizations the "movement infrastructure," and I demonstrate that long-term patterns of institutional change are shaped by variations in the emergence and continuity of a community's movement infrastructure. The cultivation of local leadership and the building of effective organizations are crucial steps in developing the capacity for ongoing social change efforts.

In this study, I employ two major research strategies to examine the trajectory and impact of local civil rights movements in Mississippi. First, I have assembled a quantitative county-level data set to examine the movement's impacts on electoral politics, primary and secondary schools, and social policies. Second, I completed intensive examination of three communities using archival data and informant interviews to examine *how* movements matter and the interaction of movements, opponents, and authorities. These strategies are complementary, and both are essential if we are to understand the complex dynamics of the civil rights movement and its legacy. The quantitative analysis allows for precise estimates of movement impacts and other forces shaping change, such as the social and economic characteristics of the community, the role of violence by whites, and the intervention of federal agencies and courts. The comparisons of all counties by level of movement activism present the broad patterns. The quantitative data described above carries the burden of making systematic comparisons across communities by summarizing major relationships, including patterns over time and among variables. The qualitative case studies explore the process of movement building, the tactical interaction between movements and countermovements, and many other dynamics that cannot be measured quantitatively across all counties. The case studies examine variations among counties, all of which had high levels of activism in the early 1960s, and demonstrate what these changes looked like and how they came about in specific contexts. The key strength of the case studies is to illustrate major characteristics of communities and organizations, to provide insight into the motivations and social relationships within those communities, and to demonstrate processes of change or mechanisms through which change occurs. (See appendix A for a more detailed description of the research design.) The following map (fig. 1.1) shows the patterning of movement activity in Mississippi and identifies the three case studies. Mississippi counties are grouped into three major categories of sustained, episodic, and non-movement counties based on indicators of movement

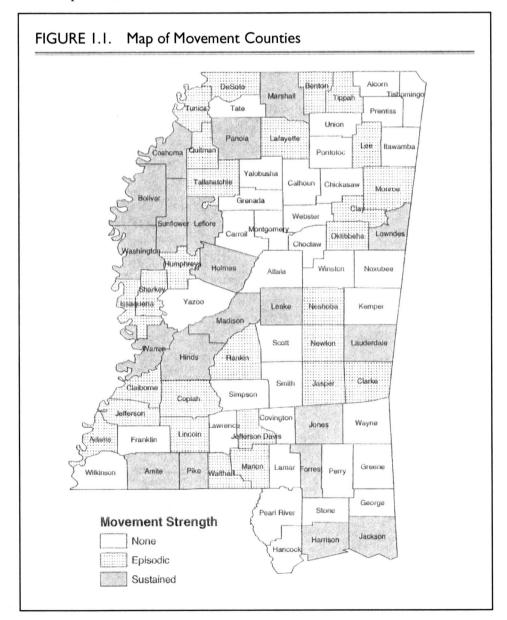

FIGURE 1.1. Map of Movement Counties

activity and organization in the early 1960s. (The indicators used for these comparisons are described in detail in chapter 4.)

## DIMENSIONS OF MOVEMENT INFRASTRUCTURE

I propose a movement infrastructure model for examining whether and, if so, how movements have enduring impacts. Three components of a movement's infrastructure must be examined to explain a movement's influence on social change: leadership, organizational structure, and resources. Strategies and tactics are shaped by the configuration of a movement's leadership, organization, and resource capacities. Leaders and organizations often carry particular repertoires of action and ideologies that influence the ability of movements to have lasting impacts. Infrastructures that allow the movement to employ multiple mechanisms of influence including disruption, persuasion, and bargaining will have the greatest impact across outcomes because movements must engage a complex and changing environment. This ability is crucial because, as Daniel Cress and David Snow argue, most of the impacts that movements have operate through "multiple pathways rather than through one surefire pathway or set of conditions" (2000, 1096). At a general level, I claim that the autonomy and continuity of the infrastructure are key factors explaining the long-term viability and impact of the movement, sustaining a movement through shifts in the broader political environment (Andrews 1997; Rupp and Taylor 1987). A strong movement infrastructure can spur political elites to initiate policy concessions in response to the perceived threat of the movement. Often that threat rests on the belief that a movement has the capacity to institute more substantial change through parallel, autonomous institutions (Clemens 1998; Schwartz 1976).

This argument dovetails with the work of scholars who have focused on the organizational survival of social movements (Edwards and Marullo 1995). I focus on the process by which organizational consolidation is achieved in one locale and organizational collapse occurs in another. This is based on the assumption that organizational survival is a key intervening link that allows activism to be sustained during periods of limited opportunity (Clemens 1998; Minkoff 1993; Tarrow 1994; Taylor 1989). As Debra Minkoff notes, "The very existence of associations in which people can participate should have some discernible, if not easily measurable, impact on society and, ultimately, social change" (1993, 905). The key limitation of the research on organizational persistence is the assumption that survival is associated with later influence—a claim that is rarely demonstrated.

In my argument, leadership is important for movement impact in ways that differ from most conventional accounts of organizational leadership. Rather than the individual properties of leaders, I give greater attention to the social relations of leaders to one another, to movement participants, and to the institutions targeted by the movement (for a general discussion of leadership in movements, see Aminzade, Goldstone, and Perry 2001). I draw on the arguments advanced by Aldon Morris and Belinda Robnett about civil rights leadership that emphasize the linkage between leaders and community institutions. For Morris (1984), successful movement leadership is rooted in "indigenous" organizations. This link makes leaders more responsive and less easily co-opted when they negotiate with authorities and opponents. Hence, the structural location of black ministers within community institutions made them an effective leadership base during many civil rights campaigns.

Leaders and organizations must be embedded in indigenous, informal networks. In her study of gender and leadership in the civil rights movement, Robnett (1996) distinguishes between formal leaders (e.g., ministers) and an intermediate layer of "bridge leaders" who stand at nodal points within the informal networks of a community. Movements with a simple structure of formal leaders and mass base are unlikely to be successful because bridge leaders are needed to expand participation throughout the community. Bridge leaders make co-optation of formal leaders less likely because bridge leaders can effectively connect to the demands and expectations of a movement's broader constituency. This type of leadership structure can generate ongoing tension within the movement. However, it also can provide advantages, such as innovation (Stepan-Norris and Zeitlin 1995). A differentiated leadership structure allows for communication to various audiences, including participants, potential recruits, opponents, and state actors (Klandermans 1997). A leadership structure with a diversity of skills and experiences will be better able to use mass-based tactics as well as routine negotiation with other groups, including authorities (Ganz 2000; Gerlach and Hine 1970).

The critical role of preexisting organizations and resources has been established in the emergence of social movements. To persist over time, movements must forge new organizational forms and establish independent resource flows (McAdam 1982; Schwartz 1976). In the mobilization process, the informal structure of relationships among activists and organizations must be expansive across communities and subgroups. In the policy-making process, formal organizations become a necessary vehicle for advancing a group's claims. Organizational structures can alter the routine operation of the political process when they are perceived as legitimate and/or threatening by established political actors (Clemens 1997; Gamson 1990).

Movements that rely primarily on the mobilization of people rather than on externally generated financial resources are more likely to continue using protest tactics (Schwartz and Paul 1992). As a result, their strategic and tactical options are often broader (Ganz 2000). Ultimately, movements require substantial contributions of participants to maintain organizations and launch protest campaigns. This is seen most clearly at the local level, where movement organizations are less likely to maintain a paid professional staff.

The importance of indigenous resources does not preclude the possibility that external resources can facilitate the movement or its efficacy. However, dependence on external resources makes movements vulnerable to shifts in the discretion of external actors (Jenkins and Eckert 1986; McAdam 1982). In addition, external resources often entail obligations that can constrain the movement's strategy and tactics and increase the chance of co-optation.

In the movement infrastructure model, strategy and tactics depend to a large degree on a movement's leadership, organization, and resources. This contrasts with alternative explanations that view effective protest and formal organization in conflict with one another or ignore the role of organization. Strategy and tactics are conceptualized broadly in the infrastructure model and range from protest to the building of counter-institutions. Consistent with this line of argument, Marshall Ganz (2000) has shown how the United Farm Workers were able to organize California farmworkers where more resource-rich organizations failed. According to Ganz, the UFW's leadership and organizational structure generated greater strategic capacity "if a leadership team includes insiders and outsiders, strong and weak network ties, and access to diverse, yet salient, repertoires of collective action and also if an organization conducts regular, open authoritative deliberation, draws resources from multiple constituencies, and roots accountability in those constituencies" (2000, 1005; see also Delaney, Jarley, and Fiorito 1996). Ganz's argument refers to the characteristics of a single organization, but these characteristics can also be properties of a broader field of organizations. For most social movements, the impact of the movement will be more closely tied to the collective properties of multiple organizations rather than a single challenger.[3] As a property of a single organization or set of groups, strategic capacity facilitates the ability of movements to develop creative solutions to collective problems.

In sum, strong movement infrastructures have diverse leaders and a complex leadership structure, multiple organizations, informal ties that cross geographic and social boundaries, and a resource base that draws substantially on contributions from their members for both labor and funds. These characteristics provide movements with greater flexibility that allows them to influence the policy process through multiple mechanisms including disruption, persuasion, and negotiation. This argument differs from the main alternatives among sociologists and political scientists. I will briefly outline three major alternatives by highlighting areas of convergence and divergence with the movement infrastructure argument.

### Disruption: Securing Concessions from Threat

One of the most common ways of conceptualizing movement efficacy focuses on the short-term potential of protest to win victories. The first two models of movement efficacy focus on protest, but they specify alternative mechanisms through which protest influences change—disruption and persuasion. In both arguments, mobilization has the momentary potential through an "action-reaction" process to leverage change by mobilizing political elites, electoral coalitions, or public opinion.

In the first argument, movements are dramatic, disruptive, and threatening to elites, which prompts a rapid response—typically either concessions and/or repression. Frances Fox Piven and Richard Cloward have been the primary proponents of this view, arguing that "the most useful way to think about the effectiveness of protest is to examine the disruptive effects on institutions of different forms of mass defiance, and then to examine the political reverberations of those disruptions" (1977, 24). The independent influence of protest is constrained by its role in a sequence of events. In *Poor People's Movements* (1977), Piven and Cloward raise questions about the independent impact of protest because it "wells up in response to momentous changes in the institutional order. It is not created by organizers and leaders" (36). Protest is one link in a sequence, and once the sequence is initiated, protesters have little control over the policy response. The authors conclude that "whatever influence lower-class groups occasionally exert in American politics does not result from organization, but from mass protest and the disruptive consequences of protest" (36).[4]

Organizations, particularly mass-based membership organizations, are doomed to failure because powerless groups can never mobilize as effectively as dominant groups in a society. As a result, organizations can only lessen the disruptive capacity and efficacy of protest (Piven and Cloward 1984, 1992; also see Gamson and Schmeidler 1984; A. Morris 1984). Elite reaction is ultimately focused in a self-interested way on ending protest. Analyzing urban policy changes in the 1960s, Ira Katznelson argues that "the targets of these public policies were not objects of compassion, but of fear born of uncertainty" (1981, 3). Policy makers caught off guard by protest attempt to quickly assemble a strategy of repression, concessions, or a combination of the two that will end the protest wave (Tarrow 1993). Disruption models focus on the limitations of protest on policy making beyond the agenda-setting stage.

### Persuasion: Generating Support Through Symbolic Protest

In the second model, movements are dramatic and generate support from sympathetic individuals and groups that take up the cause of the movement. The intervening role of "third parties," "bystander publics," or "conscience constituents" is critical. In a classic essay, Michael Lipsky argues that "the 'problem of the powerless' in protest activity is to activate 'third parties' to enter the implicit or explicit bargaining arena in ways favorable to protesters" (1968, 1145). Lipsky claims that "if protest tactics are not considered significant by the media ... protest organizations will not succeed. Like the tree falling unheard in the forest, there is no protest unless protest is perceived and projected" (1151; also see Benford and Hunt 1992).[5]

David Garrow (1978) argues that civil rights campaigns, especially in Selma, Alabama, generated momentum for the 1965 Voting Rights Act. For some theorists, repression is an intervening link. For example, Garrow contends that attacks by southern officials on civil rights activists further solidified the support of bystanders. Paul Burstein (1985) shows that the movement did not reverse the direction of public opinion on race and civil rights. He argues instead that movements are probably unable to have such a substantial impact on opinion. Rather, protest increased the salience of the civil rights issue through protest, demonstrating the injustice of southern racism and violence. As civil rights became more important in the eyes of the American public, political representatives acted on louder and clearer signals from their constituents (Burstein 1999). In this view, protest is a form of communication, and persuasion is the major way that movements influence policy (Lohmann 1993; Mansbridge 1994).

The first two arguments focus on similar aspects of movements, but they differ on key points. The disruption model emphasizes disruptive and often violent action forcing a response from political elites, and the persuasion model proposes that protest can mobilize sympathetic third parties that advance the movement's agenda by exerting influence on political elites (see also McAdam and Su 2002 on disruptive and persuasive movement activity). Both of these action-reaction arguments share the assumption that (1) large-scale dramatic events shape the process of change by (2) mobilizing more powerful actors to advance the movement's cause, and (3) that (implicitly) movements have little or no direct influence beyond this initial point. In both models, the primary focus is on the communicative aspects of public protest events rather than on organizational form or capacity within a movement.

### Negotiation: The Routinization of Protest

The negotiation model, a third major approach, argues that the determinant of movement efficacy is the acquisition of routine access to the polity through institutionalized tactics. This approach typically describes a drift toward less disruptive tactics, such as electoral politics, coalitions, lobbying, and litigation. Organization and leadership figure prominently in this model. Organizational changes parallel the tactical shift, including increasing centralization and bureaucratization of movement organizations. In order to achieve influence, social movements generate organizations that evolve into interest groups. In the negotiation model, the organizational and tactical shifts are accompanied by an increase in influence over relevant policy arenas. In contrast, the action-reaction model would predict that movement influence declines as tactics become routinized and organizations become incorporated. Most important, the access-influence model argues that disruptive tactics have little independent impact on institutional change. Rufus P. Browning, Dale Rogers Marshall, and David H. Tabb, in their study of the impacts of black and Hispanic political mobilization on a variety of policy outcomes, argue that protest and electoral strategies were used together effectively, but "demand-protest strategies by themselves produced limited results in most cities" (1984, 246).

Negotiation models also assert that securing insider status is more consequential than pursuing a single, specific policy objective. Thomas Rochon and Daniel Mazmanian (1993) argue that the antinuclear movement, by advocating a single piece of legislation, was unsuccessful. In contrast, the environmental movement, especially antitoxic groups, attempted to become a legitimate participant in the regulatory process. By gaining access, the movement has been able to have a substantial long-term impact on policy (also see Costain 1981; Sabatier 1975). In this vein, Mario Diani argues that "social movement outcomes may be assessed in terms of the movement's capacity to achieve more central positions in networks of social and political influence" (1997, 133; see also Laumann and Knoke 1987). In contrast to this negotiation model, movement organizations may achieve positions that are merely symbolic, and movements can generate leverage without directly bargaining with state actors or other authorities (Burstein, Einwohner, and Hollander 1995; Schwartz 1976).

The negotiation model has fewer proponents than the disruption and persuasion models among the sociologists who study social movements. However, the notion that "routine" tactics are most efficacious is consistent with pluralist theories of democracy that view the political system as relatively open to citizen influence. This argument would find greater support among the political scientists who study interest groups, political parties, and the policy process. From this perspective, organization building (especially professionalization, bureaucratization, and centralization) provides movements with the necessary tools to operate in the interest group system, where bargaining is the key mechanism of influence.

## COMPARING THE MODELS

The movement infrastructure model that I have proposed builds on the insights of the prior three models. First, it assumes, like the disruption and persuasion models, that there are key moments when movements can be especially efficacious. Further, it assumes that disruptive tactics are important for movements to have an impact, especially when they are creatively injected into routine political processes. The movement infrastructure model differs from the others because it emphasizes the building and sustaining of movement infrastructures as an important determinant of the long-term impacts of social movements (in contrast to short-term impacts, like agenda setting). Furthermore, unlike the access-influence model, movements have the greatest impact when they maintain their ability to use both "outsider" and "insider" tactics. Litigation, lobbying, and electoral politics can be effectively employed by social movements. However, movements lose key opportunities for leverage in the political process when they quickly adopt the strategies and tactics of "interest groups" and abandon "insurgent" forms.

Although much of the debate turns on the question of the types of organizational forms that are most efficacious, organization as a concept gets used loosely in arguments and criticisms. For example, Piven and Cloward's (1977) argument is cast as a broad critique of organizations, but their real target is national membership organizations. If we distinguish forms of organizations, we can see that there is variation, with some playing a more direct role in facilitating disruption. In his analysis of the 1963 Birmingham campaign, Morris (1993) illustrates the importance of organizing for large dramatic campaigns. Forman (1972) argues persuasively that SCLC's campaign at Selma (and Albany) depended on the organizing of SNCC field-workers in Selma and nearby Lowndes County. In many cases, especially the most repressive settings, building organizations is disruptive and can be a necessary step before other forms of collective action are possible. SNCC's own measure of success was "the extent to which the people they helped bring into political activity became leaders themselves" (Payne 1995, 318). As a result, building organizational structures was itself a strategic vehicle of the movement.[6] In this study, I pursue these questions about the efficacy of different organizational forms.

I argue that movements are most influential when they can create leverage through multiple mechanisms. The prior three models focus on a single mechanism as the primary means by which movements create change—disruption, persuasion, or negotiation. The movement infrastructure model accounts for the ability of movements to impact political change through multiple mechanisms, and this change can occur when a movement's leadership and organization allow for strategic flexibility and innovation.

The pattern of outcomes for a movement may depend on processes described by each of these models. For example, the negotiation and persuasion models focus on agenda setting as the primary outcome that movements can influence. In contrast, access-influence and movement infrastructure models examine later stages in the policy-making process. Ultimately, researchers should use these models to compare across different types of social movements and political contexts. However, the main patterns identified in this study demonstrate the utility of the movement infrastruc-

TABLE 5.1. Voter Participation and the Level of Movement Activity

| | Movement Counties | | Non-Movement Counties | State |
|---|---|---|---|---|
| | Sustained | Episodic | | |
| *Voter Registration* | | | | |
| Registered black voters, 1967 | 4,183 | 1,844 | 992 | 2,025 |
| Registered black voters, 1967 (%) | 53.1 | 53.6 | 47.1 | 50.7 |
| Registered white voters, 1967 | 10,166 | 5,753 | 5,070 | 6,493 |
| Registered white voters, 1967 (%) | 70.6 | 71.2 | 64.6 | 68.2 |
| *Black Candidates for County-level Office* | | | | |
| Black candidates, 1967 | 3.0 | 1.5 | 0.5 | 1.4 |
| Black candidates, 1971 | 6.5 | 3.6 | 1.5 | 3.4 |
| *Voter Turnout* | | | | |
| Clifton Whitley, 1966 | 1,661 | 637 | 240 | 705 |
| Clifton Whitley, 1966 (%) | 17.8 | 16.7 | 9.7 | 13.9 |
| White voter turnout, 1966 (%) | 42.4 | 48.3 | 44.2 | 45.2 |
| Differential (white voter turnout minus black voter turnout) (%) | 24.6 | 31.6 | 34.6 | 31.2 |
| Charles Evers, 1971 | 3,705 | 1,740 | 1,057 | 1,906 |
| Charles Evers, 1971 (%) | 40.2 | 41.4 | 42.5 | 41.6 |
| White voter turnout, 1971 (%) | 65.9 | 73.8 | 76.4 | 73.1 |
| Differential (white voter turnout minus black voter turnout) (%) | 25.7 | 32.4 | 33.9 | 31.5 |
| Number of counties | 19 | 27 | 35 | 81 |

*Note:* This table reports mean values for counties.

ture model as applied to the Mississippi civil rights movement and for understanding movement impact more broadly.

## LOCAL MOVEMENTS AND ELECTORAL PARTICIPATION IN MISSISSIPPI

Did counties where the movement was most active have higher levels of electoral participation in the late 1960s and early 1970s than those that did not? We can begin to answer this question by looking at the summary statistics in table 5.1. Here, there are data on three forms of political participation—voter registration, the number of black candidates running for office, and voter turnout—covering the period from 1966 to 1971. In 1967 the number of black registered voters is greater in sustained movement counties than in episodic or non-movement counties. However, the actual number is influenced by the size of the black voting-age population. The percentage measure shows that counties with sustained and episodic movements have very similar levels of voter registration.

The second set of indicators presents the number of black candidates running for county-level office in 1967 and 1971. In the South, counties are the most important local political body, and it is possible to compare the efforts to win elected office. Here, the relationship of black candidates and the level of movement activity is very strong, with movement counties having much higher levels of political mobilization. Although these candidates rarely won elections during this period, their campaigns represented an important development in the longer struggle toward greater black political power.

Finally, I estimate the voter turnout for blacks and whites in two elections by candidates for statewide office—Clifton Whitley in 1966 and Charles Evers in 1971. Both candidates had been involved in civil rights organizing. Whitley, for example, held state-level leadership positions in the Mississippi Freedom Democratic Party and was an MFDP delegate to the 1964 Democratic National Convention. Evers's relationship to the movement was more controversial. His brother, Medgar Evers, had been the NAACP's field secretary in Mississippi and was shot down outside his home by Byron de la Beckwith in 1963.Charles Evers returned to Mississippi shortly thereafter, and he began building a political base in the southwest part of the state. While he was never fully embraced by many civil rights activists, he was a prominent state-level leader by the late 1960s. In the Whitley election, we see a pattern similar to voter registration where movement counties (sustained and episodic) had higher levels of black electoral participation than non-movement counties. In the Evers election, there is very little difference between the counties based on the level of movement activity (a pattern I examine more carefully below). Finally, note the indicators of turnout differential—the gap between white voter turnout and black voter turn out. The pattern here shows that increases in voter turnout in movement counties are not offset by increases in white voter turnout. Surprisingly, this differential is narrowed in movement counties, suggesting that there are relative gains for black turnout in these counties. This evidence contradicts the expectation that local civil rights activity escalated white countermobilization.[7] In the following sections, I examine these patterns of political participation in a more systematic manner to determine whether these relationships hold under more rigorous analyses.

## Voter Registration

In much of the South, black voter registration had been increasing since World War II. However, in Mississippi voter registration campaigns produced very minimal increases in the early 1960s. The Justice Department had already filed suits against the registrars in several Mississippi counties, and the Southern Regional Council's Voter Education Project spent $12.13 for each new voter added between 1962 and 1964 (Lawson 1976, 284). Voter registration in Mississippi increased dramatically following the passage of the Voting Rights Act. The period from 1965 to 1971 saw substantial increases in black political participation but minimal increases in black office holding.

In 1968 the U.S. Commission on Civil Rights consolidated data on voter registration in a comprehensive report, *Political Participation*. The report documents the number of newly registered black voters in Mississippi counties, and it also indicates whether a county was assigned federal examiners between 1965 and 1967. Federal examiners were usually sent to counties that were known for their discrimination against black registrants. Deep South counties were the target of the vast majority of federal examiners, with Mississippi receiving examiners in thirty-one counties by 1967 (USCCR 1968, 244–47).[8] These data provide an initial indication of the emerging patterns of black political participation in Mississippi.

We have already seen that movement counties had slightly higher levels of black voter registration, but it is important to use techniques that account for additional factors that may influence registration levels. In table 5.2, I use an OLS (ordinary least squares) regression model to examine the factors that influence black voter registration. In addition to measures of social movement activity, I measure the impact of federal examiners and white violence on black voter registration. The size of the black voting-age population in 1960 is used as a control variable in analyses for the total number of registered blacks in 1967.

The Voter Education Project argued that federal examiners had a more substantial impact on black registration rates than movement organization (Black and Black 1987, 135). The analysis I present in table 5.2 shows a greater effect for local organizing than for examiners.[9] Most significantly, I find that both organizing during Freedom Summer and NAACP membership are better predictors of a county's level of black voter registration than the presence of federal examiners, with Freedom Summer being by far the most powerful predictor.[10] These findings suggest that the resources (Freedom Summer staff and volunteers) and results (NAACP organization) of the early period of organizing were primary factors in shaping higher levels of voter registration after the Voting Rights Act.

In the next sections, I examine other forms of black political participation that have received less attention—specifically, voter turnout and the campaigns by black candidates for office. Registration is an intermediate outcome because it does not reflect particular gains for the black community but is preliminary mobilization aimed at achieving other goals.[11]

### Electoral Mobilization: Voter Turnout and Black Candidates

Movement activists ran for office in several statewide elections. Often this was a strategy for unifying the local campaigns where black candidates had a much more realistic opportunity to win office. The statewide campaigns provide a way to gauge the turnout of black voters. For electoral mobilization, I have used votes cast for two black candidates, Clifton Whitley in 1966 and Charles Evers in 1971, in their campaigns for statewide office.[12]

Treating the votes cast for black candidates as an indicator of black voter turnout raises some potential questions. For example, could whites have voted for these candidates, or could blacks have voted for white candidates? Extensive research has documented the persistence of "racial bloc voting" or "racially polarized voting" throughout the South and in major cities during this period (see, for example, Loewen 1990; McCrary 1990; and Murray and Velditz 1978).[13] With votes cast for Whitley and Evers, I am assuming that only blacks voted for these candidates. Undoubtedly, some blacks voted for white candidates, as documented by the cases in which white poll watchers or employers have manipulated the black vote for white candidates (Berry 1973; Loewen 1981; Salamon 1972a), but no systematic data on such manipulation of the black vote is available by county. Moreover, votes cast for black candidates for statewide office is a useful indicator of black electoral strength because it suggests the degree to which the votes of black citizens can be coherently and effectively marshaled in support of state-level black candidates.

Like the changes in voter registration, voter turnout is examined in terms of the impact of the movement, federal registrars, and other variables noted above. The results of the analysis are presented in table 5.2. The results for the Clifton Whitley campaign are quite similar to those found for voter registration in 1967. The movement (Freedom Summer and NAACP) and federal examiners have significant positive effects on the number of votes cast for Clifton Whitley. In fact, examiners have a slightly greater effect than Freedom Summer. In 1971 the Evers campaign shows an important difference—the effects of Freedom Summer volunteers and federal examiners are no longer statistically significant. The short-term impact of federal examiners is consistent with James Alt's study of voter registration across the South that found "the absence

---

TABLE 5.2. Coefficients from OLS Regression Predicting Electoral Mobilization: Voters Registered in 1967 and Votes for Two Black Candidates for Statewide Office

$* = p < .05; ** = p < .01; *** = p < .001$ (one-tailed tests)

|  | Voter Registration, 1967 | Whitley, 1966 | Evers, 1971 |
|---|---|---|---|
| Freedom Summer volunteers and staff, 1964 | .358*** | .229* | −.003 |
|  | (51.339) | (14.864) | (−.344) |
| NAACP membership, 1966 | .135* | .138* | .191*** |
|  | (98.800) | (45.595) | (110.632) |
| Violent Resistance Index, 1960–69[a] | .100 | .115 | .022 |
|  | (15.914) | (8.235) | (2.825) |
| Federal examiners, 1965–67 | .119* | .246*** | .054 |
|  | (437.704) | (408.363) | (158.858) |
| Black voting-age population, 1970 | .400*** | .423*** | .796*** |
|  | (.190) | (.091) | (.301) |
| Percentage urban, 1970 | −.066 | −.050 | .019 |
|  | (−5.278) | (−1.785) | (1.228) |
| Constant |  | — | — |
|  | (500.937)* | (−61.768) | (149.620) |
| R-squared | .683 | .649 | .867 |
| Adj. R-squared | .657 | .621 | .856 |

Note: The standardized coefficient is presented followed by the unstandardized coefficient in parentheses. Although the index covers the period 1960–69, only 2 incidents out of 657 occurred after 1966.

---

of a significant effect [for examiners] after 1967 … [which] suggests that the relative impact of federal examiners' presence on black registration rates wore off over time" (1994, 371).

The Evers campaign for governor in 1971 appears to be a departure from the Whitley campaign in that the movement base of the early 1960s does not play a significant role; however, the NAACP variable, measuring mid- to late 1960s movement strength, does have a significant positive effect. The pattern of black political mobilization in Mississippi did not follow a linear path through the late 1960s and 1970s, underscoring the need for multiple outcome measures. As mayor of Fayette in Jefferson County, Charles Evers's political strength was concentrated in several majority-black counties in southwest Mississippi (e.g., Claiborne, Wilkinson, Jefferson) that had had little civil rights activity from 1961 to 1965 (Berry 1973).[14] While the electoral successes of these counties have continued at the local level, they represent a different pattern of mobilization than that found in pre-1965 movement counties.

The 1967 county and state elections in Mississippi were widely viewed as the first opportunity for black Mississippians to make significant gains in office holding by building on the massive gains in registered voters. Over a hundred candidates ran for office in twenty-six counties with twenty-two candidates winning office in the November general election. While the victories were important, they were also disappointing, leading Frank Parker to conclude that "the 1967 election results were a substantial victory for Mississippi's massive resistance to black political participation" (1990, 73). As we saw in Holmes County, despite the importance of Robert Clark's election, many local leaders were surprised and disappointed by the results of the 1967 election.

In which counties were blacks most likely to launch campaigns for elected office? Table 5.3 presents the results of an OLS regression analysis predicting the number of black candidates running for office in 1967 and 1971. The same set of independent variables is used from the earlier analyses with two exceptions. The control variable, black voting-age population, is now included as a percentage of the total voting-age population.[15] A measure of voter turnout for Clifton Whitley is used as an indicator of mass participation in electoral politics in the immediate aftermath of the Voting Rights Act.

The most interesting results of the analysis are that federal examiners had no significant impact, Freedom Summer and NAACP had significant positive effects, and that violent resistance had a significant negative effect. The positive effects of Freedom Summer and the NAACP are clear indicators that the movement infrastructure had expanded to support electoral campaigns and leaders.

The statistical nonsignificance of federal examiners is interesting because the presence of examiners should indicate a greater "openness" of the polity. However another dimension of the political opportunity structure is the use of repression by elites and other actors. Here we see that the use of violence by local whites decreases the number of black candidates for office. This probably operated through a variety of avenues.

Black candidates would have been more likely to experience harassment and violence in highly repressive counties, and some potential candidates may have withdrawn from elections or avoided electoral politics completely. In addition, a broader infrastructure of organizations and leaders was less likely to develop in highly repressive communities. In sum, repression minimizes the development of the movement infrastructure used to launch local campaigns.

### Racial Disparities in Voter Turnout

I have already noted the impact of white violence on the number of black candidates running for office. More routine tactics were available to white Mississippians to counter black political power, including voting for segregationist candidates for local, state, and federal office. The analyses of voter registration and turnout reported above

TABLE 5.3. Coefficients from OLS Regression Predicting Number of Black Candidates Running for Office in 1967 and 1971

$*$ = $p < .05$; $**$ = $p < .01$; $***$ = $p < .001$ (one-tailed tests)

|  | Black Candidates, 1967 | Black Candidates, 1971 |
|---|---|---|
| Freedom Summer volunteers and staff, 1964 | .369*** | .342*** |
|  | (.081) | (.161) |
| NAACP membership, 1966 | .159* | .193** |
|  | (.177) | (.461) |
| Violent Resistance Index, 1960–69 | –.192* | –.211** |
|  | (–.047) | (–.110) |
| Federal examiners, 1965–67 | –.091* | –.017 |
|  | (–.510) | (–.209) |
| Percentage vote for Whitley, 1966 | .372*** | .013 |
|  | (9.294) | (.676) |
| Proportion of the black voting-age population as total, 1970 | .371*** | .577*** |
|  | (6.119) | (20.351) |
| Percentage urban, 1970 | –.061 | .012 |
|  | (.007) | (.003) |
| Constant | — | — |
|  | (–2.081)*** | (–4.643)*** |
| R-squared | .596 | .606 |
| Adj. R-squared | .558 | .568 |

*Note:* The standardized coefficient is presented followed by the unstandardized coefficient in parentheses.

indicate absolute levels of black participation. However, electoral power is a matter of relative power, so a key indicator of change is the level of black political participation relative to white participation.

Voting patterns can be used to assess the tactical interaction between black and white mobilization. Given the persistence of racial bloc voting, we can assume that increases in white registration undermined the potential power of black voters. The trend is striking for the 1960s where "three new whites were enrolled in the Deep South for every two blacks." Earl Black and Merle Black note that "it is difficult to say how much of this huge increase ... can be attributed to racism" (1987, 139). In a multivariate analysis for the entire South, James Alt finds that white registration increases were greatest in counties with high black proportions, "suggesting a continuing fear among whites of the possibility of black electoral dominance" (1994, 354). Data on white voter registration is limited for Mississippi. Instead of using the limited voter registration data, I have analyzed white voter turnout in statewide elections—the same elections reported above: Clifton Whitley's campaign for the Senate in 1966 against the incumbent James Eastland and Charles Evers's campaign for governor in 1971. I estimate white voter turnout as the votes cast for white candidates as a proportion of the white voting-age population.

The relationship between white and black turnout is estimated by taking the difference in these two proportions. In all counties, white turnout exceeds black turnout, so this measure provides an estimate of the overall disparity in black and white electoral mobilization. This measure allows for a refinement in the earlier analysis by assessing black and white mobilization in relation to one another. For example, movement mobilization may increase black turnout and simultaneously increase white turnout at even greater levels. The same is true for federal examiners or any other of the variables analyzed above. Table 5.4 presents the results of the OLS regression models for the 1966 and 1971 elections. The primary independent variables from earlier equations are included in the analysis: early (Freedom Summer) and late (NAACP) movement organization, white violence, presence of federal examiners, and percentage urban. In addition, the proportion black of the voting-age population measures whether turnout disparities were different as the relative size of the black population increased. For the equations, negative coefficients indicate smaller differences in the level of voter turnout; in other words, the gap between black and white turnout is narrowed.

In both elections, the turnout disparity was positively related to the proportion black, which could indicate depressed rates of black turnout in these counties or increased white turnout. The latter is the case in Mississippi. In fact, black turnout is positively correlated with the proportion black in a county for both elections. For example, during the Whitley campaign, the correlation coefficient is 0.37. White turnout is related to

TABLE 5.4. Coefficients from OLS Regression Predicting White Turnout Advantage in 1966 and 1971

* = p < .05; ** = p < .01; *** = p < .001 (one-tailed tests)

| | 1966 | 1971 |
|---|---|---|
| Freedom Summer volunteers and staff, 1964 | −.332** | −.049 |
| | (−.004) | (−.0004) |
| NAACP membership, 1966 | .134 | −.231* |
| | (.008) | (−.011) |
| Violent Resistance Index, 1960–69 | .022 | .019 |
| | (.0002) | (.0002) |
| Federal examiners, 1965–67 | −.222* | −.111 |
| | (−.064) | (−.027) |
| Proportion black of the voting-age population, 1970 | .564*** | .421*** |
| | (.478) | (.298) |
| Percentage urban, 1970 | −.163 | −.350** |
| | (−.001) | (−.002) |
| Constant | — | — |
| | (.208)*** | (−.296)*** |
| R-squared | .392 | .359 |
| Adj. R-squared | .343 | .308 |

Note: The standardized coefficient is presented followed by the unstandardized coefficient in parentheses. The racial disparity measures are determined by the proportion white turnout minus the proportion black turnout. Negative coefficients indicate smaller differences in turnout rate.

the proportion black at an even greater magnitude; the correlation coefficient between white turnout and proportion black during this same election was 0.70. These results suggest that the electoral threat posed by a larger black electorate generated huge turnouts by whites in 1966 and 1971.

In the Whitley campaign of 1966, the presence of federal examiners and the civil rights movement resulted in smaller disparities between white and black voter turnout. The earlier analysis showed that these two variables predicted higher levels of black voting. Importantly, examiners and movement organization also narrow the gap between black and white voting levels. Here again, the movement has a larger impact than federal examiners on the disparity. For the 1971 elections, NAACP organization and percentage urban predict smaller disparities in turnout. In short, the results reported in table 5.4 confirm that local movement organization resulted in relative gains (by narrowing the gap between black and white turnout) as well as absolute gains (more black voters). Nevertheless, white turnout rose dramatically as the proportion black in a county increased.

## STUDY DESIGN

In this appendix, I describe the research strategy that I have used to study the various impacts of the Mississippi civil rights movement. Building on the conceptualization of movement outcomes presented in chapter 2, I present a more detailed consideration of the empirical dilemmas for research on outcomes. This initial methodological discussion applies generally to studies of movement outcomes. In addition, I consider the Mississippi movement as a case study in terms of its strengths and limitations. The majority of the chapter focuses on the two components of the research design: the qualitative case studies and the quantitative data set of Mississippi counties. The analysis that flows from these two distinct research strategies is complementary. In fact, I argue that both are essential because each answers different types of questions about the potential impacts of movements on outcomes.

## BROAD THEMES

### Levels of Mobilization and Levels of Analysis

Like many social movements, the civil rights struggle included a combination of local, regional, and national organizations and campaigns. In this study, I give primary consideration to the local dimensions of mobilization, countermobilization, and impact. This focus is important for two reasons. First, the movement itself was based in local movement centers, despite the historiographical bias toward treating the movement as if it were a nationally coordinated movement "from above" (Morris 1984).[16] Second, by examining these smaller units, we can study the variation across the state. Here, James Button's assertion that there was local variation in mobilization and impact becomes a methodological point of leverage (1989). In an assessment of strategies for improving the explanatory power of case studies, Edwin Amenta (1991) suggests that analysis of "subunits" of the case has important advantages. His example is the distribution of New Deal programs across states. Lee Ann Banaszak (1996) follows the same strategy in her comparative study of the women's suffrage movements in the United States and Switzerland by examining state-level variation in the United States and canton-level variation in Switzerland. Obviously, for this design strategy to work, there must be variation and the subunits must be "meaningful." For example, the processes that take place within that unit must be consequential for explaining variation. With the civil rights movement, this is the case, and it turns out to be a useful strategy for examining movement outcomes in many other cases.

While keeping the primary focus on the local level, there are processes that must be examined at the state and national level to understand local movements and their consequences. These include the broader dynamics of movements, such as shifts in ideology, funding, or tactics, and changes in the opportunity structures that operate at these broader levels. For example, the collapse of COFO in the mid-1960s and the MFDP in the late 1960s originated at the state level, but these changes in movement organization impacted local movements. White resistance to black electoral power through vote-dilution tactics occurred in state legislatures as well as the municipal and county political bodies. Another example is the aggregate decline of the War on Poverty funding, which has important consequences at the local level. The rule of thumb used in this study is that I have examined these types of state and national processes when they impact on the local level in important ways. A more comprehensive explanation of the rise and decline of the War on Poverty or any other of these large-scale shifts is beyond the scope of this study.

### Mobilization and Context

The questions examined in this study call for a research design that can capture the underlying dynamics of conflict and the variation from case to case. This includes the multiple actors who enter into the struggles with and against social movements. In short, the extensive collection of historical data is necessary before a balanced analysis can be made about the role of local organizing and other factors in producing social and political change. I have used two complementary research strategies for studying the movement in Mississippi, each of which corresponds to different sets of data and modes of analysis. They are as follows:

1. A quantitative county-by-county data set to examine three major groups of outcomes: (a) electoral politics, including participation and black office holding; (b) federal antipoverty programs; and (c) schools and desegregation.
2. A set of three case studies examining the variation in the patterns of movement development after 1965 at the county level. The case studies combine further archival research and informant interviews with local activists, politicians, and citizens.

The two research strategies allow for the combination of distinctive strengths found in each approach. The quantitative assessment of all Mississippi counties allows for a multivariate analysis with refined estimates of movement impact. The qualitative case studies allow us to situate these patterns in specific locales and explore the internal dynamics of the community in greater detail, especially the interplay between the movement organizations and the social infrastructure that sustains or undermines it.

### The Outcome Arenas Studied

One of the major difficulties in studying the outcomes of social movements is determining exactly what outcomes to examine. This study centers on three major "outcome arenas"—electoral politics, federal poverty programs, and educational institutions. Each of these outcome arenas falls within the overall purview of local civil rights movements; however, the relative importance of each "goal" varied within the Mississippi movement as a whole and across local movements. From its origins in the early 1960s, electoral politics was the central focus of the Mississippi movement; as such, it represents a major and enduring goal, more than the other arenas. Underlying electoral politics and many of the other strategies pursued by the movement were a concern with the economic problems facing black Mississippians. The War on Poverty, then, was another arena in which local movements directed considerable energy. However, this is a more ambiguous case because movements were reluctant, fearing possible cooptation. Finally, with educational institutions, there was far less effort placed in attacking institutional inequalities in this arena.

Within each outcome arena, I have measured different types of outcomes at different points in time (following the theoretical argument I make in chapter 2). By looking at many dependent variables, I can examine differences between outcomes (voter registration vs. black elected officials) and over time. Further, increasing the number of dependent variables in this way increases the overall reliability of the study, providing greater confidence in the theoretical conclusions (Campbell 1975).

### Mississippi as a Case Study

Mississippi is well suited for a study of the consequences of the civil rights movement in the South. First, the historical significance of Mississippi alone makes it worthy of close examination. During the modern civil rights movement, Mississippi was a trailblazer in developing strategies of resisting the emergence of the movement. In the period after the Voting Rights Act, Mississippi once again developed new strategies for minimizing the political power of black Mississippians. Hence, Mississippi can be treated as a test case for the South as a whole.

Second, there is sufficient variation among counties on all of the key variables to allow for careful generalization to the civil rights movement in other parts of the South (including the extent of mobilization and countermobilization, the size of the black population, class structure, and urbanization). V. O. Key, in his classic study of southern politics (1949), argued that there were "many Souths." I argue similarly that Mississippi is not monolithic. Examining one state poses certain limitations, but it also has the methodological advantage of "holding constant" variation at the state level. This is especially useful given my primary interest in local patterns of conflict and change.

However, Mississippi's "exceptionalism" should be noted. First, the coordination of a statewide movement in the early 1960s and the wide array of strategies pursued by the movement make the Mississippi case unique. In most other states, the movement worked on a city-by-city basis[17] rather than coordinating and confronting racial inequality statewide as in Mississippi. In terms of the data available, this is a clear advantage because it means that comparable evidence can be used to examine varying levels of mobilization across the state. Second, the strategies used to resist the movement were more intense and more varied than in other areas.

### Unit of Analysis

For the quantitative analysis and case studies, I use counties as the unit of analysis. There are three major reasons for using counties rather than municipalities. First, the movement mobilized at the county level in Mississippi. There was often variation in the county in terms of which areas had greater levels of participation in the movement. Fortunately, the case studies allow me to examine this variation. Nevertheless, counties were a primary organizational unit because they were the most important political unit in Mississippi containing, for example, the County Board of Supervisors, the most significant political body in local southern politics (see Black and Black 1987; and Krane and Shaffer 1992). This leads to a second reason for using counties as the unit of analysis—substantially important outcomes can be measured at the county level. Finally, a large body of political research uses counties as the unit of analysis dating back (at least) to Donald Matthews and James Protho's classic study *Negroes and the New Southern Politics* (1966). Following in this tradition, the results of this study can be compared to this broader body of research (see, for example, Alt 1994, 1995; Black and Black 1987; Colby 1986; Davis 1987; James 1988; Roscigno and Tomaskovic-Devey 1994; Salamon and Van Evera 1973; Stewart and Sheffield 1987; Timpone 1995 on electoral politics; Conlon and Kimenyi 1991 on schools; and Colby 1985 on poverty programs).

Counties are useful units. However, there are some measurement difficulties to be addressed especially with educational and poverty program variables. For schools, districts are the unit by which students and resources are distributed. In Mississippi many districts are contiguous with county boundaries. However, in some cases, there are multiple districts within the same county; (there is one multicounty district for Sharkey and Issaquena counties because of the low populations in these counties). For these multidistrict counties, data can be aggregated to the county level.[18] For the multicounty district, estimates can be determined using census reports for the school-age population for blacks and whites in each county. Multiple districts were not used primarily for the purposes of segregation; rather, racially separate schools were contained within each district. Typically, in a multidistrict county, there would be a district for the county seat and a rural school district. I have tested for possible bias by comparing the single and multidistrict counties.

With poverty programs, counties were again an important unit for distributing programs and resources. However, there were some statewide and multicounty programs. Where it is possible to make county-level estimates of the distribution of poverty program funds, I have done so. For a small number of cases, statewide programs cannot be disaggregated into county-level appropriations from the information included in the Office of Economic Opportunity reports.

There is one final methodological issue concerning the county data set. Hinds County includes the state capital, Jackson, and it is a statistical outlier on many variables. For this substantive and statistical rationale, I have excluded it from the quantitative date reported throughout the book.

## STATEWIDE QUANTITATIVE DATA

In this section, I describe the quantitative data set with attention directed toward the analytic issues that have been addressed with the data. The specific variables and their sources are reported in appendix D. The richness of the data set described below allows me to examine hypotheses concerning movements, conflict, and change.

First, I describe the groups of outcome measures in detail. The first set of outcomes focuses exclusively on electoral politics with four groups of indicators: (1) voter registration; (2) votes cast for black candidates in statewide elections; (3) the number of black candidates in early elections; and (4) the number of county-level black elected officials for the years between 1974 and 1984 (before this point the numbers were too low to be meaningful at an aggregate level).

The second group of outcomes examines the expansion and distribution of public services in relation to the black community. Indicators of public services include community action programs (CAPS) and Head Start programs. Frances Fox Piven and Richard Cloward argue that political elites use public expenditures to diminish protest

(1977; see also Colby 1985). Following a similar line of argument, John Dittmer argues that federal funding was initially directed toward the movement (in part because white politicians rejected the funding) but was shifted to "safer" hands as those resources became a base of power for community organizing (1993 and 1994; see also Quadagno 1994). This struggle played out over the funding for Head Start programs, and this case raises central issues concerning the constraints faced by local activists in dealing with federally funded programs. Collections of the Office of Economic Opportunity at the National Archives and Records Administration were consulted for documentation of CAP and Head Start programs in the state.

The third group of outcomes examines schools as an arena of conflict and includes measures of the extent of desegregation and the formation of private academies. The key indicator of desegregation is the dissimilarity index for selected years, and private academies are measured as the proportion of white school-age children attending these white-flight school[s]. This data provides the basis for analyzing how schools, as institutions, are shaped by the ongoing and historical residues of political conflict (see Andrews 2002).

There are two types of measures for the local movement: (1) indicators of local organizational strength and (2) indicators of the movement's capacity to mobilize the local community. Measures include the number of Freedom Summer volunteers, number of votes cast in the 1964 Freedom Vote (a mock election), number of Mississippi Freedom Democratic Party (MFDP—an independent movement-based political party) organizers in the county (1965), the number of COFO field-workers in the county prior to and following Freedom Summer, the number of NAACP members, and the amount of NAACP dues collected for the years between 1961 and 1970.

The intervention of the federal government, in this case the Justice Department, is measured by the presence of federal examiners and the number of people registered by federal examiners. This allows me to test to what extent factors external to the county impact on black electoral participation.

Measures of white resistance to the movement falls into four major categories: (1) organizations explicitly directed toward resisting the movement (e.g., Citizens' Council and Ku Klux Klan organizations); (2) violent actions taken by whites toward the movement to intimidate or stop local mobilizing; (3) the establishment of counterinstitutions to subvert the goals of the movement; and (4) "legal" resistance such as the changing of electoral procedures or boundaries.

For organizational measures, I use indicators of Citizens' Council and Ku Klux Klan organizations in the county For the summer and fall of 1964, several indicators are used that measure white harassment and violence against civil rights workers, including threats, physical assault, and shots fired at civil rights workers; here, the relative impact of different resistance strategies can be assessed. For 1960 to 1969, I have used the number of attacks of civil rights workers compiled by David Colby (1987) from organizational records and newspapers.

Finally, I have compiled many variables measuring the local social structure. In order to account for variation in demographic and economic variables among the counties, data is available from census reports and city and county data books. I have compiled data on the income and occupational structure of blacks and whites in the county, urbanization, and absolute and relative size of the black and white population (and the voting-age population).

## COMMUNITY STUDIES

In this section, I discuss the logic of case selection, describe the three communities, review the types of data used, and outline the major questions that can be answered by the community studies. Many dimensions of the development and transformation of local movements are difficult, if not impossible, to measure quantitatively for all counties. The following issues are given primary consideration through the case studies: (I) early movement strength and early participant-leaders; (2) continuity or change in the movement base leading to late movement strength or internal factionalism; (3) a changing set of participants—in terms of class position, organizational affiliations, et cetera.; (4) external movement connections—links to national organizations and resources; (5) changing demographic basis and class structure; (6) role of federal funding of poverty programs; (7) federal intervention in electoral politics—federal examiners, Justice Department suits, et cetera; (8) violent repression by whites; and (9) non-violent resistance/opposition by whites.

I utilized the same mix of data sources for each case study. Informant interviews with key participants have helped to make up for a sparse literature on the period after 1965. The interview list was constructed to tap different target groups. Major groups include movement activists from different points in time and with different organizational affiliations. In addition, elected officials and community leaders were interviewed. I employed a uniform interview protocol that focused on the level and forms of political conflict. Interview data was supplemented with a review of local weekly newspapers. Last, archival sources (described in appendix B) were examined to formulate profiles of the "movement infrastructure" that developed in the early and mid-1960s. These profiles have been assembled based on published historical work and archival research with the SNCC, CORE, and NAACP papers and the manuscript and oral history collections at Tougaloo College.

The community studies significantly strengthen the research design by focusing on the same set of outcomes (electoral politics, education, and social policies) while extending the range of data. On the question of movement strategy and infrastructure, the community studies include data about tactics that cannot be captured for all Mississippi counties, such as the formation of community centers (in Holmes and Madison), rural health clinics (Bolivar), and farming and manufacturing cooperatives (Bolivar and Holmes). It is noteworthy that the movement strategies listed here are both characteristics of mobilization and outcomes. Further, the community studies provide additional insight into the strategies used by whites toward the movement, such as the redrawing of electoral boundaries (Parker, Colby, and Morrison 1994). Last, the community studies shed light on the ways in which local social structure shaped political mobilization and consequently changes in local institutions.

## DATA SOURCES

The research for this study was derived from four major sources: (1) archival collections of participants, civil rights organizations, and government agencies; (2) informant interviews; (3) newspapers; and (4) reports and documentation of various organizations and agencies such as the United States Commission on Civil Rights. Let me describe each in turn, highlighting the limitations and strengths of each.

### *Archival Collections*

By far, the most valuable source of data for this study was the archival collections that document mobilization at the local level. The major collections consulted for this study are listed in appendix B. Nevertheless, one limitation of the archival collections is the almost exclusive documentation of major civil rights organizations (e.g., CORE and SNCC) and the early 1960s; this limitation is reflected in the historical scholarship. However, for the period from 1965 to 1970, extensive documentation is available in smaller collections. For an understanding of the Mississippi movement during this period, one of the most valuable collections is the Civil Rights Litigation Records at Tougaloo College. In addition to the original documents, there is a set of 170 microfilm reels, including the case and office files for the major civil rights legal organizations working in Mississippi. The activities of many local movements find their way into the Litigation Records. To paraphrase one of the activists interviewed for this study, there were civil rights lawyers behind every bush back then. The collections of various organizations were examined, including SNCC, CORE, NAACP, CDGM, and the MFDP. The Freedom Information Service Archives was another particularly valuable collection for the post–Voting Rights Act period. In addition, the collections of many individuals are available and were examined, including Fannie Lou Hamer, Ed King, Rims Barber,

Charles Horowitz, and James Loewen. In addition to these movement sources, I have examined the documents of various government agencies, including the Office of Economic Opportunity, the Department of Justice, and the United States Commission on Civil Rights.

## Interviews

Informant interviews provided another source of documentation that was especially important for the community studies. In each community, I conducted open-ended interviews with key participants. Individuals were selected who could comment on specific areas of the local movement and community history. In other words, I attempted to interview individuals representing different periods and organizations. A uniform interview protocol was used to provide comparable information about the internal dynamics and trajectory of local movements. Topics covered in the open-ended interview were key organizations, leadership, internal conflicts, major tactics, repression, early electoral campaigns, and participation in the War on Poverty. However, I tailored the interview to the respondent's experience and expertise, such as Head Start, the history of litigation in the community, or a specific movement organization. Using interviews to establish a community history is a difficult task, and researchers face a number of potential problems. The most important problem is the limitations of memory over an expanded time frame. This was especially acute for my study, where I was interested in establishing sequencing and detailed accounts of major events such as boycotts.

The interviews also provided data on the relations between different organizations, a (retrospective) account of the high and low points of mobilization, and the forms of repression and their effects. I conducted the interview research in tandem with the other research for this study. Like all forms of data, the interviews are strengthened when they are scrutinized in relation to other forms of data. For example, prior to conducting the interviews, a preliminary profile and history was established for each community based on archival research and prior studies. If a respondent discussed an event or organization that I did not already have documentation on, I returned to the archival collections and local newspapers to search for independent confirmation and further documentation on a particular time period or organization.

In addition to the interviews I collected, I have drawn on interviews that have been conducted by prior researchers. These include the Tom Dent Oral History Collection conducted in the late 1970s and early 1980s, the Civil Rights Documentation Project at Howard University, and Stanford University's Project South Oral History Collection of taped meetings, discussions and interviews from 1965. Because many of these interviews were conducted in the 1960s and 1970s, they help address the memory problem in my interviews. In addition, some of the recordings are with individuals who have since died or of meetings that obviously cannot be re-created.

## Newspapers

Like interviews, newspapers come with particular strengths and limitations. Newspapers were used for a number of different reasons. When reporters interviewed key informants, they can be used much as the interviews noted above to assess the ideas and tactics of key actors in the midst of conflict. In the case of Mississippi, local newspapers have to be treated with special care because they can vary widely between towns depending on the local editor. For example, in Holmes County the *Lexington Advertiser* reported extensively on movement activity, going as far as announcing meetings of the MFDP and NAACP. In Madison and Bolivar counties, local newspapers were openly hostile to the movement. In both cases, the newspapers reported infrequently on the movement. The newspapers also participated in openly repressing the movement. The *Bolivar Commercial* listed the names of parents sending their children to formerly all-white schools, inviting economic pressure and violence on these families. The *Madison County Herald* listed the names of individuals who had registered to vote in the past week as an act of intimidation. Neither paper reported movement activity beyond vague rumors. For example, in the mid-1960s, the *Bolivar Commercial* reported a rumor that civil rights activists were working in Shaw. More common were diatribes in response to events covered in the national press. The *Bolivar Commercial* pursued the "outside agitator" theory by blaming organizations like the Delta Ministry (a group sponsored by the National Council of Churches) or "Yankee" lawyers for any local activity In short, the Madison and Bolivar papers were not helpful sources for news on major campaigns (which were generally not reported) during the 1960s. For Bolivar County, the *Delta Democrat Times* from Greenville in nearby Washington County reported on movement activity. For example, the Shelby school boycott of 1968 generated numerous articles in the *Delta Democrat Times,* in contrast to the *Bolivar Commercial,* which only commented on the boycott after it ended.

For this study, I have collected extensive newspaper coverage for each of the three cases. Part of that coverage was collected from newspaper clippings in the subject files at the Mississippi Department of Archives and History (MDAH) under a broad range of topics. These subject files proved particularly helpful for the period from 1970 to 1985. By this period the major newspapers in the state, the *Clarion-Ledger* and the *Jackson Daily News*, began to report on black politics and protest more systematically. The subject files also include articles from regional and local newspapers and articles from the *Jackson Advocate* (a black-owned newspaper), the *New Orleans Times-Picayune,* the *Memphis Commercial Appeal,* and the *Washington Post.* These files, though limited, were helpful in establishing a baseline of major protest events, political battles, and litigation within each of the communities. I followed up on key events reported in state or regional newspapers (e.g., a boycott sponsored by the United League of Holmes County in 1978) by examining local newspapers and by interviewing central actors.

In addition to the subject files, I made intensive investigation of local newspapers for selected points in time. I conducted a review of newspapers in each community during the following periods: Freedom Summer, the implementation of freedom of choice school desegregation, poverty program implementation, the formation of CAP boards, and full-scale school desegregation (for this period a search was also conducted of the *New York Times*, which reported widely on the *Alexander v. Holmes* decision and the implementation of school desegregation). In addition, searches were conducted for other periods of local mobilization and local elections.

A final methodological point on the use of newspapers: generally speaking, newspapers report on events, but not on organizations, or only incidentally on organizations as sponsors of events. For example, the *Delta Democrat Times* covered in minute detail the school boycott in Shelby during the spring and summer of 1968. The coverage was especially detailed concerning legal developments such as the curfew. The Shelby Educational Committee was noted as a sponsor of the boycott, but little investigation was made concerning the origin or development of this organization. An organization like the North Bolivar County Farm Cooperative never received substantial coverage in the local or regional press. The important point is that these limitations in the data, unless duly noted and addressed, can lead to analytic errors. The most serious error is to reproduce the notion that the civil rights movement was a series of "events" without addressing the underlying organizational developments in particular locales.

### Reports and Government Documents

The last source of documentation of the Mississippi movement is reports and data generated by government agencies and other organizations. These include reports by the United States Commission on Civil Rights, the Joint Center for Political Studies, and congressional hearings. More familiar sources such as census documents are used frequently, especially for the quantitative data set; and reports published by the state of Mississippi were used for education, election returns, and other county-level data. Many of these state documents are located at the Information Services Library of Jackson State University.

## DISCUSSION QUESTIONS

1. Why did the author choose Mississippi as a case study for determining the legacy of the civil rights movement in the South?
2. Discuss a specific issue or piece of legislation that demonstrates the civil rights movement's ongoing impact on American society.
3. What were some of the variables that affected black voter mobilization in the mid-1960s?

## NOTES

1. Numerous studies have attempted to determine the impact of key court decisions and legislative changes, including Davidson and Grofman (1994) on the Voting Rights Act, Grofman (2000) on the 1964 Civil Rights Act, and Rosenberg (1991) on major Supreme Court decisions.
2. Over the past four decades, leading scholars have reviewed the relevant literature on social movements and have noted the limited amount of systematic research on outcomes (Diani 1997; Eckstein 1965; Giugni 1998; Marx and Wood 1975; McAdam, McCarthy, and Zald 1988; Tarrow 1998). Burstein, Einwohner, and Hollander observe that "the field of social movements grew tremendously in the 1970s and 1980s, but the study of movement outcomes did not. ... [The result is] that we still know very little about the impact of social movements on social change" (1995, 276). In the past five to ten years, this has been a growth area, and in chapter 2, I discuss recent trends in studies of movement impact in detail.
3. This may be one of the ways that unionization campaigns differ from other forms of contentious politics.
4. The literature responding to Piven and Cloward's thesis is quite extensive; see the 1993 edition of their *Regulating the Poor* for a bibliography. Two important critiques from movement scholars are Gamson and Schmeidler's "Organizing the Poor" (1984) and Morris's *The Origins of the Civil Rights Movement* (1984). See also Piven and Cloward's responses in (1984) and (1992).
5. These models of movement influence are connected to methodological strategies. For example, Rucht and Neidhardt argue that media-reported protest is a meaningful barometer of all protest: "Insofar as we are interested in those protests which are an input for the political system, media-reported protests have a higher validity than the whole range of actual protests" (1998, 77).

6. For more detailed discussion of movement organization, see Conell and Voss (1990), Minkoff (1995), Schwartz (1976), Schwartz and Paul (1992), and Staggenborg (1988).

7. This is true at least for the counties where the movement operated. Arguably, the movement could have had an impact on communities without a local movement, although it would be very difficult to determine whether or not this type of impact occurred.

8. See U.S. Commission on Civil Rights, *The Voting Rights Act: The First Months* (1965), for a detailed description of the role of federal examiners.

9. I measured the presence or absence of federal examiners in the county. Examiners provided a parallel registration process that was intended to eliminate discrimination. The Voter Education Project report (and other researchers) used the total number of blacks listed by federal examiners as an indicator of the effect of examiners. This conflates the outcome (number of registered blacks) with the facilitative role played by examiners and overestimates the effect of examiners.

10. Although direct effects of examiners were limited, there may have been indirect effects. For example, the presence of examiners may have moderated the resistance of examiners in other counties. If this were true, then the cross-sectional estimates would underestimate the overall impact of examiners.

11. A second reason for moving to other outcome measures is that the data on voter registration is the least reliable measure of political participation. Voter registration records are not kept by race, so the data used are estimates of various kinds either by local registrars or self-reported in census data. Even aggregate data on voter registration tends to be inaccurate because registrars fail to purge records on a regular basis for deaths, migration, and felony conviction (Lichtman and Issacharoff 1991).

12. Clifton Whitley ran for the U.S. Senate in the Democratic primary in August and in the general election as an independent candidate. Voter turnout in these two elections is highly correlated ($r = 0.797$), so I have used an average of the two as an indicator of mid-1960s black electoral mobilization.

13. "Racial bloc voting" refers to the tendency in biracial elections for whites to vote for white candidates and blacks for black candidates. In legal cases concerning discriminatory redistricting, racial bloc voting research has been important for establishing the discriminatory effect of at-large election systems.

14. These counties had no Freedom Summer projects. By 1966 Claiborne County had 1,316 adult members of the NAACP; Jefferson and Wilkinson had 924 and 889, respectively.

15. The two variables (the size and proportion of the black voting-age population) cannot be entered into the same equation without generating multi-colinearity. In table 5.2, the dependent variables require a control for the absolute size of the black electorate. In tables 5.3 and 5.4, the dependent variables require a control for the relative size of the black electorate.

16. See Payne's essay at the end *of I've Got the Light of Freedom* (1995) and Carson's essay "Civil Rights Reform and the Black Freedom Struggle" (1986) for more thorough developments of this idea. For historical analyses that focus on local patterns of mobilization, see Ceselski (1994), Chafe (1980), Dittmer (1994), Eskew (1997), and Norrell (1985).

17. The SCLC's strategy reflected this pattern by focusing on particular cities, for example, Birmingham, Selma, and Chicago. Even SNCC's work outside Mississippi was focused on one town rather than statewide.

18. Studies examining school desegregation and politics in urban areas have followed a similar strategy of aggregating across school districts to compare cities to each other.

# CHAPTER 12
## Arenas for Individual and Group Strategies

# Beyond Affirmative Action
## *Equality and Identity*

## Cornel West

*Institutionalized rejection of difference is an absolute necessity in a profit economy which needs outsiders as surplus people. As members of such an economy, we have all been programmed to respond to the human differences between us with fear and loathing and to handle that difference in one of three ways: ignore it, and if that is not possible, copy it if we think it is dominant, or destroy it if we think it is subordinate. But we have no patterns for relating across our human differences as equals. As a result, those differences have been misnamed and misused in the service of separation and confusion.*

—AUDRE LORDE, *SISTER OUTSIDER* (1984)

THE FUNDAMENTAL CRISIS in black America is twofold: too much poverty and too little self-love. The urgent problem of black poverty is primarily due to the distribution of wealth, power, and income—a distribution influenced by the racial caste system that denied opportunities to most "qualified" black people until two decades ago.

The historic role of American progressives is to promote redistributive measures that enhance the standard of living and quality of life for the have-nots and have-too-littles. Affirmative action was one such redistributive measure that surfaced in the heat of battle in the 1960s among those fighting for racial equality. Like earlier *de facto* affirmative action measures in the American past—contracts, jobs, and loans to select immigrants granted by political machines; subsidies to certain farmers; FHA mortgage loans to specific home buyers; or GI Bill benefits to particular courageous Americans—recent efforts to broaden access to America's prosperity have been based upon preferential policies. Unfortunately, these policies always benefit middle-class

Americans disproportionately. The political power of big business in big government circumscribes redistributive measures and thereby tilts these measures away from the have-nots and have-too-littles.

Every redistributive measure is a compromise with and concession from the caretakers of American prosperity—that is, big business and big government. Affirmative action was one such compromise and concession achieved after the protracted struggle of American progressives and liberals in the courts and in the streets. Visionary progressives always push for substantive redistributive measures that make opportunities available to the have-nots and have-too-littles, such as more federal support to small farmers, or more FHA mortgage loans to urban dwellers as well as suburban home buyers. Yet in the American political system, where the powers that be turn a skeptical eye toward any program aimed at economic redistribution, progressives must secure whatever redistributive measures they can, ensure their enforcement, then extend their benefits if possible.

If I had been old enough to join the fight for racial equality in the courts, the legislatures, and the board rooms in the 1960s (I *was* old enough to be in the streets), I would have favored—as I do now—a class-based affirmative action in principle. Yet in the heat of battle in American politics, a redistributive measure in principle with no power and pressure behind it means no redistributive measure at all. The prevailing discriminatory practices during the sixties, whose targets were working people, women, and people of color, were atrocious. Thus, an *enforceable* race-based—and later gender-based—affirmative action policy was the best possible compromise and concession.

Progressives should view affirmative action as neither a major solution to poverty nor a sufficient means to equality. We should see it as primarily playing a negative role—namely, to ensure that discriminatory practices against women and people of color are abated. Given the history of this country, it is a virtual certainty that without affirmative action racial and sexual discrimination would return with a vengeance. Even if affirmative action fails significantly to reduce black poverty or contributes to the persistence of racist perceptions in the workplace, without affirmative action black access to America's prosperity would be even more difficult to obtain and racism in the workplace would persist anyway.

This claim is not based on any cynicism toward my white fellow citizens; rather, it rests upon America's historically weak will toward racial justice and substantive redistributive measures. This is why an attack on affirmative action is an attack on redistributive efforts by progressives unless there is a real possibility of enacting and enforcing a more wide-reaching class-based affirmative action policy.

In American politics, progressives must not only cling to redistributive ideals, but must also fight for those policies that—out of compromise and concession—imperfectly conform to those ideals. Liberals who give only lip service to these ideals, trash the policies in the name of *realpolitik,* or reject the policies as they perceive a shift in the racial bellwether give up precious ground too easily. And they do so even as the sand is disappearing under our feet on such issues as regressive taxation, layoffs or take backs from workers, and cutbacks in health and child care.

Affirmative action is not the most important issue for black progress in America, but it is part of a redistributive chain that must be strengthened if we are to confront and eliminate black poverty. If there were social democratic redistributive measures that wiped out black poverty, and if racial and sexual discrimination could be abated through the good will and meritorious judgments of those in power, affirmative action would be unnecessary. Although many of my liberal and progressive citizens view affirmative action as a redistributive measure whose time is over or whose life is no longer worth preserving, I question their view because of the persistence of discriminatory practices that increase black social misery, and the warranted suspicion that good will and fair judgment among the powerful does not loom as large toward women and people of color.

If the elimination of black poverty is a necessary condition of substantive black progress, then the affirmation of black humanity, especially among black people themselves, is a sufficient condition of such progress. Such affirmation speaks to the existential issues of what it means to be a degraded African (man, woman, gay, lesbian, child) in a racist society. How does one affirm oneself without reenacting negative black stereotypes or overreacting to white supremacist ideals?

The difficult and delicate quest for black identity is integral to any talk about racial equality. Yet it is not solely a political or economic matter. The quest for black identity involves self-respect and self-regard, realms inseparable from, yet not identical to, political power and economic status. The flagrant self-loathing among black middle-class professionals bears witness to this painful process. Unfortunately, black conservatives focus on the issue of self-respect as if it were the one key that would open all doors to black progress. They illustrate the fallacy of trying to open all doors with one key: they wind up closing their eyes to all doors except the one the key fits.

Progressives, for our part, must take seriously the quest for self-respect, even as we train our eye on the institutional causes of black social misery. The issues of black identity—both black self-love and self-contempt—sit alongside black poverty as realities to confront and transform. The uncritical acceptance of self-degrading ideals, that call into question black intelligence, possibility, and beauty not only compounds black social misery but also paralyzes black middle-class efforts to defend broad redistributive measures.

This paralysis takes two forms: black bourgeois preoccupation with white peer approval and black nationalist obsession with white racism.

The first form of paralysis tends to yield a navel-gazing posture that conflates the identity crisis of the black middle class with the state of siege raging in black working-poor and very poor communities. That unidimensional view obscures the need for redistributive measures that significantly affect the majority of blacks, who are working people on the edge of poverty.

The second form of paralysis precludes any meaningful coalition with white progressives because of an undeniable white racist legacy of the modern Western world. The anger this truth engenders impedes any effective way of responding to the crisis in black America. Broad redistributive measures require principled coalitions, including multiracial alliances. Without such measures, black America's sufferings deepen. White racism indeed contributes to this suffering. Yet an obsession with white racism often comes at the expense of more broadly based alliances to affect social change and borders on a tribal mentality. The more xenophobic versions of this viewpoint simply mirror the white supremacist ideals we are opposing and preclude any movement toward redistributive goals.

How one defines oneself influences what analytical weight one gives to black poverty. Any progressive discussion about the future of racial equality must speak to black poverty and black identity. My views on the necessity and limits of affirmative action in the present moment are informed by how substantive redistributive measures and human affirmative efforts can be best defended and expanded.

## DISCUSSION QUESTIONS

1. What are economic redistribution policies?
2. What is the connection between affirmative action and redistributive economic policies?
3. What two forms of paralysis are raised? How does recognizing them relate to relieving suffering among the poor?

# Getting Along
## *Renewing America's Commitment to Racial Justice*

### Melvin Oliver and Thomas Shapiro

*In America, though, life seems to move faster than anywhere else on the globe and each generation is promised more than it will get; which creates, in each generation, a furious, bewildered rage, the rage of people who cannot find solid ground beneath their feet.*

—James Baldwin, "The Harlem Ghetto"

*Can we all just get along?*

—Rodney King, Los Angeles, 1992

## INTRODUCTION: THE MEANING OF MONEY

Wealth is money that is not typically used to purchase milk, shoes, or other necessities. Sometimes it bails families out of financial and personal crises, but more often it is used to create opportunities, secure a desired stature and standard of living, or pass along a class status already obtained to a new generation. We have seen how funds transferred by parents to their children both before and after death are often treated as very special money. Such funds are used for down payments on houses, closing costs on a mortgage, start-up money for a business, maternal and early childhood expenses, private education, and college costs. Parental endowments, for those fortunate enough to receive them, are enormously consequential in shaping their recipients' opportunities, life chances, and outlooks on life.

A common literary theme shows how money debases character, love, and relationships. In *A Room of One's Own* Virginia Woolf reminds us that the absence of money also deeply corrupts. As a woman, Virginia Woolf thought that her financial inheritance would be more important in her life than even gaining the right to vote. Suppose a black person inherited a good deal of money (let's not inquire about the source) at about the time the slaves were emancipated in 1863. Of the two events—the acquisition of wealth and the attainment of freedom—which would be more important in shaping the life of this person and his or her family? John Rock, the abolitionist, pre-Civil War orator, and first African American attorney to argue before the Supreme Court, lectured that "you will find no prejudice in the Yankee whatsoever,"[1] when the avenues of wealth are opened to the formerly enslaved.

Over a century and a third later Ellis Cose disagrees with this assessment in *The Rage of a Privileged Class.* His book illustrates the daily discriminations, presumptions, and reproaches to which even very successful upper-middle-class blacks are subject. Cose reminds us that the color of the hand holding the money matters. The former mayor of New York, David Dinkins, stated pointedly; "a white man with a million dollars is a millionaire, and a black man with a million dollars is a nigger with a million dollars."[2] Even highly accomplished and prosperous black professionals bitterly lament that their personal success does not translate into status, at least not outside the black community.

This notion is further elaborated in *Living with Racism* by Joe Feagin and Melvin Sikes, a book based on the life experiences of two hundred black middle-class individuals. Feagin and Sikes found that no amount of hard work and achievement, or money and resources, provides immunity for black people from the persistent, commonplace injury of white racism. Modern racism must be understood as lived experience, as middle-class blacks "tell of mistreatment encountered as they traverse traditionally white places."[3] Occasions of serious discrimination are immediately painful and stressful, and they have a cumulative impact on individuals, their psyches, families, and communities. The repeated experience of racism affects a person's understanding of and outlook on life. It is from the well of institutionalized racism that daily incidents of racial hostility are drawn.

One's sense of autonomy and security about the future is not merely or necessarily characterological; it is also a reflection of one's personal position and status. "The secret point of money and power in America is neither the things that money can buy nor power for power's sake … but absolute personal freedom, mobility, privacy,"[4] according to the writer Joan Didion. Money allows one "to be a free agent, live by one's own rules."

Mary Ellen comes from an upper-middle-class business- and property-owning black family and is well on the road to building her own wealth portfolio. She talks about how her background helped shape her attitudes toward economic security and risk-taking.

I think that growing up as I did, I think my mindset is a little different because I don't feel like I'm going to fall back. I don't feel that. A lot of people I talk to feel that. They don't see options that I see. They don't take as many risks. You know, I could always run home to my parents if something drastic happened. A lot of people don't have those alternatives.

As the twentieth century draws to a close the mixed legacy of racial progress and persistent racial disadvantage continues to confront America and shape our political landscape. Our focus in this book on assets has yielded a fuller comprehension of the extent and the sources of continued racial inequality. But how can we use this understanding to begin to close the racial gap?

This chapter steps back from the detailed examination of wealth to place our major substantive findings into the larger picture. Our exploration of racial wealth differences began with theoretical speculations about how wealth differences might force us to revise previous thinking about racial inequality. The unreflective use of income as the standard way to measure inequality has contributed to a serious underestimation of the magnitude and scope of the racial disadvantage, revealing only one of its causes. If income disparities are not the crux of the problem, then policies that seek to redress inequality by creating equal opportunities and narrowing racial differences are doomed to fail, even when such programs succeed in putting blacks in good jobs. The more one learns about pattern of racial wealth differences, the more misguided current policies appear. One of our greatest hopes is that this book brings to widespread attention the urgent need for new thinking on the part of those in the world of policymaking. Given the role played by racial wealth differences in reproducing inequality anew, we are more convinced than ever that well-intended current policies fail not simply because they are inadequately funded and prematurely curtailed but, perhaps more important, because they are exclusively focused on income. In some key respects our analysis of racial wealth differences forms an agenda for the future.

## WHY RACIAL WEALTH INEQUALITY PERSISTS

The contemporary effects of race are vividly depicted in the racial pattern of wealth accumulation that our analysis has exposed. We have compiled a careful, factual account of how contemporary discrimination along demographic, social, and economic lines results in unequal wealth reservoirs for whites and blacks. Our examination has proven insightful in two respects. It shows that unequal background and social conditions result in unequal resources. Whether it be a matter of education, occupation, family status, or other characteristics positively correlated with income and wealth, blacks are most likely to come out on the short end of the stick. This is no surprise.

Our examination of contemporary conditions also found, more surprisingly, that equally positioned whites and blacks have highly unequal amounts of wealth. Matching whites and blacks on key individual factors correlated with asset acquisition, demonstrated the gnawing persistence of large magnitudes of wealth difference. Because it allows us to look at several factors at once, regression analysis was then called into play. Even when whites and blacks were matched on all the identifiably important factors, we could still not account for about three-quarters of the racial wealth difference. If white and black households shared all the wealth-associated characteristics we examined, blacks would still confront a $43,000 net worth handicap!

We argue, furthermore, that the racialization of the welfare state and institutional discrimination are fundamental reasons for the persistent wealth disparities we observed. Government policies that have paved the way for whites to amass wealth have simultaneously discriminated against blacks in their quest for economic security. From the era of slavery on through the failure of the freedman to gain land and the Jim Crow laws that restricted black entrepreneurs, opportunity structures for asset accumulation rewarded whites and penalized blacks. FHA policies then thwarted black attempts to get in on the ground floor of home ownership, and segregation limited their ability to take advantage of the massive equity build-up that whites have benefited from in the housing market. As we have also seen, the formal rules of government programs like social security and AFDC have had discriminatory impacts on black Americans. And finally, the U.S. tax code has systematically privileged whites and those with assets over and against asset-poor black Americans.

These policies are not the result of the workings of the free market or the demands of modern industrial society; they are, rather, a function of the political power of elites. The powerful protect and extend their interests by way of discriminatory laws and social policies, while minorities unite to contest them. Black political mobilization has removed barriers to black economic security, but the process is uneven. As blacks take one step forward, new and more intransigent legislative or judicial decisions push them back two steps. Nowhere has this trend been more evident than in the quest for housing. While the Supreme Court barred state courts from enforcing restrictive covenants, they did not prevent property owners from adhering to these covenants voluntarily, thereby denying black homeowners any legal recourse against racist whites. Similarly, while the Fair Housing Act banned discrimination by race in the housing market, it provided compensation only for "individual victims of discrimination,"[5] a fact that blunts the act's effectiveness as an antidiscrimination tool. These pyrrhic victories have in no way put an end to residential segregation, and black fortunes continue to stagnate.

Our empirical investigation of housing and mortgage markets demonstrates the way in which racialized state policies interact with other forms of institutional discrimination to prevent blacks from accumulating wealth in the form of residential equity. At each stage of the process blacks are thwarted. It is harder for blacks to get approved for a mortgage—and thus to buy a home—than for whites, even when applicants are equally qualified. More insidious still, African Americans who do get mortgages pay higher interest rates than whites. Finally, given the persistence of residential segregation, houses located in black communities do not rise in value nearly as much as those in white neighborhoods. The average racial difference in home equity amounts to over $20,000 among those who currently hold mortgages.

The inheritance of accumulated disadvantages over generations has, in many ways, shortchanged African Americans of the rather dramatic mobility gains they have achieved. While blacks have made stunning educational strides, entered middle-class occupations at an impressive rate, and moved into political positions in numbers unheard of a quarter of a century ago, they have been unable to surmount the historical obstacles that inhibit their accumulation of wealth. Still today, they bear the brunt of the sedimentation of racial inequality.

## THE SUBSTANTIVE IMPLICATIONS OF OUR FINDINGS

What are the implications of our findings? First, our research underscores the need to include in any analysis of economic well-being not only income but private wealth. In American society, a stable economic foundation must include a command over assets as well as an adequate income flow. Nowhere is this observation better illustrated than by the case of black Americans. Too much of the current celebration of black success is related to the emergence of a professional and middle-class black population that has access to a steady income. Even the most visibly successful numbers of the black community—movie and TV stars, athletes, and other performers—are on salary. But, income streams do not necessarily translate into wealth pools. Furthermore, when one is black, one's current status is not easily passed on to the next generation. The presence of assets can pave the way for an extension and consolidation of status for a family over several generations.

This is not, however, an analysis that emphasizes large levels of wealth. The wealth that can make a difference in the lives of families and children need not be in the million-dollar or six-figure range. Nonetheless, it is increasingly clear that a significant amount of assets will be needed in order to provide the requisites for success in our increasingly technologically minded society. Technological change and the new organization of jobs have challenged our traditional conception of how to prepare for a career and what to expect from it. Education in the future will be lifelong, as technological jobs change at a rapid pace. Assets will play an important role in allowing people to take advantage of training and retraining opportunities. In the economy of the twenty-first century children will require a solid educational foundation, and parents will most likely need to develop new skills on a regular basis. The presence or absence of assets will have much to say about the mobility patterns of the future.

Second, our investigation of wealth has revealed deeper, historically rooted economic cleavages between the races than were previously believed to exist. The interaction of race and class in the wealth accumulation process is clear. Historical practices, racist in their essence, have produced class hierarchies that, on the contemporary scene, reproduce wealth inequality. As important, contemporary racial disadvantages deprive those in the black middle class from building on their wealth assets at the same pace as similarly situated white Americans. The shadow of race falls most darkly, however, on the black underclass, whose members find themselves at the bottom of the economic hierarchy. Their inability to accumulate assets is thus grounded primarily in their low-class backgrounds. The wealth deficit of the black middle class, by contrast, is affected more by the racial character of certain policies deriving in part from the fears and anxieties that whites harbor regarding lower-class blacks than by the actual class background of middle-class blacks. As Raymond Franklin suggests in his *Shadows of Race and Class:*

The overcrowding of blacks in the lower class … casts a shadow on middle-class members of the black population that have credentials but are excluded and discriminated against on racial grounds.

Given the mutually reinforcing and historically accumulated race and class barriers that blacks encounter in attempting to achieve a measure of economic security, we argue that a focus on job opportunity is not sufficient to the task of eradicating racial disadvantage in America. Equal opportunity, even in the best of circumstances, does not lead to equality. This is a double-edged statement. First, we believe that equal opportunity policies and programs, when given a chance, do succeed in lowering some of the more blatant barriers to black advancement. But given the historically sedimented nature of racial wealth disparities, a focus on equal opportunity will only yield partial results. Blacks will make some gains, but so will whites, with initial inequalities persisting at another level. As blacks get better jobs and higher incomes, whites also advance. Thus, as Edwin Dorn points out in *Rules and Racial Equality:*

To say that current inequality is the result of discrimination against blacks is to state only half the problem. The other half—is discrimination in favor of whites. It follows that merely eliminating discrimination is insufficient. The very direction of bias must be reversed, at least temporarily. If we wish to eliminate substantive inequality we waste effort when we debate whether some form of special treatment for the disadvantaged group is necessary. What we must debate is how it can be accomplished.

How do we link the opportunity structure to policies that promote asset formation and begin to close the wealth gap? In our view we must take a three-pronged approach.

First, we must directly address the historically generated as well as current institutional disadvantages that limit the ability of blacks, as a group, to accumulate wealth resources. Second, we must resolutely promote asset acquisition among those at the bottom of the social structure who have been locked out of the wealth accumulation process, be they black or white. Third, we must take aim at the massive concentration of wealth that is held by the richest Americans. Without redistributing America's wealth, we will not succeed at creating a more just society. Even as we advance this agenda, policies that safeguard equal opportunity must be defended. In short, we must make racial justice a national priority.

## TOWARD A MORE EQUAL EQUALITY

Our recommendations are designed to move the discourse on race in America beyond "equality of opportunity" and toward the more controversial notion of "equality of achievement." The traditional debate in this area is between fair shakes and fair shares. The thrust of our examination allows us to break into this debate with a different perspective. We have demonstrated that equal achievement does not return equal wealth rewards—indeed, our results have shown vast inequality. Of course, this may simply be another way of saying that wealth is not only a function of achievement; rather, it can rise or fall in accordance with racially differential state policies and in the presence or absence of an intergenerational bequest.

We are not left, however, with a pessimistic, nothing-can-be-done message. Instead, the evidence we have presented clearly suggests the need for new approaches to the goal of equality. We have many ideas related to this topic and several concrete suggestions for change that can lead to increased wealth for black and poor families. On the individual and family level, proposals are already on the table concerning the development of asset-based policies for welfare, housing, education, business, and retirement. On the institutional level we have a whole series of recommendations on how to tighten up the enforcement of existing laws that supposedly prohibit racial discrimination on the part of banks and saving and loans. After presenting those recommendations we shall broach the sensitive, yet wholly defensible strategy of racial reparations. Then we will reflect on the leadership role that the black community must play in closing the wealth gap.

## DISCUSSION QUESTIONS

1. What are some examples of the daily "slights" experienced by wealthy African Americans?
2. What was discovered about the wealth of equally positioned whites and blacks?
3. What role does the racialization of the welfare state play in wealth disparities between whites and African Americans?
4. What remedies do the authors offer to close the wealth gap between whites and African Americans?

## NOTES

1. Rock 1858. 172
2. Cose 1993, 28.
3. Peagin and Sikes 1994, 15.
4. Didion's 1967 essay "7000 Romaine, Los Angeles" reprinted in Didion 1968, 71.
5. Zarembka 1990,101–2. On the Fair Housing Act see ibid., 106.
6. Our emphasis on asset acquisition is not meant to discount the need for income and employment policy. On the contrary, we believe that it is imperative to institute policies that encourage full employment at wages consistent with a decent standard of living. In fact, many of our proposals assume that people have some kind of income. However, to dwell on the intricacies of this area would divert our attention from the unique implications of our argument There are several important proposals already under discussion that merit serious consideration (see Carnoy 1994; Ellwood 1988; Weir 1992; Wilson 1987).